Pastor  W9-CAH-337

Kevin Harney doesn't just write about seismic shifts, he lives them—with great exuberance and passion. Kevin and his wife, Sherry, are living testaments that with God's help we can expect more, enjoy more, become more. Dive into this book and let Kevin coach you to greater levels of faith, fulfillment, and fruitfulness.

—Mark Mittelberg, author, *Building a Contagious Church* and
Becoming a Contagious Christian

Insights that really work can lift our vision, enhance our skills, and lead to transformed lives. Kevin Harney's book *Seismic Shifts* will help you experience and manage change on a whole new level.

—Kenton Beshore, senior pastor, Mariners Church, Irvine, Calif.

Kevin Harney has the heart of a pastor, the mind of a missionary, and the hands of a servant. In *Seismic Shifts*, Dr. Harney draws from all of these to give us a practical, personal, pastoral, compassionate, forthright, and challenging guide for allowing the Holy Spirit to transform every aspect of our lives. He tells it like it is. Persons young and old will see themselves and their social systems radically transformed, healed, and empowered as they allow Jesus Christ to shift their lives in the directions Kevin describes.

—Charles Van Engen, PhD,
Arthur Glasser Professor of Biblical Theology of Mission,
School of Intercultural Studies, Fuller Theological Seminary

The greatest journey begins and continues one step at a time. With contagious energy, Dr. Kevin Harney has given us doable steps to allow the Spirit to take us on the journey of His life!

—Nancy Grisham, PhD, Livin' Ignited

If I wasn't already a personal friend of Kevin's, I would be after this read. It is refreshing to feel the heart of a pastor who truly believes what he is suggesting to the church and backs it with real-life stories. Practical wisdom, biblically based, life-proven ... *read it*!

—Dr. Jeff Porte, senior pastor,
Third Reformed Church, Kalamazoo, Mich.

Also by Kevin Harney

Ephesians: Bringing Heaven to Earth

Finding a Church You Can Love (with Sherry Harney)

Interactions Small Group Series (with Bill Hybels)

John: An Intimate Look at the Savior

New Community Small Group Series (with Bill Hybels and John Ortberg)

Old Testament Challenge (with John Ortberg)

This We Believe

the little changes that make a **BIG** difference in your life

Seismic
SHIFTS

Kevin G. **Harney**

ZONDERVAN™

GRAND RAPIDS, MICHIGAN 49530 USA

We want to hear from you. Please send your comments about this book to us in care of zreview@zondervan.com. Thank you.

ZONDERVAN™

Seismic Shifts

Copyright © 2005 by Kevin Harney

Requests for information should be addressed to:

Zondervan, *Grand Rapids, Michigan 49530*

Library of Congress Cataloging-in-Publication Data

Harney, Kevin.
    Seismic shifts : the little changes that make a big difference in your life / Kevin G. Harney.
        p. cm.
    Includes bibliographical references and index.
    ISBN-13: 978-0-310-25945-9
    ISBN-10: 0-310-25945-2
    1. Christian life. 2. Success—Religious aspects—Christianity. I. Title.
    BV4598.3.H36 2005
    248.4—dc22

                                                                    2005017302

This edition printed on acid-free paper.

Interior design by Ruth Bandstra

Printed in the United States of America

05 06 07 08 09 10 11 /❖DCI/ 11 10 9 8 7 6 5 4

Contents

Part 6

Acknowledgments

Each person mentioned in these acknowledgments has impacted my life and ministry on a seismic level. In the process of writing this book, many people have offered wisdom and insight. Though their names are not on the cover, their contributions can be found on every page.

Over the past decade, I have partnered with Zondervan on many projects. I am consistently amazed by the people who make up this remarkable company. You labor tirelessly behind the scenes, giving your skills, prayers, and abilities as sacrifices of worship to the God you love and serve. Your passion for providing books and ministry resources that honor Jesus inspires me. I thank all of you. I am honored to thank by name:

Lyn Cryderman. For believing in me as a writer and trusting that I have a message for God's people.

Jack Kuhatschek. You are a brother. Your friendship means more than you know. You have guided the development of this book from concept to completion. As iron sharpens iron, God uses you to sharpen my life.

Mike Cook. Your joyful disposition and unquenchable optimism make me think of Jesus. Thank you for lifting up the message of *Seismic Shifts* so that others might be transformed.

Christine Anderson and Brian Phipps. The editorial work you do has a refining quality that burns away what is not needed and purifies what is good.

I also want to thank my family and my church family:

Sherry. You are more than my better half; you are my better three-fourths! Your example of how God brings big transformation from small beginnings helped inspire this book. There is not a word between these pages you have not read, prayed over, and in many cases made better. Friend, wife, inspiration, lover, and so much more; I thank God for you.

Zach, Josh, and Nate. You were little boys when I began discovering the power of seismic shifts. I am humbled as I watch the little choices and changes you make that are shaping you into men of God.

7

The congregation and staff of Corinth Church. Your love for God and willingness to take seismic steps toward the Savior is impacting your community and the world. Special thanks to Don Porter for his faith-filled leadership and to Debi Rose, my ministry assistant, for her AWICS (Any Way I Can Serve) attitude.

I give special thanks to Malcolm Gladwell for his brilliant work in the book *Tipping Point.* Gladwell's insights on how little things make a big difference have had a seismic impact on my own learning about change.

I am honored to acknowledge a group of leaders and churches who believe that God has the power to change the world. These leaders have prayed for this book, read portions before it was completed, and have shared wisdom and insight as it was in development. These churches had the courage to be the first to spend six weeks learning about seismic shifts on a congregational level through preaching, small groups, and personal study of this book. For your partnership and courage, I bless you:

Beechwood Church and Pastor Jim Lankheet

Central Wesleyan Church and Pastor Paul Hontz

Day Break Church and Pastor Wes Dupin

Fairhaven Ministries and Pastor Tom DeVries

Faith Church (Indiana) and Pastor Bob Bouwer

Faith Church (Traverse City) and Pastor Peter Semeyen

Fifth Reformed Church and Pastor Jim Zinger

Fountain of Life Church and Pastor Randy Barr

Fourth Reformed Church and Pastor Tim Mendering

Gun Lake Church and Pastor Todd VanEk

Hager Park Church and Pastor Dave Lantz

Liberty Baptist Church and Pastor Paul Taylor

Orland Park Church and Pastor Howard Hoekstra

Remembrance Church and Pastor Rod Kamrath

Third Reformed Church and Pastor Jeff Porte

Thornapple Evangelical Covenant Church and Pastor Steve Armfield

Trinity Church and Pastor Jon Opgenorth

Vriesland Church and Pastor Mike VanKampen

Introduction

The Little Things Do Matter

I was on the phone with a friend who lived seven miles away. All of a sudden, she shouted, "Do you feel that?"

I said, "What?"

With excitement in her voice, she replied, "The earthquake!"

I said, "No, but I will soon!"

In a matter of seconds, our whole house began to move. I was upstairs, so the swaying was pronounced. Fortunately it was one of the smooth-rolling kind of earthquakes and not one of the jarring types. "I'll call you back when it's over," I said, and we hung up. I hurried into the middle of the cul-de-sac in front of our house, the place all of our neighbors met and hung out each time there was an earthquake. Over the next few hours, there were a few aftershocks, but the majority of the activity had passed.

In almost three decades of living in Southern California, I experienced many earthquakes. We never seemed to panic. It was just part of living in an area where seismic activity could rock your world at any time. When the earth started shaking, we just stood under a door frame and then moved outside as soon as we could.

What has always fascinated me about earthquakes is that such a relatively little shift along a fault line in the crust of the earth could have such a significant and widespread impact. In school we learned that when a small seismological movement takes place, the shock waves can roll for miles and the aftershocks can continue for days.

Throughout my life, I have thought about seismic shifts. I have seen, over and over again, that little shifts can have a big impact not only in the crust of the earth but also in every area of our lives.

Seismic Shifts Everywhere

In life, seismic shifts are small movements that have a surprisingly significant impact. These shifts can take place in our businesses, homes, churches, families, spiritual lives—almost anywhere. Each time we identify a small change that makes a big difference, we see a seismic shift in action. If we pay attention, we will discover seismic shifts all around us.

I walked into a pharmacy to pick up a prescription for one of my boys. As I stood at the counter, I laughed out loud when I saw what was sitting near the credit-card machine. Taped to the end of an ordinary ballpoint pen was a plastic spoon with a big smiley face drawn on it.

When the pharmacist came over, I asked her, "What's the deal with the happy-face spoon taped to the pen?"

She said, "People were taking our pens ... all the time! We were losing pens every single day. So I taped the spoon to the pen, drew on a happy face, and it has been sitting there ever since."

Four months later, I dropped in to pick up another prescription. Take a wild guess at what I saw sitting on the counter—the smiling spoon-pen. I asked the pharmacist if it was the same one she had made months before, and she assured me it was. This little shift, this slight change, strange as it was, would save the pharmacy countless pens in the months to come. It was a small change that had a big impact.

Seismic shifts can also have a dramatic impact on our attitudes and actions. Nancy had grown up in the church. For seventy years, the music had been led by the organ. The old hymns and traditional style of music ministered to Nancy's soul. It connected her with God. Then, a new pastor came to town. He introduced guitars into the worship service. Nancy did not like the guitar music. It didn't help her meet with God or go deep in worship. The following is part of a real conversation between Nancy (not her real name) and her pastor (me).

"Pastor Kevin, can I talk with you?"

"Of course, Nancy."

She spoke with humble honesty. "I just want you to know that I don't like the guitar music. It does not help me worship. I like the old music."

I said, "Well, Nancy, thanks for your honesty. Could I ask you one question?"

"Sure!" she said.

"Do you think we should use only the organ and not use guitar music in church?"

"Oh no!" she said. "I think we should use the guitar music. I think it will reach some of the young people and draw new people to the church. I just wanted you to know that I don't enjoy it!"

At that moment, Nancy became one of my seismic-shift heroes. She had moved from focusing on her desires and tastes and had learned that the needs of others matter too. Nancy made the shift from thinking only of herself to thinking of others. She made a choice, an intentional shift, a willing sacrifice for the sake of others. This shift transformed her heart. Rather than becoming bitter and resentful, she rejoiced that lives were being touched and a whole new generation of people was coming to love and worship Jesus.

In the church, there are many seismic shifts that create shock waves of transformation. These little changes have a wonderful impact by moving a congregation toward God's vision and purpose. These same seismological movements are at work in our personal lives, creating the potential for transformation on many levels.

Think about a husband who has a hard time telling his wife that he loves her. He has grown up believing that actions speak louder than words. He defends himself by saying things like, "I provide for my wife and family. I work hard. My life says it all; I don't need words." Then with time, he begins to look into the eyes of his wife and see her pain. He knows she longs to hear him say it and mean it. One day he looks at her, swallows hard, and says what her heart has longed to hear: "I love you!"

Not only does he say these three little words, he makes them a regular part of his vocabulary. This trisyllabic declaration redefines the relationship. It instills hope in his wife's heart and rekindles a long-lost romance. Once again, a little change makes a big difference.

Dominos Are Falling! • • • • • • • • • • • • • • • • •

Have you ever seen a display of hundreds or even thousands of dominos? When all the dominos are set up in just the right places, the anticipation is tremendous. Everyone knows that if someone takes the tip of their finger and topples the first domino, the chain reaction will be exhilarating. One by one the dominos will fall.

When I was in sixth grade, I became fascinated with dominos. I would spend hours setting up complex configurations in my bedroom. Then when everything was ready, I would topple the one key domino and watch with delight as this little motion began an avalanche that didn't stop until every single domino had fallen. Often I would invite my family to watch. I was so into the domino thing that my parents got me a special set for Christmas that included ramps, bridges, and lots of extra dominos. I suppose those hours of fun taught me more than I realized. One little push, in the right place at the right time, can start a chain reaction.

Seismic Shifts is about change. Big change. But it focuses on the small shifts we need to make if we want to experience transformation. Ask yourself the following questions. After you read each one, whisper either yes or no.

- Do you want to experience deeper levels of joy?
- Do you hunger for a growing and dynamic connection with God?
- Do you want greater discipline in your eating habits, exercise, and the care of your body, soul, and emotional life?
- Are you longing for your relationships with family members and friends to move to a whole new level of communication and closeness?
- Do you hope that one day you can have the financial and material resources you need to feel secure and happy?
- Would you like to be so comfortable expressing your faith that you can share God's love with others in a way that feels natural?

If you answered yes to any of these questions, you are reading the right book. God offers the power needed to experience transformation in every area of your life. In this book, we will look at six types of shifts: shifts that bring joy, expand faith, provide rest, build relationships, unleash riches, and change the world. In my two decades of pastoral ministry, I have discovered that these are some of the main areas in which people desire transformation but have the hardest time experiencing it. In the pages of this book, you will discover the little changes that make a big difference in your life. I believe, with all of my heart, that you are beginning a life-impacting journey that can send out shock waves of blessing for years to come.

In each of the chapters of this book, we will look at a specific aspect of God's dream for our lives. Our creator has a plan for each of us. We need to learn to take the baby steps needed to move toward his purposes. As we make seismic shifts, we will be amazed at the joy and growth God brings.

Just as pushing one domino over can begin a chain reaction, the practical ideas in the pages ahead will transform your life. Every chapter of this book includes Seismic Shift Suggestions. These are practical little changes you can make that can have a big impact on your life in the area covered in that chapter. At the end of each chapter are a couple of questions for reflection as well as directions for prayer. These are provided to help you go a little deeper into each topic.

God is ready to move in your life in powerful ways. It all begins with little changes. If we're willing, God will show up and bring transformation into every part of our lives.

My prayer is that as you read *Seismic Shifts*, you will be amazed by the presence of God, moved by the power of God, touched by the grace of God, and changed by the hand of God.

Part 1

Shifts That Bring Greater Joy
Than You Can Imagine

Does God think we have too much fun? Is he worried that his children are in danger of exploding with joy? C. S. Lewis didn't think so. He believed God has far more joy in store for us than most of us imagine or dream. Lewis writes, "We are half-hearted creatures, fooling around with drink and sex and ambition when infinite joy is offered us, like an ignorant child who wants to go on making mud pies in the slum because he cannot imagine what is meant by the offer of a holiday by the sea. We are far too easily pleased." What Lewis believed is supported over and over again in the Bible.

King David lived in an agricultural setting where a good harvest brought celebration for the whole community. When grain was plentiful and grapes were heavy on the vine, joy was close at hand. Yet David boldly writes, "You have filled my heart with greater joy than when their grain and new wine abound" (Ps. 4:7).

In the very next psalm, David, who had often run to God for protection in hard times, writes, "But let all who take refuge in you be glad; let them ever sing for joy. Spread your protection over them, that those who love your name may rejoice in you" (Ps. 5:11).

Throughout his years of following God, David experienced the heights of amazing victories as well as the depths of heartbreak. As a young man, he became a fugitive and was hunted from cave to cave in the wilderness by a mad king who wanted nothing more than to pin him to the wall with a javelin. Later in life, David sat on the throne of Israel, but he was forced to flee from his palace in Jerusalem when his own son Absalom launched a military coup d'état and ousted him. Through all of this, he understood God was, and always would be, his source of joy. Through tears and times of joy, David could boldly declare, "You turned my wailing into dancing; you removed my sackcloth and clothed me with joy" (Ps. 30:11).

If we turn the clock ahead many centuries, we see an angel appear to a band of shepherds to announce the coming of the long-awaited Messiah. The news of Jesus' birth is characterized as "good news of great joy": "But the angel said to them, 'Do not be afraid. I bring you good news of great joy that will be for all the people'" (Luke 2:10).

Thirty-three years later, this Messiah had been crucified, had died, and had been placed in a tomb. After three days, Jesus rose from the dead in glory, triumphant over death and the grave. When Mary Magdalene and the other Mary went to the tomb, they met a heavenly messenger.

The angel said to the women, "Do not be afraid, for I know that you are looking for Jesus, who was crucified. He is not here; he has risen, just as he said. Come and see the place where he lay. Then go quickly and tell his disciples: 'He has risen from the dead and is going ahead of you into Galilee. There you will see him.' Now I have told you."

So the women hurried away from the tomb, afraid yet filled with joy, and ran to tell his disciples. Suddenly Jesus met them. "Greetings," he said. They came to him, clasped his feet and worshiped him.

—**Matthew 28:5–9**

Years later, a man named Paul was in jail for preaching about this resurrected Jesus. While incarcerated, Paul wrote to the Christians in the city of Philippi. In his short letter, Paul used various forms of the word joy fourteen times. Even while imprisoned, he understood that overflowing joy was still his because of faith in Jesus. He writes, "Rejoice in the Lord always. I will say it again: Rejoice! Let your gentleness be evident to all. The Lord is near. Do not be anxious about anything, but in everything, by prayer and petition, with thanksgiving, present your requests to God. And the peace of God, which transcends all understanding, will guard your hearts and your minds in Christ Jesus" (Phil. 4:4–7).

From the Old Testament to the New, the Bible declares this message: in the good and hard times, those who walk closely with God can and should experience life-transforming joy.

Many people would be surprised to discover that the words joy, rejoice, rejoicing, and joyful appear more than three hundred and fifty times in the Bible. A study of these passages makes it clear that the natural condition of a person in relationship with God is joy. Some of these passages talk about people facing a time of joylessness, but it is clear that it is not the natural and ongoing condition of a Christian's heart.

God is ready to let a river of joy flow into our hearts and lives. But too often we are content with only a sip or a thimbleful. We settle for too little. Maybe C. S. Lewis was right about our being like children content to make mud pies in the slums while God offers us a holiday by the sea.

Could it be that God has more joy in store for us than we ever imagined? Is it possible that God expects his children to live with such a deep level of celebration that even hard times, loss, struggle, and the pain of this life seem small compared with his supply of joy?

Enough with mud pies and living in the slums of joylessness. It is time for a holiday by the sea!

Chapter ONE

The Seismic Shift from Infancy to Adulthood

> Then we will no longer be infants, tossed back and forth by the waves, and blown here and there by every wind of teaching and by the cunning and craftiness of people in their deceitful scheming. Instead, speaking the truth in love, we will in all things grow up into him who is the head, that is, Christ.
>
> —Ephesians 4:14–15 TNIV

> In fact, though by this time you ought to be teachers, you need someone to teach you the elementary truths of God's word all over again. You need milk, not solid food! Anyone who lives on milk, being still an infant, is not acquainted with the teaching about righteousness. But solid food is for the mature, who by constant use have trained themselves to distinguish good from evil. Therefore let us leave the elementary teachings about Christ and go on to maturity.
>
> —Hebrews 5:12–6:1

Babies are cute. They can do the smallest thing and adults cheer with delight, laugh with joy, and stare in amazement. Think about it, parents actually talk with pride about how their little boy holds his head up or how their little girl smiles on command. They act as if these relatively common activities rival the exploits of great athletes.

It's the same story with toddlers. They are in a season of development in which everything they do seems to impress someone. First steps evoke praise from family and friends. Speaking just a few words is viewed as a major accomplishment. Some parents of toddlers actually clap and celebrate as their little girl or boy uses the "potty chair" for the first time.

It should not amaze us that people get excited when a baby or toddler does these things. Affirmation in these moments makes perfect sense. When little ones take baby steps of growth, they should be celebrated. Seemingly little accomplishments really are a big deal because they reflect God's plan for growth and maturity.

On the other hand, it would be strange to see people standing around cheering for a healthy fifteen-year-old girl just because she rolled over from her stomach to her back. It would be outright bizarre to see a fully grown and capable man who expects someone else to wipe his nose and tie his shoes because he does not want to do these simple tasks. In short, it would be sad to see an adult choose to continue acting like an infant.

We all agree that a normal and healthy life leads a person from infancy to adulthood along a course of consistent steps of growth. When this process is stunted, something is wrong. We know this is true when it comes to physical growth, but we often forget this same natural process in our spiritual lives. God expects his children to grow up in faith in a way that leads from spiritual infancy to maturity. This process will bring joy and excitement to our lives when we learn to see ourselves as God sees us.

God Has a Dream ●

When God looks at his children, he has a dream. Just like earthly parents dream about what their little boy or girl will grow up to be, God dreams about his children and their future. His dream is for us to move from spiritual infancy to become more and more like his Son, Jesus Christ. In the letter to the Hebrews, we read that God is working to help us "reach unity in the faith and in the knowledge of the Son of God and become mature, attaining to the whole measure of the fullness of Christ" (Eph. 4:13).

In the same way that a parent helps a baby learn to walk, talk, and feed herself, God wants to help us take steps toward spiritual maturity. God longs to see his children make serious and consistent efforts toward growth. God offers us instruction through the Bible, support through his people, and strength through his Holy Spirit, but he will not force us to grow. We must respond to his invitation and promptings and take action that will result in maturity.

God's dream is to see us taking steps toward him. And when we stumble or fall, God rejoices when we get up and keep trying. He does not promise that we will never struggle, but he longs for us to keep striving as we grow to be more like Jesus.

Some years ago, when our first son was learning to swim, I experienced something I think is similar to what God feels when he watches his children. We had heard of a woman who gave swimming lessons in her back-yard pool. She was legendary in our area because she had never met a child she couldn't teach to swim. She was also a nurse, so we felt safe having her help our son through this challenging learning experience.

With confidence and excitement, we took Zach to his first lesson. After some preliminary greetings and instructions, it was time to get the kids in the pool. Zach ran straight for the fence and locked his fingers in the chain links with white-knuckled fury. He had no intention of getting in the pool and "swimming for Mrs. Rita." He explained to her, as only a terrified little boy can, that he appreciated her offer, but he was going to take a pass on this whole swimming lesson thing. Maybe some other day.

Sherry and I looked on and had to make a decision. We could explain to our little boy that he would have to take this step toward maturity. Or we could pack him in the minivan and drive home. We wanted to see him press through his fear and succeed at swimming, even if it was hard for him. We knew we could not force Zach to swim, but we could give our strongest encouragement for him to try.

After we pried his viselike fingers from the fence, we explained to Zach that we expected him to give his best effort. We assured him we loved him. We promised he would not sink to the bottom of the pool. Then we placed him in Rita's arms and left. To make a long story short, by the end of the week, Zach was jumping off the diving board in the deep end and swimming the full length of the pool. We rejoiced in the growth we saw in our son and were thankful we had pressed him to take this scary step. We were also proud of him for trusting us and growing through his fears.

God looks at us, his beloved children, and rejoices each time we take a baby step forward on our spiritual journey. He is proud when we face our fears or overcome hurdles so we can grow to be more like Jesus. He also experiences sorrow when we won't grow in faith. When we cling to the chain-link fences of life and refuse to let go, he wants to gently pry our fingers free and remind us that he will be with us and we won't sink to the bottom of the pool. God cheers each time we experience the victory and joy of spiritual growth. He celebrates these steps because he knows we will find lasting joy as we grow up in faith.

What does God dream about? He dreams about you and me! He dreams about our taking steps closer to him. He dreams about our getting up when we fall and trying again, even when we scrape our knees. He dreams about our discovering deep and lasting joy on each step of our journey. He dreams about what we could become if we will simply commit ourselves to the process of moving from spiritual infancy to adulthood.

Rapid or Normal Growth?

Has it ever struck you that some people seem to experience unusually rapid spiritual growth? They come to a place of authentic faith in Jesus Christ and begin to grow immediately. It is almost as if they are taking spiritual steroids. In a matter of days and weeks, a passion for God blossoms in their lives. Over weeks and months, these new followers of Jesus begin to devour God's Word like a starving person who is invited to an all-you-can-eat buffet for the first time. These relatively new believers naturally find a place to serve in the church, begin to share their resources with those in need, and freely tell others about God's love and how he is changing their lives. At a freakish mutantlike pace, they grow in spiritual maturity so quickly that they pass many who have been Christians for a much longer time.

On the other hand, there are people who believe in Jesus and attend church faithfully, but year after year, they seem to stay the same. They listen to the pastor's sermons, but nothing seems to sink in. They show few signs of spiritual progress. They seem to tread water, staying in the same place month after month, year after year, and even decade after decade. Maybe they experience an occasional moment of spiritual inspiration, but the flame quickly flickers and they resume the familiar posture that has characterized their spiritual lives for so many years.

The question at hand is this: what should normal spiritual growth look like? Should we be surprised and amazed by those who grow rapidly, or should we see this as normal for those who follow Jesus? Is it right to watch people in the church go year after year showing no signs of spiritual growth, and look the other way, pretending this is normal? And here's an even more personal question: if we look at our own spiritual lives and realize we are treading water, what should we do about it?

How do parents feel when they realize their child's growth is stunted? The answer is obvious: they are deeply concerned. If their little boy or girl has a physical problem, they call a doctor. They will go from specialist to specialist and do all they can to help their child overcome this obstacle. If their son or daughter is dealing with an emotional or mental hurdle, they will contact a Christian counselor or a psychologist to get help. Any loving parent who sees something hampering the growth of their child will take action.

Seismic Shifts That Lead Us toward Spiritual Maturity

One Sunday morning, I was preaching about God's desire to see us grow into mature followers of Jesus. To make the point, I showed a video clip of a dad and mom teaching their little boy to walk. I borrowed a home video from a woman who works in our church office. This sixty-second clip of John and Chrisann teaching their firstborn to walk communicated more clearly than I could have hoped to with mere words.

Little Evan was doing his best to keep his balance, putting both arms straight up in the air. In his white T-shirt and diaper, he took wobbly steps across the kitchen floor until he got to the little mat by the sink. As he stepped on it, the mat shifted ever so slightly, and he lost his footing and dropped to the floor. His mom cheered him on, "Great job, Evan! You're doing great." He struggled to his feet and kept crossing the floor, arms in the air, a look of determination on his face. Then with no warning, he pitched straight forward and fell with a thud to the cold tile floor. The congregation gasped. You could sense that everyone wanted to reach up to the screen and help this little guy back to his feet.

There he was, sprawled with his nose just an inch off the floor, his little butt sticking up in the air. Then his father spoke, "Evan, stand up and walk to Daddy." He lay there, frozen for a moment. Then from somewhere deep inside, Evan found the strength to push himself up, turn around, and begin walking toward his father. The congregation watched, wanting to cheer but absolutely silent. Step by step, he crossed the floor until he fell into his daddy's arms. The response from the congregation was both joy and a huge sigh of relief.

This video clip illustrates something God wants all of us to understand. He looks at us and sees beloved children. When we lose our balance and fall flat, he is right there. He says, "Stand up and walk to Daddy."

That's the heart of God for you and me. He wants us to get back up each time we fall and continue the glorious journey across the linoleum tile of life until we reach the arms of our Father.

Maybe you are lying on your belly in the middle of the kitchen floor. You are tired, discouraged, and don't feel you can get up and press on. It feels better to just stay right where you are.

Your Father is there. Can you hear him? "Stand up and walk to Daddy. Stand up and walk to Daddy." He is so close. His arms are open. Don't give up. Stand up one more time and keep on trying.

When the apostle Paul wrote to the church in the city of Corinth, he lamented the fact that they were not growing up spiritually. They had slipped and fallen, but they refused to get up and try again. He writes, "Brothers and sisters, I could not address you as spiritual but as worldly — mere infants in Christ. I gave you milk, not solid food, for you were not yet ready for it. Indeed, you are still not ready" (1 Cor. 3:1–2 TNIV). In common language, Paul is calling the believers in the city of Corinth a bunch of spiritual babies. Ouch! He then goes on to tell them about some of the signs of their spiritual infancy and challenges them to enter a process of growing up in faith.

The Holy Spirit invites every Christian to enter the joy of spiritual growth. We accept by learning to identify signs of spiritual adulthood and committing to take consistent steps toward maturity. These seismic shifts propel us to deeper places of intimacy with God. Along the way, if we listen closely, we will hear our heavenly Father cheering for us and celebrating each step.

In the rest of this chapter, we will look at seven key indicators that we are moving toward spiritual maturity.

Seven Indicators of Growth • • • • • • • • • • • • • • • • •

■ Learning to Feed Ourselves

When a baby is born, we know he needs help eating, at least for a time. He can't find his own food and prepare it. A mother offers her milk as the basics of life. But if Mom and Dad refuse to provide for the baby, he will die. Someone must spoon-feed this little guy for many months. But all parents expect a healthy little boy or girl to learn how to eat on their own eventually. If they don't, the parents know something is very wrong.

|||||| **Seismic Shift Suggestion** ||||||

This Week's Menu. For many people, a great step toward spiritual maturity is simply spending a little time in God's Word each day. Block out at least five minutes for personal Bible reading each day for the coming week. Find a quiet place, open God's Word, and read. If you are not sure where to start, you can use the six-week daily reading guide provided in the back of this book.

In the same way, our heavenly Father wants his children to learn how to dine regularly on his Word, the Bible. It is our primary source of spiritual sustenance. Those who are moving toward spiritual adulthood learn that they can't expect others to feed them forever. It is certainly helpful to have spiritual mentors, Sunday school teachers, mature family members, pastors, and teachers who assist us in our growth. But we need to learn how to study the Bible on our own. This movement from relying on others to feed us spiritually to developing an ability to feed ourselves is a seismic shift each of us should make. When we do, our movement toward spiritual maturity accelerates rapidly and we discover amazing joy. One key indicator that a person is growing spiritually is when they make regular Bible study a part of their spiritual journey.

Learning to Talk and Listen

It is exciting to watch a child speak their first words, mimic noises, and eventually discover they can communicate what they want, need, and feel. Learning to talk is an important measure of growth. When a child begins to listen and respond to what they hear, their parents are thrilled.

In the same way, it is a clear sign we are growing spiritually when we develop our ability to talk with God and listen to him. Prayer is foundational for all who follow Jesus. Once, when Jesus was trying to help people understand who he is, he used an illustration that would have made a lot of sense to people in his day. He referred to himself as a shepherd and his followers as sheep. He said, "He calls his own sheep by name and leads them out. When he has brought out all his own, he goes on ahead of them, and his sheep follow him because they know his voice" (John 10:3–4). Jesus made it clear that his followers can recognize his voice and follow his directions just like sheep follow a shepherd. A growing prayer life in which we talk with God and listen to him is another sign we are moving forward in our spiritual journey.

⠓ Sharing

One of the biggest challenges for every parent is teaching their little one to share. Once a child learns to talk, one of their first and most emphatic words is, "Mine!" Children say this often and forcefully. Parents have to consistently pry a toy out of their child's pudgy fingers, hand it to another child, and gently say, "Honey, you need to share with your friend." The child naturally looks at Mommy and says, "You are right and so very wise. Thank you for reminding me of what I already know and truly desire in the deepest part of my heart. From now on, I will seek to be an example of generosity in the way I share my toys with others." Right? Wrong! The battle to grow in generosity is one every child and adult faces. The journey of learning to share lasts a lifetime.

> ||||| **Seismic Shift Suggestion** |||||
>
> **Honest Evaluation.** In the coming week, take note of any way you share your resources with others. Think specifically of your money or material goods. Are you sharing freely? Are you looking for ways to help and support others? If you are, celebrate this and pray for strength to continue. If you sense you need to grow in your ability to share, pray for courage and a generous heart.

An indication that we are growing from spiritual infancy to adulthood is when we take steps forward in our generosity toward people and God. The Bible reminds us over and over that everything we have is a gift from God. In the letter of James, we read, "Every good and perfect gift is from above, coming down from the Father of the heavenly lights" (James 1:17). God wants us to discover the joy of giving freely to him and also sharing our resources and abilities with those who are in need. As we learn to do this in a natural way, we can be assured we are making the journey from infancy to adulthood.

⠵ Helping Others

A newborn baby can't do chores around the house, earn income to help pay the bills, or lend a hand mowing the lawn. They need someone to help them with everything. But as a little boy or girl grows up, they discover that part of being in a family means helping. Eventually they reach an age when they can take out the trash, set the table, and clean their room. A loving parent will challenge them to do their share of chores, even when they don't feel like it. We need to move from being helped to helping others in our spiritual journey as well.

Another clear sign we are moving forward in maturity is when we stop saying, "Take care of me," and begin saying, "How can I help you?" We all need the support of others. But as we grow up in faith, we come to a place where we actually experience what it feels like for God to use us as his instruments to extend love, care, and support to others. The Bible says, "Carry each other's burdens, and in this way you will fulfill the law of Christ" (Gal. 6:2). God expects us to come to a place in our spiritual lives where we are not always demanding that someone carry our burdens but are willing to support others in their time of need.

It is helpful to note that some followers of Christ break this mold and are very good at serving. In some cases, they are quick to serve but do not want to let others help bear their burdens. Their growth curve includes allowing people to come alongside them in times of need.

Loving People

Imagine the frustration and disappointment of a young woman who looks forward to having a baby so she will have someone to love her. Some young parents imagine a precious little one who will reciprocate their affection immediately upon exiting the womb. But piles of diapers, late-night feedings, and bouts of colic shatter the illusion and introduce the hard reality: babies need lots of love and offer very little back. The truth is, as they grow up, they must be taught how to love. It does not come naturally.

This is why Jesus spent so much time teaching his followers about loving others. He knew that expressions of authentic love come as we learn to be more like him. Jesus said, "A new command I give you: Love one another. As I have loved you, so you must love one another. By this everyone will know that you are my disciples, if you love one another" (John 13:34–35 TNIV). In just two short verses, Jesus says, "Love one another," three times. It is quite apparent that he believed our love for each other is a sign of spiritual maturity. When Jesus was asked about the greatest commandment, he said that the first and most important commandment is to love God, but a close second is, "Love your neighbor as yourself" (Matt. 22:39). As we grow from spiritual childhood to adulthood, we learn to love people in ways that reflect the heart of Jesus.

Loving God

Parents seek to lavish their children with love. From the day they are born, through childhood, into their adolescent years, and even into their adult lives, a loving father and mother will continue to express affection to their children. The hope and prayer of every parent is that one day their children will reciprocate. This is why it is so painful when a toddler screams, "I hate you!" or a teenager rejects their parents' effort to have a close relationship. Every dad and mom longs to hear their child express authentic words of love.

God, our heavenly Father, also longs for his children to love him. Jesus said, " 'Love the Lord your God with all your heart and with all your soul and with all your mind.' This is the first and greatest commandment" (Matt. 22:37–38). Jesus made it clear that of all the things we can do with our lives, loving God is on the top of the list. Growing in this relationship with our Creator is an essential sign that we are making the journey from spiritual infancy to adulthood.

Living in a Bigger World

Before we are born, we are in a small and safe place, the womb of our mother. Once we are delivered, our world stays quite limited—a car seat, crib, or playpen sets the parameters of our universe. With time, toddlers can roam the house, and their world gets bigger. But once they get outside and start riding a bike, the world seems massive! That is, until they get a license and start driving. At this point, only the price of gas limits how far they can wander.

|||||| **Seismic Shift Suggestion** ||||||

Start with Prayer. One of the greatest ways to expand your heart for the world is through prayer. Make a list of people you love who don't yet have a relationship with Jesus. Also, write down the names of countries where many people are far from God. Then take a few moments each morning or evening to pray for the love of God to pour over these people and places.

We experience this journey from a small to a big world in our walk of faith as well. God is in the business of expanding our hearts with a love for the world. He wants us to get a glimpse of how he feels about people all over the globe, and this is why the Bible says, "For God so loved the world that he gave his one and only Son, that whoever believes in him shall not perish but have eternal life. For God did not send his Son into the world to condemn the world, but to save the world through him" (John 3:16–17). Brand-new followers of Jesus spend time focusing on their own growth and lives. This is a natural starting point. But with spiritual maturity comes an expanding heart for those who do not know the love of Jesus. As our world gets bigger, our hearts begin to ache for others to enter a living and saving relationship with God through faith in Jesus. When this happens, we are seeing a clear indicator of our movement toward spiritual adulthood.

The Joy of Growing Up

When a baby takes their first step, joy overflows. Parents cheer. Friends join the celebration. Often the baby smiles or squeals with delight! God also watches and smiles. When his children take steps toward spiritual maturity, God rejoices, and he wants us to celebrate with him. He made us for growth. In this chapter, we have surveyed seven signs that we are on a trajectory from spiritual infancy toward adulthood. We will investigate each of these more closely in the coming chapters. The question is, Do you desire to grow in joy as you take steps forward in your walk with God? How is your joy quotient today? If it is at a low ebb, maybe it is time to make a seismic shift!

FOR REFLECTION • • • • • • • • • • • • • • • • • • • •

- As I look at the seven indicators outlined in this chapter, what is one area in which I need to take a step toward maturity, and what action can I take to begin this journey?
- Who is one person God has used to help me grow toward spiritual maturity? What qualities in their life inspired me to move from infancy toward adulthood in my journey as a follower of Jesus? How can I develop one of these characteristics in my life so God can use me to inspire others?

FOR PRAYER • •

- Thank God for the way he has helped you move forward in your spiritual journey. You might want to think back to when you first became a follower of Christ and identify some of the landmarks along the way.
- Ask God to help you continue on an upward and joy-filled trajectory of spiritual growth.

Chapter TWO

The Seismic Shift from Doing to Being

For you created my inmost being;
  you knit me together in my mother's womb.
I praise you because I am fearfully and wonderfully made;
  your works are wonderful, I know that full well.
My frame was not hidden from you
  when I was made in the secret place.
When I was woven together in the depths of the earth,
  your eyes saw my unformed body.
All the days ordained for me were written in your book
  before one of them came to be.

—**Psalm 139:13–16**

I still remember nap time in kindergarten. Most of the kids were very good at lying still on their little foam mats. If they were being graded, they would have received an A+ for their fine napping skills. They would take their little mats from their cubbyholes, roll them out on the hard classroom floor, and lay down quietly. Their self-control was staggering to me. There they would lie, quiet as little church mice. Still as stones. Pretty as a picture. Some of them would actually fall asleep. And when nap time was over, Mrs. Snow would pick one of these good little children to be the wake-up fairy. All through the year, I dreamed that one day I would be able to be so good during nap time that I would be the one chosen to wake up the other children from their slumber.

All year long I tried to lay still. There I was, on my little mat, doing my best to pretend I was asleep. But in reality, I was a seething bundle of nerves ready to jump out of my skin! It must have shown, because when the year was over, my dream had never become a reality. I never got to take that magic wand (okay, it was a ruler) and gently tap each class member on the shoulder to wake them from their nap. I never got to be the wake-up fairy. Everyone knew it, especially me—I was a failure.

Even at a very young age, the measure of who I was could be seen by all. My behavior dictated my place, my status, my station in life. If I had been in kindergarten in the 1990s, they would have labeled me ADD and given me a pill. If it had been the 2000s, I would have gotten another consonant in my diagnosis and been called ADHD. I would have received medication and maybe some counseling. But my kindergarten nap times came in the 1960s, and back then the only diagnosis for a wiggly, squirmy, and overly energetic little boy came in one simple word: naughty! There was no pill for that, only punishment. And you could be sure my squirrelly behavior during nap time would never be reinforced by the honor of being exalted to the high place of wake-up fairy.

From my earliest days, I understood that my behavior determined my worth. It was all about doing the right things in the right way at the right time. There were good kids and naughty kids, and there was no question which category I fell into.

The Message of Our World • • • • • • • • • • • • • • • •

At a young age, most of us discover that what we do determines our value. This reality intensifies as we become adults. Our performance, victories, accomplishments, and steps up the ladder of success determine our place in the social structures and pecking orders of our world. Sadly, for many people life becomes a journey of trying to do enough good things to finally feel valuable.

Before we ever realize what is happening, we are scored, graded, and measured. Right when we are born, we get our first score. The doctors and nurses give us an APGAR rating. We are weighed, measured, and the tone of our skin is evaluated. You would think we might get a little more time to snuggle with Mom and Dad, but no! We are already being evaluated from the moment we draw air into our lungs.

These weights and measures become very important to parents. It is not unusual to hear a father proudly declare that his son weighed ten pounds, eight ounces (huge girls are not quite as brag-worthy). To hear the tone in some fathers' voices, you might think this was akin to landing a huge bass or bagging an eight-point buck! While some dads are quick to celebrate the sheer size of their offspring, most mothers are less enthusiastic about having delivered a kid with a head the size of a watermelon.

This pathology continues into our childhood. Performance on a cheerleading squad, the football field, or in the classroom often determines our worth in the eyes of others. The world sets standards, and if we are not careful, we can spend a lifetime trying to prove our worth.

It would be comforting to believe that all of this ends when we enter adulthood, but it does not. In many cases, the demand to perform and to prove our worth only increases. As adults, we simply face a new list of accomplishments and new standards for success. What kind of house do you own? What model of car do you drive? How much money do you make? How many promotions have you gotten? How much do you weigh? The answer to these questions, and others like them, can define how others view us and how we see ourselves. What equation determines our net worth? It is simple; with an emotional calculator, add up the diplomas, trophies, possessions, and all you have done in this life and discover the painful fact that the numbers never add up to success and a deep sense of self-worth. Never! The world's math won't lead to a place of joy and lasting peace.

A View from God's Throne • • • • • • • • • • • • • •

The good news is that our worth is not based on an APGAR rating, a GPA, or an ACT score. Our value is not based on income, a savings account balance, our looks, or the car we drive. God wants us to know our net worth does not determine our value in his eyes. It never has, and it never will.

God has something very different in mind. The Creator of heaven and earth does care about what we do, but his greater concern is who we are and who we are becoming.

Our vantage point is from the muck and mire of this world. We buy the lie. We accept the assessments, scores, account balances, report cards, and psychological assessments as valid indicators of our worth. God has a radically different perspective. From his heavenly throne, he sees us as we really are. What he wants is for us to see ourselves through his eyes.

If we make this seismic shift, our lives will overflow with peace and joy! When we see ourselves as God sees us, life takes on new meaning. The staggering reality is that God sees us as so valuable that he gave everything so we could be restored to relationship with him. He sees us as beloved and precious children. John expressed this truth with these words: "How great is the love the Father has lavished on us, that we should be called children of God! And that is what we are!" (1 John 3:1). He loves us more than our minds can imagine and our hearts can contain.

The problem is that at some point in our past, we each made a decision that is still impacting us today, a secret choice made deep in our hearts. In some cases, it was so secret that we can't remember when we made it. But somewhere along the line, we decided to view our lives and assess our worth through the eyes of a certain person or a group of people. It might have been the eyes of a parent, a friend, an employer, a peer group, or even our own eyes. But from that moment on, we based our worth on how we performed in the eyes of this person. And we adjusted our behavior to fit their perceptions.

My wife, Sherry, learned this at a young age. When she was still in the early years of grade school, she overheard one of her music teachers comment to another teacher that she had a monotone singing voice. Because she was a young girl, this devastated her. Sadly, for the next decade, Sherry never sang loud enough for anyone else to hear, including herself! Because of this one thoughtless comment, she spent over ten years in school and church afraid someone would hear how bad she sounded when she sang.

Then, many years later, Sherry was invited to lead a children's choir at church. She felt God wanted her to do this even though she "could not sing." God gave her the courage to press beyond her fear. With time, God helped Sherry understand that he made her voice and loved the way she sounded. As Sherry received God's affirmation about her singing, she discovered two surprising things: she loved singing, and God had definitely not given her a monotone voice. Her grade school teacher had been wrong. Over the next two decades, she taught hundreds of young children how to sing praise to God with joy in their hearts. As she led children's choirs, she helped these little ones know that God loves each of their voices and their songs of praise.

God longs for each one of us to make a seismic shift. He wants us to see ourselves through his eyes, not through the eyes of the people around us. He does not look primarily at what we do or how we perform. He is concerned with who we are. When we get a glimpse of ourselves through his vision, we discover that his fatherly love overflows with unspeakable grace. He is patient, understanding, and loving beyond description. When we see ourselves through his eyes, we are staggered by the simple, pure, and piercing reality that we are loved. Even with our frailties, struggles, and sins, God's passion for us never wanes.

Maybe someone once said that your voice was monotone, that you would never amount to anything, or that you were a failure. Somewhere along the way, you began to believe that lie. It is time to hear from God. He knows where you have been hurt and all the ways you have tried to measure up. He wants you to stop performing and come to him as you are. Let your heart hear God's word for you today: "For God so loved the world that he gave his one and only Son, that whoever believes in him shall not perish but have eternal life. For God did not send his Son into the world to condemn the world, but to save the world through him" (John 3:16–17), and, "But God demonstrates his own love for us in this: While we were still sinners, Christ died for us" (Rom. 5:8). Jesus is still speaking, "Greater love has no one than this, that he lay down his life for his friends" (John 15:13). After these words, Jesus proved the depth of his love by giving his life on the cross as the payment for our sins.

We experience life-changing seismic shifts when we finally feel the waves of God's amazing love come crashing over our hearts. We are freed from society's demands to perform and measure up. We are released from the generational bondage of families that place expectations on us that we can never meet. We no longer see ourselves through the eyes of the people around us, or even through our own eyes. When we make this joy-giving shift, we see ourselves the way God sees us.

I Am His Beloved, He Loves Me That Much • • • • • •

When we make the seismic shift from doing to being, we begin to see ourselves as God sees us. We start to realize that God's greatest revelation of love came when Jesus, the Son of God, left the glory of heaven to come to this earth and show us the way home. It is hard to imagine God loving us that much, but it is a fundamental truth every Christian must accept.

This reality hit home for me many years ago when I heard a pastor tell a story about some wayward geese. As the story goes, there was a woman who attended church faithfully and was a sincere follower of Jesus. She believed in God and accepted that Jesus had entered human history as a man and that he had died to pay the price for sins. Everyone who knew her could see that her faith was authentic and that she understood God's love for her.

Her husband was a kind man and loved her very much. He did not believe in God or Jesus, but he never held his wife back from her faith. He could see it was real for her, so he encouraged her "religion" but did not embrace it for himself.

Every so often, the woman would invite her husband to attend church with her. "Honey, could you come with me just once?"

His response was always the same. "It makes no sense to me! Why would God leave heaven and come as a human being? If there is a God, I can't comprehend why he would ever become a man and walk on this earth. I just don't get it."

The woman felt sad, but she would head off to church alone and pray that one day her husband would understand and accept that Jesus really did come to show the way to God. Her prayer was that the love she experienced each day as she walked with Jesus would one day fill the heart of the man she loved.

One Christmas Eve, the woman thought, *I will try one more time. I will invite my husband to the Christmas Eve candlelight service.* When she gently extended the invitation, he gave the same response he had always given.

As she headed off to church, snow began to fall and the wind began to blow. Her husband sat by the fire to read a book. After almost an hour, he heard a thump on the window, then another and another. He got up to see if some of the neighborhood kids were throwing snowballs at the house. When he looked out the window, he saw that the light snow had turned into a heavy storm. Then he noticed a flock of geese on the ground under the window.

They had become disoriented in the storm, seen the light in the window, and tried to fly into the house. He could see that they were injured and confused, so he put on a coat, a hat, and boots and quickly went out to see if he could help. When he came near the geese, they scurried away, more fearful of him than concerned about their pain. He opened the door to his barn and tried to shoo them in. Every time he got near, they scattered in the other direction. He could not get them to go toward the safety of the barn.

Finally, he was exhausted and no closer to getting the injured geese into the barn. At that moment, he had a thought. *If only I could become a goose, just for a short time. I could lead them to safety. They are hurt, confused, and scared of me. If I could become one of them, I could lead them to safety.*

At that moment, a church bell rang in the distance, and he fell to his knees in the snow. He prayed for the first time in his life. "Dear God, I think I am beginning to understand why you had to come as a man and what Christmas really means. I think, for the first time, I am beginning to see who Jesus is and why he came. Jesus, if you are trying to lead me to safety, please teach me to follow you. If you are out there and love me that much, I give my life to you!"

The man finally came to a point where he realized it was the love and concern of God that initiated Jesus' coming into the world. If we are gong to live with enduring joy, we must receive this truth: we are God's beloved children.

This truth is expressed over and over throughout the Bible. Take a moment to read the following passages from 1 John slowly and reflectively. Ask God to help you hear what he wants to say about the greatness of his love for you.

> How great is the love the Father has lavished on us, that we should be called children of God! And that is what we are!
> —1 John 3:1

> This is love: not that we loved God, but that he loved us and sent his Son as an atoning sacrifice for our sins. Dear friends, since God so loved us, we also ought to love one another.
> —1 John 4:10–11

> God is love. Whoever lives in love lives in God, and God in him.
> —1 John 4:16

⊪⊪⊪ Seismic Shift Suggestion ⊪⊪⊪

Worth Remembering. We forget how much God loves us. All through the Bible, God teaches his followers to set up reminders and memorials to help them stay focused on his truth. Write one or more of the following passages on a card or sheet of paper. Then post this reminder somewhere you will see it every day. You might want to put it on the refrigerator, on the bathroom mirror, or in your purse or wallet. Each time you see this reminder, read it slowly and celebrate how much God loves you. As you meditate on how God feels about you, commit to follow his will and not the expectations of people.
Passages: John 3:16; Romans 8:38–39; 1 John 3:1; 4:10–11

Have you come to faith in God through his Son, Jesus? If you have, you are God's beloved. If you have not, his arms are open, and he longs to lavish love on you. Receive his love, believe it, and walk in joy knowing that through faith in Jesus Christ, you can be declared the beloved of God! Hear the words of Scripture echo through the centuries: "No, in all these things we are more than conquerors through him who loved us. For I am convinced that neither death nor life, neither angels nor demons, neither the present nor the future, nor any powers, neither height nor depth, nor anything else in all creation, will be able to separate us from the love of God that is in Christ Jesus our Lord" (Rom. 8:37–39).

God Is My Father, and I Am His Child • • • • • • • • • •

When we see ourselves through God's eyes and discover who we really are, we discover we are his precious children. It is one thing to be loved by a stranger, but the love of a heavenly Father meets a deep need in each of our hearts.

Over the years, I have ministered in jails and prisons. It still sends chills down my spine each time I hear door after door slam shut and lock behind me. In our local jail, the guards lead us into the "pod" where the prisoners live, then they lock us in and leave. Once we are in the pod, the main guard opens all the cell doors by pushing a button from his remote location. The men come out and join us if they want to be part of the service.

One of the Sundays I was scheduled to preach happened to be Father's Day. In my training, I had been informed that many men in jail did not have a father involved in their lives. Or if their father was around, he might have been abusive or neglectful. I had been told, in no uncertain terms, not to refer to God as Father and that imagery of God as a father could be counterproductive to our efforts to minister to these men.

As I prepared for this Father's Day message, I felt convicted that these men needed to know they are children of a loving heavenly Father. I knew I would be taking a risk, but I felt in my heart that God wanted them to know his fatherly love. When I began preaching, I said a quiet prayer, and then I told these hurting and lonely men what I knew God wanted them to hear.

As I preached, I said, "Today is Father's Day. I know some of you might not have fond feelings for your father. I know others might have been deeply hurt by your dad. I also want you to know that I have been told I am not supposed to refer to God as Father when I preach here in the jail, but today I am going to break that rule!" I think they liked the fact the preacher was being a little rebellious.

|||||| **Seismic Shift Suggestion** ||||||

Say It Every Day. Each morning when you wake up and look in the mirror, say these words out loud:

I am loved by God!

Even if you have bed-head and sleep dust in your eyes, even if you don't believe it the first time you say it, stay there, looking at the reflection of a child loved by God and say it until you know it's true:

I am loved by God!

I am loved by God!

I went on to say, "None of us has a perfect father. Not one of us. The good news is, we do have a perfectly loving Father in heaven. Maybe your earthly father let you down, but your heavenly Father will not! Your earthly father might have abandoned you, but your heavenly Father promises, 'I will never leave you nor forsake you' (Josh. 1:5). Your earthly father might have been downright mean or even abusive, but God loves you more than you can begin to know. Through his Son, Jesus Christ, God invites you to come home to him."

I told them about the rebellious, wandering son who left home with his dad's money, wasted it, and eventually came back home, broken and penniless. I explained that the dad's response reflects the heart of our heavenly Father, and how when the father in the story saw his son, he was "filled with compassion for him; he ran to his son, threw his arms around him and kissed him" (Luke 15:20). I can't print the whole text of my prison message, but what happened as I spoke to these men was nothing short of a miracle. They did not get angry because I told them about their heavenly Father. Some of them had tears streaming down their faces. Others were smiling from ear to ear. They were warm and responsive.

Since that day, I have been profoundly aware that these men were no different than you and me in our need to know that the God of heaven wants to embrace us as his precious children. We are all broken; we are all imprisoned by our sin. None of us has a perfect earthly father. But we have a Father in heaven who loves us ferociously!

He will not stop. He will never relent. His love can't be quenched!

When we wake up each morning aware and amazed that we are God's beloved children, we are making the shift to a new way of living. People might get angry with us and treat us poorly. Things might not go our way. We might not get the performance evaluation we want. Life can be hard and even painful. But through faith in Jesus Christ, we become children of God. No struggle in this life, no judgment by another person, and no prison wall can keep God's fatherly love from filling our hearts and lives.

The Joy of Being

We can travel one of two paths in this life. One is doing, and the other is being. We can get on the fast track of doing and spend our whole lives trying to measure up. We can perform, work hard, and give all we have to try to become what others feel we should be. This path leads to an anxious life in which we are forever chasing the proverbial carrot on the stick. This is clearly not God's plan for his children.

The path God wants us to take leads to a deep understanding that we are his precious children. This pathway of being leads to joy because we discover our worth and meaning in who we are in Christ rather than in what we do. You might never be the president of a multinational company, win a beauty contest, or be chosen to be the wake-up fairy. But when you know the love of God, all of these things pale in comparison.

Our world is filled with signposts pointing down the road of doing. From the cradle to the grave, the constant message is the same: perform, measure up, be a winner, succeed! God has also posted signs along the way. He sent his only Son to show us that we are more valuable than we have ever dreamed. Sometimes God is more subtle than the world. He often whispers. If we slow down and listen, we will hear his voice: "I love you my child. Your value to me is not based on what you do. Rest in me. Receive my love and grace. Find joy in the simple reality that my love for you will always be enough."

FOR REFLECTION • • • • • • • • • • • • • • • • • •

Sometime in the next few days, set aside ten to fifteen minutes. Find a quiet place where no one will interrupt you. Then ask yourself the following questions:

- What standards or criteria do I use to determine my personal value?
- When I think about my life and what makes me feel valued and worthwhile, whose eyes am I looking through?

FOR PRAYER •

- Ask God to help you learn to see yourself through his eyes and not through your own eyes or the eyes of others.
- Thank God that his love for you is based not on your goodness but on his grace.

Chapter THREE

The Seismic Shift from Somberness to Celebration

Rejoice in the Lord always. I will say it again: Rejoice!

—Philippians 4:4

Nehemiah said, "Go and enjoy choice food and sweet drinks, and send some to those who have nothing prepared. This day is sacred to our Lord. Do not grieve, for the joy of the LORD is your strength."

—Nehemiah 8:10

I consider that our present sufferings are not worth comparing with the glory that will be revealed in us.

—Romans 8:18

Joy is a choice! It really is.

If you're not sure, just ask Esther and Betty. Both of these women discovered that life does not always work out the way we plan and that joy rarely flows freely throughout a lifetime. As a little girl, Esther experienced the pain of severe burns on her chest and neck when her clothes caught on fire while playing with fireworks on the Fourth of July. The scars never went away, and her self-consciousness because of them lingered for over seven decades. As a young woman, she fell in love and got married, but she ended up going through a painful divorce. Esther's second marriage ended when she received a telegram from the United States government informing her that her husband, who had been missing for six months, was confirmed killed in action in World War II. Although he had poor vision and was not supposed to go into battle, he was mistakenly sent to the front lines and paid the ultimate price. At the tender age of thirty, Esther was divorced, widowed, and a single mom. In her later years, she had a stroke that paralyzed half of her body. Though she lived for another decade, she was never able to walk or take care of herself again. No one would question that Esther faced genuine pain and suffering in her life.

Like Esther, Betty fell in love and married young. Sadly, her husband fell deep into alcoholism, abandoned his family, and eventually died while living on the streets of New York. At only thirty-one, Betty became a widow and was left to raise three little boys alone. Eventually she remarried and had four more children. This presented unique challenges as Betty raised five boys and two girls in a blended family, long before the term *blended family* had been invented and before there were books to help navigate these challenging waters. She faced another tragedy when her second son was killed in a car accident. Later in life, Betty had a severe heart attack. She battled to recover and lived for many more years, but the attack had clearly taken a toll. It is fair to say that Betty also experienced her share of pain and sorrow in this life.

As a young single mom, Esther left her home in Flint, Michigan, and moved to Pasadena, California. Betty also transplanted to Pasadena from Scranton, Pennsylvania. In this new place, each had the chance to experience a fresh beginning. As the years passed, these two women both became "little old ladies from Pasadena." But that is where the similarity ended. Although both experienced significant loss and pain, they had radically different responses.

Esther pulled away from people and gave most of her attention to stray cats in the neighborhood. She didn't smile much. Joyous was not a word people used of her. Betty, on the other hand, opened her heart and home to every stray boy and girl who needed a smile, a warm meal, and a hug. Laughter filled her home. Even after her heart attack, Betty's compassionate love and joyful spirit drew people to her. At almost any time, if you walked into Betty's home, you could hear her singing or whistling joyfully.

Though Betty and Esther lived in the same little town for more than four decades, they might never have met if Betty's son hadn't asked

Esther's daughter for her hand in marriage. The merger of these two families provided me with a study in the contrast between joy and joylessness. You see, these two women were my grandmothers.

Every Christmas, my parents would pack my sisters and me into our blue station wagon and drive to Pasadena. We would always go to Betty's house first. We affectionately called her Granny, and her house was filled with light, cheer, laughter, and true Christmas joy. My granny had survived a heart attack, the losses of a husband and a teenage son, and much more, with an enduring commitment to see the good in each day. Her contagious joy overflowed to every person she encountered. And her authentic love for God impacted all of her relationships.

Later each Christmas Eve, we would make the short drive across town to see my grandma, Esther. The feeling in her house was very different. Although we knew deep down that Grandma loved us kids, her home was not a place of smiles, mirth, or joy. As a little boy, I could not explain it, but I knew we all wanted to get back to Granny's as soon as we could. And I can honestly say I think Grandma Esther felt the same way. Going to her house was not an experience to be treasured but a duty to be endured.

||||| Seismic Shift Suggestion |||||

Find a Betty and Learn. Have you ever noticed we become like the people we hang around? This is why parents are so concerned about the friends their children connect with early in life. This principle continues into our adult years. Identify someone in your life who has an enduring, unquenchable joy. Then make a point of spending time with them at least once a month. Watch this person's face and gestures, and soak in their attitude toward life. Ask God to help you become more like them. Let this "joy mentor" lead you to a new way of seeing life.

Looking back, I realize these two women faced many of the same pains and losses. In one case, the furnace of life's suffering produced a heart of compassion, love, and joy. In the other, the struggles and losses of life led to a joyless, isolated, and lonely existence.

As I grew up, I got to see, in living color, that joy is a choice. Some people face incredible pain and suffering in this life and emerge from the ashes like the mythical phoenix with a greater appreciation for what they have and a renewed commitment to joy. Others face similar circumstances and respond with anger and bitterness. For them, a joyful heart and lasting happiness seem impossible to attain, so they stop trying. What is even more staggering is when you meet someone who has countless blessings, abundant financial resources, and more than they could ever need, yet they still can't seem to discover joy. In a day of plentiful resources, great freedoms, longer life spans, and multiplying forms of entertainment, many people still don't experience lasting joy.

God has good news. He is the source of joy and wants to share it freely with us. Joy is the natural disposition of God's heart, and he wants us to be surprised by joy every day of our lives. No matter what we face, if we make the right choices and follow God with our whole hearts, we can experience more joy than we have ever imagined.

The Delight of God

When was the last time you went to a wedding and saw the bride walking down the aisle with a frown on her face? The answer is probably, "Never!" Joy fills a heart in love. A bride's smile lights up the whole room as she walks down the aisle toward her beloved. When love is real, joy flows freely.

Christians, above all people, can live in joy. Why? Because we are loved — deeply, passionately, and eternally! The love of God pours over our lives in such surplus that it cascades into the lives of those around us. There should be a bounce in our step inspired by joy. Our eyes should beam like a child's on Christmas morning. The very tone of our voices ought to reflect the inexpressible delight we carry in our hearts.

Followers of Jesus are people of joy. There are certainly times for sobriety, but the natural disposition of our hearts is unbounded rejoicing. The apostle Paul taught that when the Holy Spirit of God is unleashed in our lives, fruit grows naturally. The first two fruits of the Holy Spirit are love and joy (Gal. 5:22). These two go hand in hand. When love overflows, joy is the natural by-product. Consider these words of David: "You turned my wailing into dancing; you removed my sackcloth and clothed me with joy, that my heart may sing to you and not be silent. O Lord my God, I will give you thanks forever" (Ps. 30:11–12).

God is delighted when he sees his children walk in joy. He celebrates when we dance, sing, and take off our sackcloth. One of the greatest gifts we can give our heavenly Father is a life freely flowing with joy.

Never Alone •

When Jesus entered human history, God walked among us. He knew loneliness, hunger, the unspeakable physical pain of the passion, rejection by friends, temptation, and every hurt we experience. Jesus also felt depths of pain we can't imagine. He felt the crushing weight of bearing the sin of all humanity when he was crucified. God sees and understands our pain more than we know. Yet he still calls us to live in joy.

One of God's greatest servants, the apostle Paul, stands as an astonishing model of joy in the midst of a life filled with challenges and pain. In his letter to the Christians in the city of Corinth, he gives a partial list of the suffering he faced as a result of following Jesus. He writes,

> I have ... been flogged more severely, and been exposed to death again and again. Five times I received from the Jews the forty lashes minus one. Three times I was beaten with rods, once I was stoned, three times I was shipwrecked, I spent a night and a day in the open sea, I have been constantly on the move. I have been in danger from rivers, in danger from bandits, in danger from my own countrymen, in danger from Gentiles; in danger in the city, in danger in the country, in danger at sea; and in danger from false brothers. I have labored and toiled and have often gone without sleep; I have known hunger and thirst and have often gone without food; I have been cold and naked. Besides everything else, I face daily the pressure of my concern for all the churches.
>
> —2 Corinthians 11:23–28

This same man, while imprisoned for preaching about Jesus, writes, "Rejoice in the Lord always. I will say it again: Rejoice! Let your gentleness be evident to all. The Lord is near. Do not be anxious about anything, but in everything, by prayer and petition, with thanksgiving, present your requests to God. And the peace of God, which transcends all understanding, will guard your hearts and your minds in Christ Jesus" (Phil. 4:4–7).

A modern reader might wonder if Paul had some kind of personality disorder. How could a man who suffered what he did still declare, "Rejoice in the Lord always"? Maybe he had been beaten one too many times and his words were just the rants of a body and mind pushed past the boundaries of human endurance. How is it possible for a person to undergo high levels of physical and emotional pain and still live with an authentically joyful heart?

For Paul the answer was obvious. Joy is based on a life-changing, hope-giving relationship with Jesus, not on the circumstances we face. Our situation might change from day to day, but Jesus is always present, loving, and faithful. When we know Jesus, even the greatest suffering of this life can't begin to compare. Paul writes, "I consider that our present sufferings are not worth comparing with the glory that will be revealed in us" (Rom. 8:18).

Joy Busters

Why isn't there more joy in our lives, in the church, and in our world? If God's natural disposition is joy, and if his children are called to be like him, why so little celebration and so much somberness?

For one thing, the presence of real pain and suffering in this life dampens our joy. Because God understands our pain, he knows there will be times of sorrow and heartache. He does not want us to pretend we are joyful during times of loss and pain. Just read the book of Psalms, the prayer book of God's people, and this becomes apparent. Over a third of the psalms are what scholars call laments. These are painfully honest expressions of hurt, loneliness, sorrow, fear, spiritual struggle, and even anger. God has given us a record of these prayers to help us in times of mourning. God never asks us to put on a false front. The key is knowing that these times will come to an end. Joy can and will return.

God wants us to know that joy, thankfulness, and confidence in him can remain deep in our hearts even in the midst of life's valleys. If you read the lament psalms closely, you will be struck by the presence of amazing expressions of joy and confident trust right in the middle of some of the most heart-wrenching prayers of all time!

Another reason joy is in short supply today is that we trade authentic joy for cheap imitations. Too often we settle for entertainment as a substitute. We want our fancy tickled, our eyes dazzled, and our libido caressed. But we don't want to take the journey of faith that leads to enduring joy. A late night of TV seems like what the doctor ordered after a hurried day of investing in everyone else, but in the end, we feel emptier than when we flopped down on the couch. A discrete sexual encounter holds the promise of lost romance and indescribable excitement but ends up giving birth to the twins of guilt and loneliness. Many people lack joy because they are looking in all the wrong places.

God wants every one of us to experience the seismic shift from somberness to celebration. We don't have to walk through life dominated by sorrow. If we make some adjustments in our hearts and lives, joy will be our constant companion.

The Journey to Joy

Since the apostle Paul experienced profound levels of joy through significant suffering, his example can help us on the journey of joy. This is not a one-way street with only green lights. There will be bumpy roads and traffic jams, and sometimes we will head in the wrong direction. But if we follow Jesus, we will learn more and more about what it means to travel through this life with a growing experience of delight in God. What follows are some lessons from the apostle Paul that will help each of us on our journey.

Forget What Lies Behind

One shift Paul understood was taking our eyes off of the things of the past. In Paul's day, as in ours, people often lost their joy because they were trapped in the muck and mire of the past. Failures, poor choices, or even victories can keep us from walking in the present.

In the movie *Napoleon Dynamite*, Napoleon's uncle Rico lives every day thinking of one thing and one thing only: his desire to return to 1982, which was the best time of his life. It was the year he almost became a high school football hero. He ends up living in emotional limbo because he can't let go of the past. He spends hours filming himself throwing a football to imaginary receivers as if this exercise could recapture the glory of his past. But sadly, it never can.

God wants us to move beyond our successes and failures and to live in the joy-filled opportunities of the present. As we do this, we can press forward to what God has in mind for us today and tomorrow. Paul writes, "Not that I have already obtained all this, or have already arrived at my goal, but I press on to take hold of that for which Christ Jesus took hold of me. Brothers and sisters, I do not consider myself yet to have taken hold of it. But one thing I do: Forgetting what is behind and straining toward what is ahead, I press on toward the goal to win the prize for which God has called me heavenward in Christ Jesus" (Phil. 3:12–14 TNIV).

The language of this passage comes from the sports arena. Paul writes of straining ahead and winning a prize. He paints a picture of runners racing to the finish line. Their eyes must be focused ahead, not on the runners behind or even beside them. In the movie *Chariots of Fire*, there is a powerful scene in which Harold Abrahams, one of the fastest runners who competed in the 1924 Olympics, is winning a race by just the slimmest of margins. At the last moment, he turns his eyes off the finish line and glances back. In that fraction of a second, another runner passes him and Abrahams loses the race. As he and his coach look at the photo finish, he realizes the prize would have been his if he had kept his eyes on it. In that moment, he vows never to look back again.

The apostle Paul records these words as a reminder to every generation. When we spend our time living in the past, we risk losing the race God has set before us. When we forget what is behind and focus on what lies ahead, we find unspeakable joy.

Accept God's Forgiveness

As we live free from the past and race toward the future, we declare we are forgiven, washed clean, and made new through faith in Jesus Christ. Paul puts it this way: "Therefore, if anyone is in Christ, he is a new creation; the old has gone, the new has come!" (2 Cor. 5:17).

These words are shocking when we understand Paul's past. Before coming to faith in Jesus, Paul had been an enemy of the church. He had given approval for the public stoning of an early church leader named Stephen. Paul bore the guilt of knowing that this godly man had died as he looked on and gave approval for mob violence (Acts 6:1–10; 7:54–8:1). He had traveled from town to town with the goal of persecuting Christians, imprisoning followers of Jesus, and devastating the church. Later in life, Paul looked at all he had done before he knew Jesus and wrote, "Here is a trustworthy saying that deserves full acceptance: Christ Jesus came into the world to save sinners—of whom I am the worst. But for that very reason I was shown mercy so that in me, the worst of sinners, Christ Jesus might display his unlimited patience as an example for those who would believe on him and receive eternal life. Now to the King eternal, immortal, invisible, the only God, be honor and glory for ever and ever. Amen" (1 Tim. 1:15–17).

Paul's life was transformed when he realized there was no sin, rebellion, or hard-heartedness that can't be overcome by the love of God. The apostle learned what we all learn when we accept the forgiveness of sins that comes through Jesus Christ: God's grace is undeserved. But when it is received as a gift, the worst of sinners is washed whiter than snow.

Some followers of Jesus struggle to understand and live in the greatness of God's grace and love. Rich came to my office to talk about his struggle to accept God's forgiveness. He had fought in the Vietnam War and had done things he did not want to remember, much less tell others about. These things were done in the line of duty, but he still felt guilt and shame. He knew God forgave him, but he had times when he struggled to forgive himself. As Rich shared his story, I longed for this brother to walk in the freedom and joy of forgiveness. I had no idea what to say. There is no easy answer or quick fix for a man struggling with such deep guilt. During our conversation, the Holy Spirit put a thought in my mind and words on my lips that helped this struggling man.

I asked Rich if he was certain God had forgiven him. He gave an emphatic, "Yes!" I asked him again, if he was confident, in the core of his heart, that the forgiveness of Jesus Christ on the cross was enough to wash his sins away. He looked at me as if I was a bit dense and said, "I have no problem understanding God's forgiveness; my problem is I can't forgive myself."

|||||| Seismic Shift Suggestion ||||||

Let It Sink In. Maybe you have a sin or secret from the past that you just can't let go. You know God forgives you. Through Jesus he has promised that your sins are washed away, and you believe him. But you can't seem to forgive yourself. Commit to memorize these three short passages from the Bible:

- Psalm 103:12
- Isaiah 1:18
- Galatians 2:20

Then, when the sins of the past creep up and poison your present, meditate on these verses. Remind yourself that God has forgiven you and that you are not in a place to argue with him. Simply accept his verdict, "Not guilty!"

What I said in response to his assertion could have angered or offended him, but it did not. I said, "You have to forgive yourself. You have no other option. If God has forgiven you, and you refuse to forgive yourself, you are placing yourself above God."

He stared at me in stunned amazement. "I never looked at it that way. That's true. I do have to forgive myself."

Since then, Rich has started a joyful journey of self-forgiveness that is leading to freedom and the lifting of the depression that would descend on his life with no warning and steal his joy. He committed to memorize a few Bible passages about forgiveness and meditate on them any time the darkness of guilt came over him.

All who follow Jesus learn to walk in joy because we know our sins have been taken far away from us. How far? Try to get your mind around this reality. The psalmist says, "As far as the east is from the west, so far has he removed our transgressions from us" (Ps. 103:12). How far is the east from the west? The answer is shocking. They are infinitely far from each other. When this truth sinks in, joy is on the horizon.

Keep Things in Perspective

One more lesson we learn from Paul is that making comparisons can be helpful, when it is a comparison between the struggles of this life and the joy-filled blessings God gives to his children. Though Paul had faced multiple beatings, the breaking of trust in his friendships, persecution from his own people, and more suffering than most of us can imagine, he could still boldly state, "Therefore we do not lose heart. Though outwardly we are wasting away, yet inwardly we are being renewed day by day. For our light and momentary troubles are achieving for us an eternal glory that far outweighs them all. So we fix our eyes not on what is seen, but on what is unseen. For what is seen is temporary, but what is unseen is eternal" (2 Cor. 4:16–18).

Paul also said, "I consider that our present sufferings are not worth comparing with the glory that will be revealed in us" (Rom. 8:18).

Paul lived with an unyielding commitment to joy. He knew that the heavenly home awaiting him was greater than any dwelling place on this earth. He understood that the glory he would receive in eternity was already spilling into the present and that it was far superior to the praise of people in this life. Paul was convinced that if the struggles, suffering, and pain of this life could all be placed on one side of some heavenly scale, and the unseen blessings of God in this life and eternity could be placed on the other side, it would be no contest. The scale would tip with infinite weight toward the eternal blessings and joy God promises to all who follow him.

A Community of Joy

If God's people are joy-filled, the church should be the happiest place on the face of the earth. People should be drawn to congregations because of the sheer overflow of love, celebration, and joy that cascades into the community. The church should be famous, even notorious, for the excessive and extravagant joy experienced every time they gather.

Just as restaurants all over the world that specialize in barbeque boast "Best Ribs in the World" or "World-Famous Ribs," the church should be able to post a sign that says, "Most Joyful Place in the World" or "Need Joy? Inquire Within." And a world starved for authentic joy would flock to congregations to experience the refreshment their souls long to receive.

The problem is that many churches would be accused of false advertising if they posted such a sign. If we are honest, many of our congregations are joy-impaired. But it does not have to be this way. As we grow in joy, our congregations will naturally reflect the spirit of those who attend. The church is simply the gathered people of God. If we come together as people of joy, the church will be a place of delight.

|||||| **Seismic Shift Suggestion** ||||||

Bring It In. When you gather in your church, is there an overflowing sense of joy? If not, commit to bring it with you. With Jesus at your side, greet people with a smile. Give a friend a hug. Sing with gusto! Smile at the pastor. Tell someone "God loves you!" Find a first-time visitor or someone you have never met and let them know you are glad they came to worship. Make it your mission to carry the joy of Jesus in your heart and let it show on your face. You might be surprised to discover that joy is contagious. Commit to be a carrier!

Joy can't be bought, manufactured, rented, or hyped up. Every Christian congregation should take time to evaluate their joy quotient. What do visitors feel when they walk into our gathering place? What is their experience when they participate in our worship service? Is there a cold somberness, or an overflowing and contagious joy? Does your worship service cry out, "He is risen! He is alive! The God of love is here!"? Do people experience the power and passion of the living Savior as they gather week by week in your congregation?

Our welcome should be joyous. The way we greet each other and the way we welcome visitors should reflect the heart of our Savior. Our music should ring with rejoicing. This is not a commentary on styles of music; it is about the heartbeat of worship. Great and ancient hymns of the church can be sung in a joyful manner, just as contemporary praise songs are.

Of course, there are times when the appropriate posture and tone of worship is quiet reverence. Some themes, passages of the Bible, and songs can lead us to a place of reflection, repentance, and introspection. But the basic disposition of the Christian heart and congregational worship is joy.

How does God want his children to live? Does the maker of the universe expect his people to have long faces, heavy hearts, and sober dispositions? The answer is an emphatic no! Of all people on the face of the earth, the followers of Jesus should live with the greatest levels of joy. The writer of Ecclesiastes says, "There is a time for everything, and a season for every activity under heaven … a time to weep and a time to laugh, a time to mourn and a time to dance" (Eccl. 3:1, 4).

FOR REFLECTION

- What is one joy buster in my life, and how can I get past this roadblock?
- What is one specific way I can help develop a spirit of joy among the people at the church I attend?

FOR PRAYER

- Ask God to help you walk in freedom from the past. Pray for the ability to know his forgiveness and for the strength to forgive yourself.
- Make a list of ten sources of joy in your life, and use this list to guide you in prayers of thanks.

Part 2

Shifts That Expand Your Faith

Cameron was only nine years old, and his family was planning to fly on a big jet to Florida. In his young heart, he was torn. On the one hand, he was going to Disney World; this was exciting. On the other hand, he had to get on an airplane; this was scary. Anticipation filled his heart because the trip included a cruise with his favorite Disney characters; this was a dream come true. But fear filled his mind when he thought about leaving the ground and going very high in the air. Cameron was preparing to take a family vacation he would never forget, but he could not shake the thought that once the airplane was in the air, it had to come down.

Since he is a thoughtful and creative boy, Cameron came up with a plan to deal with his fear of flying. He made a list of the things he could do that would help him make it through the experience. He would keep his eyes off himself and on something else. In the days before the trip, he told his parents, and many other people, how he would be dealing with the whole flying thing.

"When the plane takes off, I will look at all the other people. While we are in the air, I will hold onto the two armrests really tight. Then when we are coming down, I will grab my dad's arm as tight as I can and look up at him."

That was Cameron's plan.

After the trip, his father, Mike, gave an update on how the flight went. The truth is, all of Cameron's tactics except for one went out the window as soon as the plane started to move. He never looked at the other travelers to distract himself at takeoff. He did not create imprints of his little fingers in the armrests while the plane was in the air. The only part of the plan he used was holding onto his father's arm and looking up at him. The way this little boy made it through this scary experience was to cling to his father and take his eyes off himself.

I think Cameron's final flight strategy is a great way to get through the highs and lows of life. The best thing we can do is hold onto our Father and keep our eyes riveted on him. This is the essence of faith. When we focus on ourselves or on the things that cause us fear, the trip will always be bumpy and fear-filled. But when our eyes shift from ourselves to God, though the journey might still have bumps and fearful experiences, we have a whole new perspective.

In this section, we will look at three ways we can keep our eyes focused on our heavenly Father. Each of these will expand our faith and grow our love for God. They are:

1. Going deeper in worship.
2. Feasting on the Word of God.
3. Learning to communicate with God in prayer.

When we make shifts that help us grow in these areas, we experience high levels of personal transformation, and the trip through this life feels a lot safer.

Chapter FOUR

The Seismic Shift from Me to God

In the year that King Uzziah died, I saw the Lord seated on a throne, high and exalted, and the train of his robe filled the temple. Above him were seraphs, each with six wings: With two wings they covered their faces, with two they covered their feet, and with two they were flying. And they were calling to one another:
"Holy, holy, holy is the Lord Almighty;
the whole earth is full of his glory."

—Isaiah 6:1–3

He must become greater; I must become less.

—John 3:30

Therefore, since we are surrounded by such a great cloud of witnesses, let us throw off everything that hinders and the sin that so easily entangles, and let us run with perseverance the race marked out for us. Let us fix our eyes on Jesus, the author and perfecter of our faith, who for the joy set before him endured the cross, scorning its shame, and sat down at the right hand of the throne of God. Consider him who endured such opposition from sinful men, so that you will not grow weary and lose heart.

—Hebrews 12:1–3

Myopia is a form of nearsightedness in which a person has a hard time seeing things unless they are very close. Those who struggle with myopia understand that their vision of the world is greatly affected by the condition of their eyes. In extreme cases, a person can see things only when they are right in front of their nose, and so their perspective is limited. Their world becomes small.

We live in a time when people are myopic in their attitude toward life. For many folks, all that matters is the very small world of "me" and "mine." Spiritual myopia develops when we see things only from our limited perspective. When we get this disease, the world begins to revolve around us, in smaller and smaller circles. There are many symptoms of this sickness of the soul. If a worship service isn't just what we want it to be, we become critical and negative. We expect others to serve us and don't think often of sacrificing for those in need. We complain freely. In chronic cases, we no longer have room for God; we are wholly centered on our desires, dreams, tastes, and whims. If there is a space for God in our lives, it is only a tiny pigeonhole we squeeze him into, leaving him there until we call on him to fix something we have broken.

Jesus performed many miracles, even healing the blind. God still works this miracle today. He can touch our eyes and remove our spiritual myopia. When this happens, we see his face and learn that the world is a much bigger place than we realized. Our faith expands, and God is no longer just a lucky rabbit's foot we keep in our pocket.

The more we focus on ourselves, the smaller our world becomes. But if we turn our eyes upward from the dusty paths of this world to the glory of heaven, our world becomes bigger, richer, and filled with glory we never imagined. It is time for followers of Jesus to discover the power of shifting our vision from me to God. When we make this seismic shift, our eyes begin to heal, and we start seeing things we never dreamed were possible.

Turn Your Eyes toward Heaven • • • • • • • • • • • • •

The Bible is filled with stories of people who made the seismic shift from me to God. They learned that when their eyes moved from self to the Savior, all of life took on new texture and meaning. The prophet Isaiah experienced personal transformation when he "saw the Lord seated on a throne, high and exalted" (Isa. 6:1). In this moment, his vision of God grew and his awareness of his need for grace became profound. When

Isaiah saw the Lord lifted up in splendor and glory, his life took a new trajectory.

John the Baptist spent years waiting for the Messiah. He was a messenger sent ahead to prepare the way for the Savior. But when his eyes saw Jesus, God in human flesh, he went through a seismic shift. He declared, "He must become greater; I must become less" (John 3:30). John watched as his disciples, men who had become his spiritual protégés, left him to follow Jesus. When this happened, he did not become resentful or angry; he rejoiced. As a matter of fact, he pointed them toward Jesus. In the New Testament, we read, "The next day John was there again with two of his disciples. When he saw Jesus passing by, he said, 'Look, the Lamb of God!' When the two disciples heard him say this, they followed Jesus" (John 1:35–37). John's joy was pointing others to the Savior, not drawing them to himself. This is a shift every Christian must make, and it comes as our eyes move off ourselves and onto God.

Everyone who follows Jesus wants their faith to grow. We want to know that Jesus' teaching about the mustard seed is still valid today. Jesus taught, "I tell you the truth, if you have faith as small as a mustard seed, you can say to this mountain, 'Move from here to there' and it will move. Nothing will be impossible for you" (Matt. 17:20). How big can our faith grow? The answer is simple. Our faith can grow as big as the God we know.

‖‖‖‖ Seismic Shift Suggestion ‖‖‖‖

Create Reminders. Create a daily reminder to turn your eyes back on Jesus. It can be as simple as deciding to recalibrate your focus each time you check your e-mail, hang up the phone, or finish a meeting or a class. Create a regular trigger by picking something you do often during a day. Let this thing remind you to stop and ask God to turn your eyes back where they should be: on his throne.

If we worship a tiny and powerless god of our own making, one we keep tucked away in a box on a shelf, our faith will be small. Those who reduce God to what they can manage find themselves living in fear. But those who worship the Creator of heaven and earth, the mighty God of eternity, have a different vantage point.

C. S. Lewis, in his book *The Silver Chair*, paints a picture of this desire to reduce God to a manageable size. In this portion of Lewis's Chronicles of Narnia, a young girl named Jill has met Aslan, the great lion, face to face. She wants to get to a stream so she can have a drink. But Aslan, the figure of Jesus in Lewis's stories, is blocking the way. So Jill makes a request:

> "May I—could I—would you mind going away while I drink?"
>
> The lion answered this only by a look and a very low growl. And as Jill gazed at his motionless bulk, she realized that she might as well have asked the whole mountain to move aside for her convenience.
>
> The delicious rippling noise of the stream was driving her nearly frantic.
>
> "Will you promise not to—do anything to me, if I do come?" said Jill.
>
> "I make no promise," said the Lion.
>
> Jill was so thirsty now that, without noticing it, she had come a step nearer.
>
> "*Do* you eat girls?" she said.
>
> "I have swallowed up girls and boys, women and men, kings and emperors, cities and realms," said the Lion. It didn't say this as if it were boasting, nor as if it were sorry, nor as if it were angry. It just said it.

What are we to do with a God so big we can't manage him? How do we relate to a Savior who does not follow our instructions? We do what Christians have done for centuries; we fall on our knees and worship. We turn our eyes toward him with confidence that in his sovereign wisdom, he can be trusted. We make the seismic shift from myopic living to placing our full confidence in God.

Overcoming Myopia in Our Worship

Who is the focal point of worship? For far too many people, the honest answer would have to be, "I am!" In particular, when we gather for corporate worship, we can become myopic and think more about ourselves than the God we claim we are worshiping. We can enter a worship service with the goal of being "blessed," "fed," or even "entertained." When this happens, our main concern is, "What will I get out of the experience?" Sadly, there are churches that cater to this self-centered perspective.

Many communities have a number of dynamic and flourishing churches. They preach the Word faithfully and experience the work of the Holy Spirit in their midst, and people joyfully declare, "This is my church home." But in these same communities, there is also a sickness that runs deep in the souls of far too many people. I call it the Church Hopper Syndrome—people jumping from church to church to get what they want out of the experience.

If you asked one of these people, "What church do you attend?" their answer might sound a bit self-centered. "Well, I go to Church A to hear my favorite preacher, but I go to Church B for my small group because they have a great program, and then I like to visit Church C for their fellowship activities, and I go to concerts at Churches D and E." If you probed further and asked if they have a home church, you might hear something like, "I am actually a member of Church F, but I haven't gone there for years."

If you got real personal and asked, "Where do you put down your spiritual roots? Where do you serve? Where do you give? Where do you invest yourself in the lives of others?" you would probably get a confused stare. You see, these people actually believe that the church exists to serve them, meet their needs, and make them happy. And this is the reason most of them are so miserable and empty!

It's like the contrast between the Sea of Galilee and the Dead Sea in Israel. Both are fed by the same source, the Jordan River. The Sea of Galilee is fresh and teeming with life. It receives water but also in turn gives up water. Fresh water flows into and also out of the Sea of Galilee. The Dead Sea is different. It receives fresh water, but it has no outlet. It never gives but only takes. Consequently the water is bitter, poisonous, and cannot sustain life.

I remember traveling through the Holy Land and experiencing this difference firsthand. The day we first stayed by the Sea of Galilee was sunny and warm, and the sky was a piercing blue. I left our tour group, went to my room, and put on my swim trunks. Then I went out and sat on a large stone at the shore. I imagined I was one of the disciples in the first century and had spent the whole day fishing. Then I stood up and jumped into the sea. It was fresh, invigorating, pure. I opened my eyes underwater and could see a great distance. A few days later, we went to the Dead Sea. Before we entered the mineral-filled water, we were warned not to let it splash in our eyes. As we got in, we realized the water was so thick we could actually float on top of it. A group, led by my wife, put together a mock water-ballet show for those on the shore. All of a sudden, a shriek filled the hot afternoon air. A woman had gone underwater and accidentally opened her eyes. The water burned like acid. For over fifteen minutes, this woman cried, howled, and flushed fresh water into her eyes to relieve the pain.

What a dramatic contrast. Two bodies of water fed by the same source. One gives back and stays fresh and alive. The other only takes and earns a much deserved name.

The same is true of those who take and take and then demand more. They become bitter and lifeless. They bounce from one church onto the next looking for something that will meet their ever-rising standards and expanding needs. But they are always disappointed. As you talk with them, it becomes painfully apparent they view church as a place to get their dose of teaching, inspiration, and entertainment, a weekly feed bag strapped to their neck. If they're not getting what they want, it's time to move on. If no one church can meet all of their standards and desires, they will attend two or three in the course of the week.

When the idea of giving back to, investing in, or caring for others is far from our minds, myopia has set in. Worship is no longer about giving God glory and lifting up his name; it is about our wants, needs, and desires.

Imagine if every follower of Christ functioned with this self-centered view of worship. Churches would fold in a matter of weeks. Congregations would be filled with people who demand that their tastes be catered to. True worship would never erupt in our midst.

We are not the center of worship. Worship is about God's glory, his name being lifted up, and his praise being expressed. If we are the center, then it's not worship; it's idolatry. But imagine a worship gathering in which every person has one thing in mind—the glory of God. The consuming passion of each person would be to praise, exalt, and lift up the one true God, the maker of heaven and earth. Dream about a church in which those gathered are committed to learn under the leading of the Holy Spirit, give freely and joyfully, sing with passion, pray with humility, fellowship with tenderness, and glorify God wholeheartedly. What might happen?

Revival would break out. God would show up in power. The world would be drawn to this authentic and anointed worship.

What is most amazing about worship is its upside-down nature. If we gather with our eyes on self and with a desire for personal gain, we will find ourselves empty. If we enter worship with our eyes turned toward heaven and with a single-minded commitment to glorify God, we discover joy and purpose. It's time for God's people to make a seismic shift in our worship as we turn our eyes away from ourselves and onto the one who is exalted on the throne of heaven. Until we do, we will never meet God and share the intimate communion he wants to have with us.

Growing as Worshipers

As we turn our eyes to Jesus, our lives and priorities come into focus. In this process of growing as worshipers, we discover who God is. Then in the light of his glory, we understand who we are. God is looking for worshipers. Jesus said, "Yet a time is coming and has now come when the true worshipers will worship the Father in spirit and truth, for they are the kind of worshipers the Father seeks" (John 4:23). Don't miss those words: "they are the kind of worshipers the Father seeks."

If anybody ever asks, "What is God looking for?" you now have the answer. He is seeking those who will worship him.

One of the greatest gifts we have as followers of Jesus is the joy of worshiping God in the community of his people. We might meet in a small house-church with fifteen or twenty people. Our congregation might be many thousands who gather in a huge auditorium. Size is not the issue. Worship is about God's people meeting for the purpose of giving glory, honor, and praise to the Lamb of God who sits on the throne.

For the rest of this chapter, we will look at some suggestions for engaging more fully when we meet with God's family for corporate worship.

Prepare for Worship

Our experience in worship is greatly impacted by what happens before we meet. If you want to have a Spirit-filled and meaningful worship experience, do all you can to come rested and refreshed. There are some seasons of life in which this is more challenging than in others. When our boys were one, three, and five years old, refreshed had a different meaning than it does today. But there are things we can do to be intentional about preparing for worship. If you attend church on Sunday morning, don't stay up until 2:00 a.m. on Saturday and then wonder why you can't focus during the sermon. Make a point of getting to bed on time and waking up fresh and ready to give your best to God.

||||| **Seismic Shift Suggestion** |||||

Plan. Treat the weekly worship service as a sacred experience, because it is. Decide how you will prepare for worship. Make sure you are rested. If you attend in the morning, get to bed on time the night before. Put a bookmark in the Psalms of Ascent (Psalms 120–134) so you can read a couple before you head to church. Leave early so you are not rushed. Use your drive time as prayer time. Sit down five or ten minutes before the service begins, and use this time to quiet your heart. If this preparation helps you to worship, make it a regular part of your lifestyle.

Plan to meet God before your time of gathered worship. Ask God to speak in power and for the Spirit to be present. Lift up those who will be leading in music and preaching the Word. Invite God to do whatever he wants to do in your life through the worship experience. If you drive to worship with others, use the time to pray together and read Scripture. If you have little children, this can be a precious time for learning to pray together. Some people like to arrive early and sit quietly in the worship space as they prepare their hearts to meet with God and his people. If you want to prepare your heart by reading the Bible, try meditating on the Psalms of Ascent (Psalms 120–134). These are the songs that for centuries the people of God sang as they traveled to Jerusalem for special times of worship.

Along with being rested and prepared, come with joyful expectancy. This was the heart of David when he wrote, "I rejoiced with those who said to me, 'Let us go to the house of the Lord'" (Ps. 122:1). When we gather for worship, God will be present, the Holy Spirit will be at work, Jesus will be lifted up; we can rejoice in this. To help build anticipation, reflect on the amazing things God has done in biblical history and in your personal history. If you want a primer for this experience, read Psalm 136, which gives an overview of many memories the Israelites held in their hearts.

Enter into Worship

Once we have prepared and have arrived at the place of worship, it is time to enter in with our whole hearts. Worship is not a spectator sport. We don't come to sit in an audience while a group of people perform for us. There is an audience in worship, but it is not the congregation; it is

God. We, the people of God, are all on the stage, and God alone is the recipient of the praise we express. This means we should engage our hearts fully as participants. When songs of praise are sung, we join the chorus with passion.

What about the person who says, "I'm not really into the whole singing thing"? It's time for this person to hear the Word of the Lord: "Sing joyfully to the LORD, you righteous; it is fitting for the upright to praise him" (Ps. 33:1). "Praise the LORD. Sing to the LORD a new song, his praise in the assembly of the saints" (Ps. 149:1).

God does not merely suggest or hope that we praise him; he calls us to sing songs of worship. Even if you don't like your voice, you can be sure that God loves it. He made you, including your vocal cords, and he delights when you sing to him.

‖‖‖‖ Seismic Shift Suggestion ‖‖‖‖

Get a Notebook. Buy a journal or a small notebook and for a month keep notes during the sermon. Write down what you learn, and review these notes during the week. Studies show that our learning retention goes up considerably when we not only hear but also write down what we hear.

He also looks for us to open our hearts as the Word is preached. We are to be humble and receptive as the Holy Spirit speaks through the sermon. Commit to bring your Bible when you gather for worship. If it will help you stay focused, take notes during the message. Write down key lessons and how you believe God wants you to respond to his Word.

As prayers are lifted, don't tune out and make a shopping list for the coming week. This is a time to engage and to agree in prayer together. If you ever find yourself shifting into autopilot during corporate worship, cry out to God to help you enter in with all your heart, soul, mind, and strength. Speak to God openly and freely as you worship. Tell him your joys and your sorrows.

Worship is about giving of ourselves to God. He takes delight in you as you sing, receive his Word, pray, and praise God. Also, be ready to give of your resources as an offering of praise. We will look at this topic later, but it is important to remember that giving tithes and offerings is a privilege and an important part of our worship.

Finally, our worship does not end with the closing prayer or benediction. Worship is a condition of our heart. We can't confine worship to a set time of the week in a certain place. We are God's worshipers at all times and in all places. But in those special times that we gather with other followers of Jesus for community worship, our vision is changed. God performs spiritual surgery to cure us of our myopia, and we see the world through his eyes, not ours. We are freed from fixating on ourselves and are swept into the majesty of the God who made us, loves us, and deserves our worship. This is a faith-expanding experience we can have over and over. What a gift!

FOR REFLECTION

- How has spiritual myopia impacted my vision? What can I do to battle this?
- Have I been swept into the Church Shopper Syndrome? If so, what can I do to shift my attention from myself and to God?

FOR PRAYER

- Ask God to heal your vision so you can see him more clearly and learn how to keep your eyes off yourself and fixed on him.
- Ask the Holy Spirit to move in powerful ways in and through those who preach the Bible, lead worship, pray, and serve in any way during your church services.

Chapter FIVE

The Seismic Shift from Snacking to Feasting

Your word is a lamp to my feet
and a light for my path.

—Psalm 119:105

All Scripture is God-breathed and is useful for teaching, rebuking, correcting and training in righteousness, so that all of God's people may be thoroughly equipped for every good work.

—2 Timothy 3:16–17 TNIV

How sweet are your words to my taste,
sweeter than honey to my mouth!

—Psalm 119:103

Do not merely listen to the word, and so deceive yourselves. Do what it says. Anyone who listens to the word but does not do what it says is like a man who looks at his face in a mirror and, after looking at himself, goes away and immediately forgets what he looks like. But the man who looks intently into the perfect law that gives freedom, and continues to do this, not forgetting what he has heard, but doing it—he will be blessed in what he does.

—James 1:22–25

In the movie *Hook*, a modern telling of the Peter Pan story, there is a scene in which the lost boys and Peter sit down at a banquet table. The boys are licking their chops and drooling, ready to dig in. Peter, who has grown up and forgotten what it is like to be a boy, is looking at a table that appears to be set with empty bowls, dry goblets, and huge platters with nothing on them. Peter can't see the feast.

After a very short "prayer," the lost boys begin to devour the food. The smorgasbord is open, the banquet has started, the feast is on! Moans and groans of approval fill the air, and the boys grin from ear to ear as they partake of the bounty of Neverland.

There sits Peter, nothing on his plate. Everyone else is celebrating and gorging themselves on turkey legs, lamb chops, mashed potatoes, fresh fruit, steaming corn on the cob, and desserts of every color imaginable. Peter has a feast set before him, but he can't enjoy it because he does not believe it is there.

This picture is frightfully familiar. There has never been a time when the Bible has been more accessible than it is today. But there have also been few times in history when people were more biblically illiterate. Here we sit, with a feast of God's Word spread in front of us, and we are starving spiritually. The banquet table has been set for us, but we rarely dig in and enjoy the plentiful provision of God's Word.

In the days of the prophet Amos, God spoke of a time when a famine would strike the land. It would be a famine worse than the times when food and water were scarce. It would be the worst kind of famine ever. Amos records these words of God: " 'The days are coming,' declares the Sovereign Lord, 'when I will send a famine through the land — not a famine of food or a thirst for water, but a famine of hearing the words of the Lord' " (Amos 8:11).

Our generation is facing a famine of God's Word. This is not because the Bible is inaccessible but because we fail to see the feast God has placed right under our noses.

Christian publishers have given the church a gift. We don't have to learn Greek or Hebrew to read the Bible. It is in our common language. And we don't even have to understand all of the thees and thous of older versions; the Bible has been translated in a way that makes sense to modern readers. To make things even more accessible, publishers have provided versions geared to certain age groups. Then, as the cherry on top of the banana split, there are a variety of study and devotional Bibles. We can read Bibles that have daily reflections for men, women, teens, seniors, and even for those who are in a time of recovery. There are giant Bibles that can adorn a living-room table, and little pocket Bibles we can carry wherever we go. It has never been easier to open the Bible and feast on the banquet of truth contained in the pages of this glorious book.

So why is there a famine? Why do so few people actually read the Bible faithfully and seriously? Because when we look at the table, we see empty dishes and cups. We fail to realize that the greatest banquet in history is the Bible, God's Word. Nothing is more satisfying. Nothing will fill us like God's truth revealed in the Scriptures.

In *Hook*, Peter finally sees the breads, roasts, and puddings covering the table. His eyes are opened. It is time for God's children to see his Word as the sustenance our hearts long for. Let the famine come to an end and the banquet begin.

An Invitation to the Feast

The Great Wall of China and the Berlin Wall are historical symbols of division. To a Jewish person in the first century, the curtain that hung in the temple in Jerusalem was just as impenetrable a barrier. This curtain hung in place year after year as a constant reminder that ordinary people could not enter the most holy place. Once every year, the high priest was allowed to pass through the curtain to bring an offering for the sins of the people. When the high priest entered this most holy place, he had a rope tied around his ankle in case he passed out. Then the people could drag him out by the rope, since they were not allowed access to this sacred part of the temple. Though it was only made of cloth, the curtain in the temple might as well have been made of iron.

It was this dividing curtain that was torn in two when Jesus died on the cross. This powerful action signifies a profound spiritual truth. We have full access to our creator God through Jesus' death on the cross. Those who follow Jesus have the same access to God that the priests in the Old Testament experienced: "But you are a chosen people, a royal priesthood" (1 Peter 2:9). This means that Christians have full access to the very throne room of God. Through our relationship with Jesus Christ, nothing stands in the way of our meeting face to face with God anytime and anywhere.

We read that when Jesus died on the cross, "the curtain of the temple was torn in two from top to bottom" (Matt. 27:51). In this life, we will receive many invitations. Wedding invitations tend to be fancy, with multiple envelopes, raised letters, and an RSVP card. For birthdays, the invitations are fun, colorful, and often humorous. When God wrote his invitation for us to come to the banquet table, he sent his only Son. The message came wrapped in human flesh.

> ||||| **Seismic Shift Suggestion** |||||
>
> **A Personal Prayer.** We are transformed when the truth is in our hearts and on our lips. Take time every day for a week to personalize the truth of Hebrews 10:19 – 22 with this prayer:
>
> I have confidence to enter the most holy place by your blood, Jesus. You have opened the way for me through your crucified body. You are both my High Priest and the sacrifice for my sins. So I draw near with a sincere heart, with faith-filled confidence, and with the assurance that I have been cleansed. Thank you for the amazing truth that I am invited into the very throne room of God through your sacrificial death on the cross! Amen.

The apostle Paul tells us, "In him and through faith in him we may approach God with freedom and confidence" (Eph. 3:12). The writer of Hebrews gives this amazing invitation: "Therefore, brothers and sisters, since we have confidence to enter the Most Holy Place by the blood of Jesus, by a new and living way opened for us through the curtain, that is, his body, and since we have a great priest over the house of God, let us draw near to God with a sincere heart in full assurance of faith, having our hearts sprinkled to cleanse us from a guilty conscience and having our bodies washed with pure water" (Heb. 10:19 – 22 TNIV). Again and again the Bible teaches that God's dream for us is to grow in an intimate relationship with him. His arms are open. He is ready to speak to us through his Word, in prayer, and by the still, small voice of his Holy Spirit. The curtain has been torn in two, and we are invited to the table to partake of his goodness.

It is as easy as taking some time each day to open the Bible and read it. As a priest of God, you don't have to wait until Sunday for the pastor to tell you what the Bible says. Those who partake only of the spiritual food provided in the Bible on Sundays at a church service will end up spiritually malnourished. No one can live on a single meal a week. God sets the table for us every day by providing his Word, the Bible. We need to get beyond a Sunday meal and partake every single day.

Ask God to be your teacher, and dig in! But remember, it is important to plan and prepare what we are going to eat. When we want to enjoy a good homemade meal, we have to shop for groceries, prepare and cook the food, and set the table, and then we get to partake in the feast! As we grow in spiritual maturity, it is important to plan what we will read in the Bible and when we will spend this time with the Lord, and to follow through with studying God's Word regularly.

Don't get me wrong, I am a preaching pastor, and I believe that gathering with God's people for worship and study of the Word is a key part of our spiritual growth. But a meal once a week is not enough! Daily time in God's Word is a key to a growing life of faith. Maturity comes when we learn to feast on God's Word. This daily food will help us become strong and healthy. In the same way that failing to eat for many days can cause malnutrition, failing to feed on God's Word can make us spiritually weak.

Three People Who Almost Missed the Feast • • • • • •

Brian said, "I can't read the Bible. It is way over my head. There is nothing in it that has anything to do with my life."

His pastor felt bad about Brian's statement but listened and prayed for wisdom. Then he made a suggestion. "Brian, why don't you read just one chapter of the book of Proverbs a day and see what happens. There are thirty-one chapters, so you can read one a day for a month." The pastor knew Brian had never really tried to dig into the Bible. He had just sat in church for years and had decided there was nothing in the Bible for him.

Brian took the challenge. He committed to read Proverbs. After a few weeks, he met with his pastor.

"Well, Brian, did you learn anything?"

Brian looked a little embarrassed and also a little wiser. He said, "Yes, I learned that I am a fool, and so are most of my friends!"

"Why do you say that?" asked the pastor.

Brian's response was honest and insightful. "Because most of the things Proverbs says about a fool apply to me and those I hang out with. Very few things it says about a wise person sounded like me and my friends."

The pastor asked Brian two questions. First, "What are you going to do about it?" Brian had lots of answers that led to some great conversation with his pastor, but more important, they led to changes in his lifestyle.

Then the pastor asked, "Do you still think the Bible has very little to say to your life?"

Brian smiled and admitted, "Now I'm worried it has too much to say!"

. . . .

Susan was talking with her youth leader. She was a new Christian and had made a decent effort to read the Old Testament but had given up. Her youth leader asked her to explain why she had stopped. Susan simply said, "I can make some sense of the New Testament, but I don't get the Old Testament."

In an effort to give Susan a new look at the value of the first two-thirds of the Bible, her youth pastor said, "Why don't you pick any of the thirty-nine books in the Old Testament, and we will open it and read together. Maybe we will discover something that relates to our lives." Susan accepted the challenge and opened to the table of contents in her Bible. She picked a book that sounded particularly ancient and irrelevant. "Let's try Haggai," she suggested. They turned there and read the first verse: "In the second year of King Darius, on the first day of the sixth month, the word of the LORD came through the prophet Haggai to Zerubbabel son of Shealtiel, governor of Judah, and to Joshua son of Jehozadak, the high priest."

"See, that's what I'm talking about," said Susan. "A bunch of ancient people whose names I can't even pronounce!" Her youth leader invited her to give it a few more verses and see if anything connected with her. They read on.

> This is what the LORD Almighty says: "These people say, 'The time has not yet come for the LORD's house to be built.'"
>
> Then the word of the LORD came through the prophet Haggai: "Is it a time for you yourselves to be living in your paneled houses, while this house remains a ruin?"
>
> Now this is what the LORD Almighty says: "Give careful thought to your ways. You have planted much, but have harvested little. You eat, but never have enough. You drink, but never have your fill. You put on clothes, but are not warm. You earn wages, only to put them in a purse with holes in it."
>
> —Haggai 1:2–6

When they hit verse 6, Susan said, "Stop! Read that again.

"That's how I feel all the time," Susan said. She began to pour out her heart. "I feel empty. I feel like I drink but my thirst is never satisfied. I never feel full. I don't ever have enough. And worst of all, I feel like I will never be truly satisfied."

Wow! What insight. Susan and her youth leader dug into the book of Haggai to find out why the people were feeling so empty. Why had they planted so much but harvested little? Why did these people feel like there were holes in their pockets and their souls, just like Susan did?

In their study, they concluded that the people of Israel had their priorities all wrong. They were putting the full force of their time, energy, and resources into themselves. They were building their own houses when God's dwelling place was in shambles. And the prophecy of Haggai made it clear that until they got their priorities straightened out, their pockets would remain full of holes.

At the end of a two-hour conversation, both Susan and her youth sponsor had fallen in love with the book of Haggai. This was not because reading it had made them feel good. It was because it had turned on a floodlight that allowed each of them to see how their priorities had slipped out of line. Through this encounter with God's Word and through the Holy Spirit's conviction, both made some seismic shifts. They also discovered that the first two-thirds of the Bible, the Old Testament, is powerful and relevant.

. . . .

Bill had made a wholehearted commitment to follow Jesus. He had grown up in a home with no faith but had met Jesus and become a new man. Upon his conversion, he fell in love with the Bible. He read it every day and gave his best effort to following what it taught. Then one day, he put down his Bible and refused to read anymore.

When a Christian friend asked him why, he was honest. He said, "I really like reading the Bible, but when I read it, sometimes I feel uncomfortable. It keeps pointing out things I am doing that I should not do. Or sometimes it tells me to start doing things I don't think I really want to do. I started feeling uncomfortable, even a little guilty, so I thought I would stop reading."

Bill's response is both sad and refreshing. It is sad because he gave up reading the Bible, at least for a time. It is refreshing because Bill said what many people feel but rarely articulate. He admitted that the conviction of God's Word can be hard to face. It was Mark Twain who wrote, "It's not what I don't understand in the Bible that worries me; it's what I do understand." This is how Bill felt. He did not complain that the Bible was unclear or ambiguous; his problem was that the words of Scripture cut like a knife and revealed things he did not want to see.

. . . .

Brian, Susan, and Bill all have something in common with the rest of us. If we are not careful, we can miss out on the amazing banquet God has set before us. If we settle for a weekly snack at church and never dig into God's Word between Sundays, it costs us more than we realize. We need to get past all of our excuses and fears, belly up to the table, and partake of the good things God has set before us.

The Action-Packed, Life-Changing, Soul-Moving Word of God

Every time we open the Bible, God is at work. But we don't always feel it. It is much like drinking milk. No one throws back a cold glass of milk and declares, "Wow, do my bones feel stronger!" Strengthening your bones happens over time, not in a moment.

In the same way, as we learn to feast on God's Word, we grow spiritually. There's no stopping it. The wonder and beauty of reading, studying, and meditating on God's Word is that we don't always feel something happening. We don't know what God will do when we sit down at the banquet table of his Word. But the Bible will always impact our life.

There are all kinds of images the Bible uses for itself. Each one points out a unique way the Holy Spirit moves and speaks through the Word. Although there are many more, we can look at five vivid pictures to give us a glimpse of how God works when we dine at the table of his Word.

A Lamp: The Bible Illuminates

Your word is a lamp to my feet
    and a light for my path.
        —Psalm 119:105

In a dark world in which it is easy to trip, stumble, and fall into all kinds of trouble, we need a light to shine on our path. The Bible is this light. When we read God's Word, he shines a light to show us the way. However, we need to remember the context in which this passage was written. In those days, a lamp was usually a small wick in a little bowl of oil. It provided no more light than a candle. If we get the idea that God wants to give us high beams so we can see way down the road, we are missing the point. The light of a single flame illuminates and shows us what lies ahead, but usually only one or two steps down the road.

Sometimes when we read the Bible, it becomes the tool the Holy Spirit uses to give us direction for the next step in our journey. It is amazing how often a follower of Jesus will discover that what they read in God's Word on a specific day provides exactly the wisdom, insight, and illumination needed for what they are about to face.

A Taste of Honey: The Bible Is Sweet

How sweet are your words to my taste,
    sweeter than honey to my mouth!
        —Psalm 119:103

Sometimes we just need to enjoy the sweetness of God's love, grace, peace, and the encouragement he wants to give. There are times when we open the Word of God and it is sweet like the taste of honey. On the days when this is our experience, we might not come away with any life-changing application. We might not nail down some deep theological truth. There are times we won't even remember exactly what we read. All we know is it was good to be in God's presence, and the truth he spoke to our heart was sweet and wonderful.

A Training Manual: The Bible Equips

All Scripture is God-breathed and is useful for teaching, rebuking, correcting and training in righteousness, so that all of God's people may be thoroughly equipped for every good work.
        —2 Timothy 3:16–17 TNIV

The Bible is God's training manual to prepare us for the life he wants us to experience. Notice the key words Paul uses as he writes to his friend Timothy. He says that God's Word will teach, rebuke, correct, and train us. These are active words. The result is that God's people become equipped, ready to do God's work.

There are times when we read the Bible and God specifically prepares us for something he wants us to do. These are wonderful moments when we stand amazed at how practical, relevant, and personal God's Word can be. In these moments, the Bible feels like an instruction manual, giving us guidance for our lives. We might not even know why we need the specific training we are receiving. At that moment, the pieces might not fit together, and our spiritual boot-camp experience makes no sense. But down the road, we discover God's wisdom and look back with thankfulness for the equipping we received through daily study of the Bible.

A Surgeon's Scalpel: The Bible Cuts to Heal

For the word of God is living and active. Sharper than any double-edged sword, it penetrates even to dividing soul and spirit, joints and marrow; it judges the thoughts and attitudes of the heart. Nothing in all creation is hidden from God's sight. Everything is uncovered and laid bare before the eyes of him to whom we must give account.

—Hebrews 4:12–13

This is a tough image but one that is absolutely necessary. There are times when we read the Bible and the truth of God's revelation comes to us like a surgeon's scalpel. We feel the Word cut deep to reveal the cancer of sin that dwells in us. But what we must remember is that God cuts not to wound but to heal. Like a skillful surgeon, he penetrates deep and removes attitudes, uncovers actions, and cuts out evil motives. Nothing is hidden from God, and he will take the razor-sharp edge of his scalpel and operate for our own good.

Those who have gone under the knife and had a successful operation know how thankful they are afterward. It is the same way with the scalpel of God's Word. The Holy Spirit uses it to cut, but after we have healed, we thank God for removing attitudes and behaviors that were killing us from the inside out.

A Sword: A Weapon for Spiritual Warfare

Take the helmet of salvation and the sword of the Spirit, which is the word of God.

—Ephesians 6:17

When Jesus was tempted by the Devil in the wilderness, he pulled out his sword and fought back. In response to each of the Devil's three temptations, Jesus quoted specific passages to counter the attack (Matt. 4:1–10; Luke 4:1–13). We must learn from Jesus' example. We know that each one of us will face spiritual battles. The apostle Paul writes, "For our struggle is not against flesh and blood, but against the rulers, against the authorities, against the powers of this dark world and against the spiritual forces of evil in the heavenly realms" (Eph. 6:12). He goes on to list all kinds of defensive armor. But the primary weapon for this spiritual war is "the sword of the Spirit, which is the word of God" (Eph. 6:17).

When we read the Bible regularly and feast on the truth of God's Word, we are training for the battles that lie ahead. Owning a sword does not make a person a warrior. Having ten swords around the house does not make someone more powerful. Only practice will prepare us for battle. Reading, studying, and knowing God's Word prepares us to stand strong against spiritual attacks. Too many people today have a stack of Bibles around the house but no idea how to use them. It is time to train to fight the "spiritual forces of evil in the heavenly realms." We don't have what it takes to win this battle in our own strength, but when we are armed with the Word of God and are trained to use it, we are ready to fight.

. . . .

How do we know what will happen when we pick up our Bibles and read them? We don't! What we can be sure of is that something will happen.

Maybe one day you open the Word and the surgeon's scalpel works deep in your heart. Another day you open your Bible and feel like you just took a bite of your favorite fruit, a big scoop of great salsa, or a sweet taste of honey. All you know on that day is that it tastes good and you feel blessed! The next day, you open the Scriptures and God places a sword in your hand for a battle you are facing. Another time you read and the light comes on, illuminating the next step in an area of your life. These things, and so much more, can happen when you sit down for a feast of God's Word. We don't ever know what God has planned, but when the Bible is open, seismic shifts are in our future.

Dining Ideas

There are many ways to begin to dig into the Bible. The first step is making time to read it. When we take this step, the Holy Spirit moves in and begins to work. But here are some ideas for how anyone can make the shift from snacking to feasting on God's Word.

A Meal a Day

The best way to grow in God's Word is to take time every day to open the Bible, pray for the Spirit to speak, and then begin reading. This might sound very obvious, but it is essential. If all you do is read one chapter of the Bible or read for ten minutes a day, this constant intake of spiritual sustenance will change your life.

|||||| **Seismic Shift Suggestion** ||||||

Dinner Plans. Make a plan for a daily feast on God's Word. Lay out seven days.

- When will you dine?
- Where will you eat?
- What will be on the menu?

Once you have decided the when, where, and what of your Bible study, tell someone else about your goal and ask them to pray for you. At the end of the week, share with this person what you learned. If you are feeling spiritually nourished from your daily feast, make a dining plan for the next week.

It is wise to pick a place that feels comfortable and a time when you won't be distracted. For some people, the best time is early in the morning. For years, my father-in-law spent his lunchtime in his truck, turning on some quiet worship music and reading his Bible. The cab of his red Chevy became a holy place where he met with God. For others, the evening works best. The key is finding a time when your body is fresh and your mind is sharp.

There are many ways you can study the Bible. Here are just some samples:

- *Read one chapter a day.* If you don't know where to start, begin with Matthew, Proverbs, or the book of James.

- *Read ten minutes a day.* Pick a book of the Bible and plan to read for ten minutes each day.

- *Use a devotional Bible.* Buy a daily devotional Bible that provides passages to read and also devotional reflections. If you use this kind of a Bible, be sure you make the biblical passages your main reading and the devotions a support tool to your Bible reading. Devotions are wonderful, but they are written by people. The Bible is God's Word, so we need to make this the main dish in our spiritual meals.

- *Use the reading guide provided in appendix 1 of this book.* This reading guide will give you six weeks of Bible readings which follow the themes of each of the six sections in this book.

Lock It in Your Heart and Brain

One great discipline is memorizing verses, passages, or sections of the Bible that really speak to your heart. If you are reading and a verse jumps out at you, write it down on a card or a piece of paper. Carry it with you through the day, and go over these words again and again until they are locked in your heart. Doing this pays amazing dividends in our spiritual growth.

The first time I experienced the value of memorizing Scriptures was when I was at the bank, taking care of my checking. I am not one of those people who do weekly finances. I let them pile up and do everything at once. So by the time I had taken care of everything, I had spent about five or six minutes at the window. What I had not noticed was that the teller I was working with was the only one serving the walk-up counter. So while we were conducting our business, a line had formed behind me.

As I walked out of the bank, a man waiting in line called me a name I won't repeat. He muttered it under his breath just loud enough for me to hear. In the next few seconds, a whole world of activity passed through my heart and mind, and I had what I have come to call a Proverbs Moment.

Here is how it transpired. I walked past the man. He made his comment. I paused midstride and began to turn toward him. I was ready to ask him if he wanted to clarify what he was trying to express with his comment. Just as quickly as I hit the brakes and stopped walking, a verse from Proverbs popped into my mind: "A fool shows his annoyance at once, but a prudent man overlooks an insult" (Prov. 12:16).

As this deep truth cut through my heart and mind, I decided to keep walking. All of this happened in a matter of seconds. The only thing those standing in line would have noticed was the man's comment, and my walking past after briefly pausing to glance at him. When I got outside, I actually put both fists up in the air like I had just scored the game-winning points at the buzzer in a big basketball game. I said to myself, *Who's the fool now? And who is the wise man?* Although I was asking myself in a rhetorical manner, the Holy Spirit answered quietly in my heart, *You are growing in wisdom.* This would have never happened had I not committed this passage to memory and allowed it to dwell in my heart.

▪ Praying the Bible

It is a wonderful experience to use the Bible as a prayer guide, using appropriate passages to direct your prayer. You can use the passage as your prayer or just as a springboard to direct you in prayer. (For an example of how to do this, look at the model of praying the Lord's Prayer in the next chapter.) If you have never tried this, some good passages to start with are:

Matthew 6:9–13 (the Lord's Prayer)

Psalm 23

Psalm 19

Psalm 51

Psalm 63

Psalm 123

Ephesians 1:1–10

Colossians 1:3–14

John 17

Let the Word of God guide and shape your prayer life.

▪ Carry Your Bible

No soldier in Jesus' day would have been caught without his sword. In the same way, those who walk with Jesus and who understand they are in a spiritual battle that rages 24/7/365 would not be found without their Bible. We never know when it might be helpful to look up a passage. You can't be sure when your schedule will afford a few moments to open the Bible. You might want to get a small Bible that you can keep in your car, purse, or even in your pocket.

▪ Talk about What You Are Learning

One of the best ways to reinforce what God is teaching you is to share it with others. If you want to revolutionize your spiritual life, find one or two people who are willing to tell you what they are learning in their study of the Bible and who want to hear what you are learning. Imagine what can happen when you know that every day you will be opening God's Word, learning, and then telling one or two other people about what God has said to you.

If you do this regularly, you not only learn from your own studies but also gain the wisdom and insight of others. This habit also creates lines of accountability for each person involved.

⠰ Be a Doer

In the book of James, we read, "Do not merely listen to the word, and so deceive yourselves. Do what it says" (James 1:22). If all we do is accumulate more information, we are missing the point of opening the Bible. God wants to see transformation along with the information. Each time you read the Bible, ask God to show you some way the truth you have learned could impact your life. Maybe it leads you to a prayer of praise. It might cause you to extend a word of encouragement to someone, to serve in a new way, or to adjust an attitude. Sometimes your reading of God's Word will lead to confession and changed behavior. What James is saying is that God's Word has the power to change us. It is the ultimate source of seismic shifts. When we read the Bible and the Holy Spirit speaks to us, and when we are willing to respond, transformation is inevitable.

FOR REFLECTION

- When is my prime time? When is my body fresh and my mind sharp? How can I work to make some of this time available for study of the Bible?
- How have I experienced the Bible as each of the following:

  - A lamp
  - A taste of honey
  - A training manual
  - A surgeon's scalpel

  - A sword

FOR PRAYER

- Ask God to use his Word as a lamp in a dark area of your life.
- Invite the Holy Spirit to use the Bible to operate on your heart. Tell God you desire for him to use the scalpel of the Word to cut for the sake of healing.

Chapter SIX

The Seismic Shift from Monologue to Dialogue

Very early in the morning, while it was still dark, Jesus got up, left the house and went off to a solitary place, where he prayed.

—Mark 1:35

"I tell you the truth, the man who does not enter the sheep pen by the gate, but climbs in by some other way, is a thief and a robber. The man who enters by the gate is the shepherd of his sheep. The watchman opens the gate for him, and the sheep listen to his voice. He calls his own sheep by name and leads them out. When he has brought out all his own, he goes on ahead of them, and his sheep follow him because they know his voice. But they will never follow a stranger; in fact, they will run away from him because they do not recognize a stranger's voice." Jesus used this figure of speech, but they did not understand what he was telling them.

—John 10:1–6

I was fifteen the first time God spoke to me. It happened on a houseboat in the Sacramento Delta in California. That same night, I had received Jesus as Savior and the leader of my life. As I went to bed, I thanked God for his love and gave praise to Jesus for dying on the cross, and then the Holy Spirit spoke. I can still remember exactly what he said: "Spend the rest of your life telling others what you have learned about Jesus or you will be miserable."

I know, it does not sound deeply profound, poetic, or even very much like the kind of thing one expects God to say. But that is what I heard. It did not feel like a threat or an ultimatum, but simply a statement of reality, and it made perfect sense to my young heart.

It was not an audible voice. The words came gently and quietly deep in my heart. I had no doubt who was speaking. The message made perfect sense to a self-centered teenager who had no plans to serve the Lord. I didn't know a lot of things for certain at fifteen years old, but I knew for sure I did not want to be miserable the rest of my life!

I grew up outside the church, and the concept of being a "religious professional" never crossed my mind. However, when God spoke these words, I knew I would spend the rest of my life teaching, preaching, and telling others about Jesus. The next morning, I asked my youth leader what I had to do to become a minister someday. He gave two suggestions. First, he said, "Get a haircut." Then he said, "On a more serious note, you might want to graduate from high school." He knew I had a 0.75 GPA at the end of my sophomore year, and he wanted me to know I should start studying a little harder.

That night on the Sacramento Delta, I was not surprised to hear God speak. I did not question who was talking to me. It seemed natural. Since Jesus had risen from the grave and the Holy Spirit was at work in the world, it made perfect sense that God would speak. I had been told God was like a perfect loving Father. That kind of Father would certainly talk with his kids. Why wouldn't he?

As the years passed, my prayer life was a natural two-way conversation with God. I would tell him my dreams, fears, needs, and praises. He would encourage, redirect, challenge, bless, and teach me. I assumed everyone who knew Jesus engaged in this kind of interaction.

With time I started talking with other Christians who loved Jesus deeply and were passionate about their faith. I discovered that many of them saw prayer as a one-sided conversation in which they told God what was on their hearts or what they needed. They did not expect to hear him speak to them. These people did not lack faith; they just never thought of prayer as a dialogue.

On our first anniversary, Sherry and I had a conversation about this topic. As we were having our morning devotions, we got to talking about prayer. Out of the blue, Sherry asked me, "Why do you talk as if you have ongoing, two-way conversations with God?"

I responded, "Because I do."

She was perplexed and somewhat skeptical. She said, "I have been a Christian most of my life, and my prayer life is not like that. I believe God leads us in the big decisions and at special times, but I don't feel like God speaks to me on a regular basis."

I said, "Have you asked for this kind of communication? Do you expect it? Do you wait on God and listen for him to speak? Do you respond to his promptings?"

She told me this was not how she had learned to pray, but her heart longed for deeper communication with her heavenly Father. I encouraged her to seek this and to ask the Holy Spirit to speak to her in new, fresh, and recognizable ways. She committed to do this.

In the coming months and years, Sherry's prayer life took on radically new dynamics. She grew to recognize God's voice. She listened for his promptings. And she made the seismic shift from a prayer life that was a monologue to one that was a dialogue. Sherry would tell you she has never heard God speak in an audible voice, but she does hear him speak to her consistently and personally.

Do You Believe God Still Speaks?

Most Christians are confident God spoke to people back in Bible times. But for some reason, many have the sense that God stopped speaking a couple of thousand years ago. Or that he speaks only when it comes to the really big life-decisions. The problem is, the Bible does not teach that God stopped speaking at some time in history. God continues to communicate with us in many wonderful ways. And if we learn to listen, we will be surprised at how God can guide our lives.

Jesus taught that sheep recognize the voice of their shepherd. "The sheep listen to his voice. He calls his own sheep by name and leads them out. When he has brought out all his own, he goes on ahead of them, and his sheep follow him because they know his voice" (John 10:3–4). He is our Good Shepherd and still speaks to his followers. He expects us to listen and to follow his direction. Hearing God speak and sensing his leading should be normative for those who call Jesus Savior.

The world might not understand this, but Christians should. Years ago comedian Lily Tomlin asked, "Why is it that when we talk to God it is called prayer, but when God talks to us it is called schizophrenia?" The truth is, talking to God and listening to God are both acts of faith. They are two sides of the same coin. It is time for those who call Jesus their Good Shepherd to learn how to recognize his voice and to follow where he leads.

Hearing God's Voice ●

Some people hear God speak with their ears; others with their heart. Still others simply feel promptings or divine nudges. God chooses to speak in various ways to different people. The key is for us to recognize his voice and follow his leading.

■ The Bible

The primary way God speaks to his followers is through the Bible. It is his Word at all times to all people. The truth in the Bible never changes. As we read the Scriptures, hear a sermon, participate in a small-group Bible study, or talk with others about God's Word, the Holy Spirit speaks to us.

Remember the time you were reading the Bible and a passage came alive in a fresh way? That was God speaking. The time you read a section of the Bible and experienced a deep conviction of sin, maybe even tears of repentance? God was talking. When you read the Bible and experienced a sense of God's blessing and favor, this was a word from the Lord. These same things happen during a sermon or in a Bible study with friends. The Holy Spirit of God speaks through the words of the Bible. We need to be ready to hear and respond.

■ Other People

Another way God speaks to us is through the words, lives, and example of others. God will give us a word of conviction, challenge, or rebuke through another person. They don't even have to be a Christian.

"What?" you ask. "Can God work and speak through someone who is not yielded to his lordship?" If you are not sure, just read about how God used King Cyrus, a pagan leader, to accomplish his purposes (Ezra 1:1–4; 5:13–16; Isa. 44:28–45:1). Or consider how God spoke through Balaam's donkey in the book of Numbers (Numbers 22). God can use anyone he wants to speak a word to his children. Our part is to listen and to learn to recognize his voice.

Many years ago, my wife and I sensed that God might be leading us to move from our home and church in California to begin a new season of ministry. We had not talked to very many people about this because we were just starting to feel this prompting. Though God spoke in many ways to give us direction, one of the most profound moments came when a hard-core atheist friend told us, out of the blue, "You won't be at this church in six months!" When we asked him where he came up with that, he just said he knew it. Although this man did not know Jesus, he loved us because we had cared for his children through the church youth ministry. The last thing he wanted was for us to move out of state and out of his kids' lives. But the word he spoke was clearly from the Lord, and we recognized what he said as another confirmation that God was preparing us for a move.

Although God can speak through anyone, it is the better part of wisdom to listen closely for God's voice when you are with godly people he has placed in your life. Make it a point to talk and listen to those who have walked with Jesus for many years. When you sense God's leading in your life, ask these people to pray for you and to share anything God places on their hearts. You will be amazed how often they hear some of the same things you are sensing from the Lord. This will help confirm that God is at work.

Circumstances

God also speaks through circumstances. He is good at closing and opening doors. God will throw up a roadblock, and in doing this he is saying, "Don't go that way." At other times, God will kick a door wide open and the circumstances give a clear indication you ought to move forward. It is critical to realize that an open door is not always a call from God. But it should certainly cause you to pray and to investigate how God might be leading.

|||||| Seismic Shift Suggestion ||||||

Time to Remember and Recognize. Think back over your life. Identify some of the ways God has spoken to you and led you through the Bible, other people, circumstances, his still, small voice, and any other way. Thank him for leading you. Also, reflect on how you heard his voice in the past so that you will recognize it with greater clarity in the future.

At one point when our family made a major move, we were investigating the possibility of buying a house. For the first eight years of our marriage, we had lived in an apartment and then in a church-owned house. We did not think we would ever be able to own a home of our own. But a man in the church told us he felt God wanted him to help us get into our own place. One option he gave was for his company to build a house at their cost. We still took time to pray about this, but it sure had the sound of being a word from God. Our prayers confirmed what circumstances seemed to be indicating, and that home became a blessing to us and our three boys.

A Still, Small Voice

Another way God speaks is through the still, small voice of his Holy Spirit. It might not be a voice you hear out loud, but it is the Spirit speaking. This can be a word to lift our spirits during a hard time. It might be a conviction of hidden sin and a call to repentance. Sometimes it is an affirmation of God's love. In many cases, it will be a word giving direction in a specific area of life. Every follower of Jesus needs to learn how to recognize the way the Holy Spirit speaks, prompts, and directs. With time, the voice of the Spirit will be just as recognizable as the voice of a good friend who calls on the phone. You know who it is right when they begin talking.

Dreams and Visions

The Bible teaches that God can speak through dreams and visions. This was true in the Old Testament and confirmed again in the New. In Peter's sermon at Pentecost, he quoted the prophet Joel: "In the last days, God says, I will pour out my Spirit on all people. Your sons and daughters will prophesy, your young men will see visions, your old men will dream dreams" (Acts 2:17).

Although some Christians today do not feel comfortable with the idea, the Bible makes it clear that visions and dreams are still valid ways for God to speak. I have never had a dream or vision that I felt was God speaking to me, but very godly people I respect have heard God speak in these ways. We need to be careful not to limit our understanding of how God communicates with his children. He is much bigger than we are, and his ways are high above ours.

Learning to Listen to God ● ● ● ● ● ● ● ● ● ● ● ● ● ● ● ●

A leader in the church came to talk with me. He asked, "How can I know when God is speaking to me? How can I be sure a prompting is really from him?" Usually a question like this is provoked by something, so I asked what started him thinking about this topic. He told me that a week earlier, he felt God was calling him to do something. He didn't do it because he was not positive this prompting was from God. He worried it was just his own idea and that he had attributed it to God.

I told him most of us have felt the same way. I suggested a fairly simple four-step process for determining if something is really a word from God.

Step 1: Identify the Source

The first thing to do when we sense God is speaking is to determine the origin of what we are hearing. In most situations, there are three possible sources. The voice speaking can be of God, Satan, or self. We need to ask, Is what I am hearing the kind of thing that I would say, that God would say, or that the Enemy would say?

||||| **Seismic Shift Suggestion** |||||

Asking Good Questions. Spend some time listening in prayer. Ask specific questions and wait quietly for God to answer. Here are some questions to get you started:

- Who is one person in my life that needs a word of encouragement?
- What would you have me say to this person?
- What is one way I need to express your love by serving others?
- What is one area of sin in my life you want me to turn from?
- What do you want to say to me about your love today?

In the case of the man I was speaking with, I asked him, "What did you feel God was calling you to do?"

He said, "I felt a very strong leading to spend time praying and fasting for a need in someone's life."

I asked him, "Do you feel Satan would push you to do this?"

He said, "No way!"

Then I asked if he was prone to fasting and praying in his own power. He laughed and said, "Never!" So we both came to the fairly logical conclusion that this leading most likely came from God.

Step 2: Use the Scripture Test

Once we have reflected on the source of what we are hearing, we need to test it against the teaching of the Bible. God's Holy Spirit will never lead us to do anything contrary to his will revealed in the Scriptures. Never! We need to evaluate what we have heard against the standard of God's Word.

As I talked with my friend who felt led to pray and fast, we asked the question, Is this prompting consistent with biblical teaching? The answer was a strong affirmation. The Bible is filled with examples of people praying and fasting during times of need. So we moved to step 3.

Step 3: Take Action

Once we have determined that God is the most likely source of what we are hearing and we have tested it against Scripture, we are ready to move into action. This could be performing an act of service, changing a behavior, giving a sacrificial gift, seeking reconciliation in a broken relationship, or countless other things.

|||||| Seismic Shift Suggestion |||||

Learning to Listen. Growing in our ability to hear from and follow God is a skill we must acquire. We will never sharpen this ability unless we use it. So the next time you feel God is prompting you, use the four-step process outlined in this chapter. You might want to invite a wise Christian friend to pray for God's leading in this area of your life. And seek their input as you press forward.

For my friend, it meant he needed to commit to a time of prayer and fasting for the need God had placed on his heart. It was as simple as that.

Step 4: Evaluate, Reinforce, and Remember

After you have taken action, be sure to evaluate what happened. Was there fruit? Was God glorified? Were people blessed and edified? If there is fruit and God was lifted up, you can be confident it was the voice of God speaking. This is not to say there is always measurable fruit. Sometimes our obedience is the fruit. Sometimes the blossoms come much later. The key is that we learn to look back and remember how God communicated. What did his voice sound like? Just like a sheep, record this in your memory bank so the next time God speaks, you recognize his voice with greater clarity.

It is vital that you stop anywhere along the way in this process if it becomes clear God is not leading. In step 1, if you feel that the voice you are hearing is the Enemy's, stop. Don't take the process any farther. If it is your own voice, use caution and wisdom. God can speak through our hearts, but our motives are not always pure. In step 2, if you look at the Bible and the prompting you think is from God is contrary to Scripture, stop. The Bible is right and you are wrong. At any point along the way, you can pause to pray for additional insight and the direction of God's Holy Spirit.

Finally, when you look back and are confident God was leading, give him praise. When you see the fruit and blessing of submission to God's direction in your life, be sure he gets the glory. Then keep your heart, life, and ears open and be ready to follow God again.

Learning to Pray with Jesus

One summer, our whole family went on a mission trip to Amsterdam. Each day, we had our three boys read a short portion of the Bible and write down one thing they learned. As they recorded what they learned through their ministry experience, Bible study, and prayer time, they came up with a number of insights.

One of our sons wrote, "Every time we pray, something happens." Wow! He was right. We can't dictate what will happen, but we can create a climate in which God unleashes his power and we are transformed. The problem is, our prayers are often so limited that we never get to see God move in power.

If our prayers are simply a wish list of stuff we want, we will never plumb the depths of communication with God. Those who see prayer as a time to tell God what they want are missing the glory of communication with God. So much more can happen when we enter a time of intimate conversation with God.

It is time for those who walk with Jesus to develop prayer lives that are bigger, richer, and more powerful than simply giving God a Christmas list and waiting for him to deliver the goods. One of the best ways to keep our prayer lives fresh is by using the model Jesus gave.

The Lord's Prayer was never meant to be a mindless chanting of the words Jesus taught his followers. As a matter of fact, just two verses before the Lord's Prayer, Jesus warned his followers not to heap up piles of words and act as if incessant repetition means anything to God. Too many people repeat the same words over and over in prayer, but their mind is in neutral and their hearts are disconnected from what they are saying.

The purpose of the Lord's Prayer (Matt. 6:9–13) is to give direction, a starting point, a springboard for meaningful prayer. Jesus gives examples and basic categories to help us keep our focus on what matters most. In this exemplary prayer, take note that Jesus begins with worship and adoration.

Adoration

Our Father in heaven, hallowed be your name. Praising God and adoring his name should always be central in our prayers. Jesus started here, and so should we. He focused on the holiness of the Father's name. Make space in your prayer life to take delight in God. Meditating on his character can help give shape to your prayers. As we reflect deeply on God's attributes, our eyes move from self to our heavenly Father.

||||| Seismic Shift Suggestion |||||

Learning from the Master. For the next week, use the structure of the Lord's Prayer to guide you as you speak with God. Don't just recite it from memory, but move deep into each area of prayer. If you have time, go through each area of the Lord's Prayer in one day. Or spend a day on each part of the prayer.

One easy way to do this is to walk through the alphabet as a prompt for reflecting on the nature of the God you worship. Begin with the letter A and list attributes of God starting with this letter. "God, you are amazing, awesome . . ." Don't just list the characteristic but reflect on what it means. How have you experienced God's awesome presence in your life? When you have exhausted a letter of the alphabet, move on to the next one. "I celebrate you because you are beautiful, compassionate, delightful, excellent, fearful, good, holy, immeasurable . . ." Use this or some other approach to press you toward exploring the wonder and greatness of God.

Submission

Your kingdom come, your will be done, on earth as it is in heaven. Prayer is about submission. Jesus taught us this when he prayed, "Not my will, but yours be done" (Luke 22:42). If Jesus humbly laid his will and life before the Father in prayer, how much more should we? Do you want to eliminate myopia from your prayer life? Make a seismic shift and stop presenting your wish list to God as if he exists to fulfill your every demand. Rather, pray for his kingdom to come and his will to be done. As you discover his will, let your life and dreams be shaped by God's desires.

When we pray for God's will to be done on earth, this includes in our lives, families, churches, and all that matters most to us. This is a dangerous prayer. We are subjugating our desires and dreams to the will of God. What an amazing posture of humility! Yet there is no better place to be.

Supplication

Give us today our daily bread. It is right to bring our needs before God. This part of prayer is called supplication, presenting our needs to God and trusting him to take care of us. We are his children, and he wants us to tell him whatever is on our hearts. When we see Jesus' example of praying for daily bread, our minds should turn to the Israelites wandering in the wilderness. God provided the manna they needed, but he did it one day at a time. In the same way, Jesus models a prayer that expresses trust in God for our daily bread as well as for other provision. Too often we want to have provision so plenteous that we are secure for weeks, months, or years. But if we were to have this, we would trust in ourselves and myopia would set in.

God promises to provide bread for the day. When the next day dawns, we come with our needs and trust God to provide again. Each day, we come before our heavenly Father and tell him what we need. These needs can be monetary, physical, relational, emotional, or of any kind. When we live with the understanding that our daily bread is provided by God, we learn contentment and gratitude.

Confession

Forgive us our debts, as we also have forgiven our debtors. Humbly confessing our sins is central in a prayer life that honors God. As we present our struggles, failings, and sins to God, we are reminded that "if we confess our sins, he is faithful and just and will forgive us our sins and purify us from all unrighteousness" (1 John 1:9). As we lift our heartfelt confession, we also listen for the Holy Spirit to speak to us. Are there people we are failing to forgive? Are we harboring anger or resentment? Our prayers of confession lead us to seek restored relationships with those who have wronged us and those we have hurt.

⚂ Protection

And lead us not into temptation, but deliver us from the evil one. God is a loving heavenly Father. He wants to protect and watch over us. We are faced with pitfalls of temptation and evil all around. In prayer we seek God for his protection. We acknowledge that he is "my rock, my fortress and my deliverer; my God is my rock, in whom I take refuge. He is my shield and the horn of my salvation, my stronghold" (Ps. 18:2). We also face head-on the reality of temptation and spiritual battles. As we pray for protection from temptation and deliverance from the Evil One, we acknowledge the reality of the spiritual world and our need for God's power in order to stand strong. Victory is found in Jesus because "the one who is in you is greater than the one who is in the world" (1 John 4:4). But Jesus reminds us of our need to call to God for strength in the midst of the battle.

. . . .

The Lord's Prayer is a gift. As we use this template for our prayers, we discover beautiful places of intimacy and honesty with our heavenly Father. If you want to follow an outline for using the Lord's Prayer, one can be found in appendix 2 in the back of this book.

There is so much we can say about prayer and about learning to dialogue with God. Many excellent books have been written on this topic, and I have listed a few in the recommended reading section in the back of this book.

In the Arms of Jesus ● ● ● ● ● ● ● ● ● ● ● ● ● ● ● ● ● ●

I want to close with a picture that captures the heart of prayer. It comes from a confession I have heard many Christians make over the years: "I feel guilty because there are many evenings I try to pray but end up falling asleep right in the middle of my prayer time." These people feel they let God down each time they doze off before uttering their official amen for the day.

This is what I tell them, and I hope it speaks to your heart.

Imagine a mother cradling her five-year-old girl in her arms. It is the end of the day, and the two are talking. The mom is telling her about the plans for tomorrow. The little girl is talking about the fun she had that day. As the daughter talks, she yawns and rubs her eyes. They keep chatting, but the little girl is fading quickly. The mother looks down at the one she loves so tenderly. As they are talking, in midsentence, her little girl falls asleep, right in her arms.

How does the mother feel? Is she angry? Disappointed?

As the mother looks on her precious daughter, she smiles and rejoices. There is no other place she would rather have her little girl fall asleep.

When we end our day talking with God and we happen to doze off, he is not angry or disappointed. He holds us in his arms, embraces us, and gives us a kiss on the forehead. God loves to be with us, to speak to us and hear what is on our hearts. And if we happen to fall asleep in his arms, it brings joy to his heart. There is no better place for us to end a busy day.

FOR REFLECTION

- How do I hear God speak to me? What can I do to listen more often?
- Jesus wants me to pray for his kingdom to come on this earth. What can I do to help usher in his kingdom in my home, workplace, or church?

FOR PRAYER

- Thank God for the ways he has spoken to you and led you in the past. Pray for open ears to hear his direction in the future.
- Spend time confessing an area of sin in your life. After you have done this, read and meditate on 1 John 1:9.

Part 3

Shifts That Bring Health and Rest

Acomedian stood on stage and said, "There is one simple way you can know you have crossed the line between childhood and adulthood. A child must take a nap but does not want to. An adult would love to take a nap but just doesn't have the time!" The audience laughed, but I felt a piercing sadness. The joke was funny because it hit close to home, maybe too close.

We live in a culture filled with people who long to feel rested and healthy. Many adults would love to unplug, relax, and take a nap. This desire is deeper than a longing for physical rest. The real hunger is for a sense of peace, order, and meaning in life. But as the years speed past, the dream of health and rest seems farther and farther away.

Life spans are getting longer, but for many people, the quality of life is not getting better. We have more medications, treatments, surgical options, and therapies available than at any time in history, but people do not seem to be feeling healthier. According to the Daily Health Policy Report, medical spending in the United States went up by over $314 billion dollars between 1987 and 2000. With all the money spent on medical care, recreational activities, and self-help programs, it would seem people today should feel rested, healthy, and at peace.

Sadly, this is not true for many of us. Like George in the introduction to the old Hanna-Barbera cartoon *The Jetsons*, we are stuck on a high-speed treadmill and we can't reach the off button. We scream, "Jane, get me off this thing!" while we run for dear life. We have become like the little girl who declared with exasperation, "The faster I go, the behinder I get."

God wants us to know that from childhood to adulthood, he has called us to be people of rest. Our souls, bodies, and minds should be refreshed and our lives filled with health and strength. God does not promise a life free from sickness and stress. But he does show the road to peace in the midst of all the complexities we face. He wants us to know there are seismic shifts we can make that will rejuvenate our souls, strengthen our bodies, and bring us peace of mind.

Jesus said: "Come to me, all you who are weary and burdened, and I will give you rest. Take my yoke upon you and learn from me, for I am gentle and humble in heart, and you will find rest for your souls. For my yoke is easy and my burden is light" (Matt. 11:28–30).

When the Savior declared these words, they came like a remedy to the people of his day. They are just as powerful now as they were two thousand years ago.

The rest we long for is available to us. We can experience the health we dream about. We can take hold of the glorious peace which seems just out of our reach.

Jesus pointed out an action that leads to the rest only he can offer. He invited us to come to him. He gave this invitation to the weary and the burdened. If you fall into either of these categories, here is good news: Jesus stands ready, offering rest. If you happen to fall into both of these groups, if you are weary and burdened today, a double blessing is on the horizon. The peace and refreshment Jesus offers can strengthen your soul and bring the rest your heart longs to experience.

CHAPTER 7

The Seismic Shift from Rushing to Slowing

This is what the Sovereign Lord, the Holy One of Israel, says:
"In repentance and rest is your salvation,
   in quietness and trust is your strength,
   but you would have none of it."

—Isaiah 30:15

Remember the Sabbath day by keeping it holy. Six days you shall labor and do all your work, but the seventh day is a Sabbath to the Lord your God. On it you shall not do any work, neither you, nor your son or daughter.... For in six days the Lord made the heavens and the earth, the sea, and all that is in them, but he rested on the seventh day. Therefore the Lord blessed the Sabbath day and made it holy.

—Exodus 20:8–11

Come to me, all you who are weary and burdened, and I will give you rest. Take my yoke upon you and learn from me, for I am gentle and humble in heart, and you will find rest for your souls. For my yoke is easy and my burden is light.

—Matthew 11:28–30

The RPMs are at the red line. Robert has no spare time in his schedule. From the moment he pops out of bed and hits the floor running, he knows there is no way he can move fast enough to accomplish everything on his schedule for the day. Breakfast is on the fly—three big swallows of orange juice and a granola bar he grabs as he rushes out the door at 7:00 a.m. sharp. His day is a blur of one commitment backed up against the next.

At 7:30 in the evening, Robert rolls into his driveway after being in constant motion for over twelve hours. He can't relax yet because he still has at least two solid hours of work to do that night. Robert knows the drill; it is nothing new. He will sit at the dining room table and shovel down a reheated dinner while he cranks out a couple more hours of work. Finally, exhausted, Robert will flop onto the couch, turn on the TV, and shift into neutral. Eventually he will drag himself to bed, hit the pillow, and put his frazzled mind to rest.

In the quiet of the night, as the silence surrounds him, Robert reflects on his life. Day after day he feels spent, exhausted, and emotionally wiped out. What makes his situation so desperate is that he can't imagine any way out of this daily cycle.

What is most shocking about Robert's frenzied life is that he is not some protégé working for a Fortune 500 company. He is a normal high school freshman who works hard to get good grades, plays an instrument in the school band, and excels at two sports in the course of the year. By the time he gets home from his soccer game after a day of school, he still has homework for three classes. This young man has learned from a young age that he has to run full speed just to stay up with the pace of life.

We live in a pathologically busy culture, and the "Robert Syndrome" is impacting too many young people and adults. We run from event to event from morning to night. We can't see any way out of this vicious cycle, this proverbial rat race. The problem is, there is no finish line. To make things worse, our culture cheers us on and inspires us to run even faster. We get awards and rewards for busyness. In the end, many of us come to believe this is the way life has to be.

Many people wear their overburdened schedules as badges of honor. Not only do they flaunt their busy pace with pride, they tend to look down on those who do not live with the same intensity. Yet in the middle of the full days, fitful nights, and endless to-do lists, most of us have an unspoken sense that something is wrong. Our bodies, minds, and souls long for rest. Deep inside, we know something must change.

A God of Rest •

Into this frantic context, God speaks with startling hope. Jesus says, "Come to me, all you who are weary and burdened, and I will give you rest. Take my yoke upon you and learn from me, for I am gentle and humble in heart, and you will find rest for your souls. For my yoke is easy and my burden is light" (Matt. 11:28–30). God asks a few core questions: Do you feel weary? Is your burden too heavy? Are you tired of carrying your load alone? Do you need rest for your soul?

If you answer yes to any of these questions, God has good news. He wants you to slow down. Take a nap. Discover that the Lord is still the Shepherd who can lead you to green pastures (Psalm 23). If you are soul-fatigued and long for rest, God wants you to know that he has established a way for you to order your life so there is always space for play, worship, refreshment, and community with those you love.

If we find ourselves wondering if God wants us to discover rest deep in our souls, all we have to do is look at his example. In the opening scene of the Bible, God is at work, creating, shaping, carving, gardening, painting, and speaking the world into existence. At the end of each day, God declares his work good and gets ready for another day of creating. Until the seventh day. On this day, God decides to take a Sabbath. He rests. In the book of Genesis, we read, "By the seventh day God had finished the work he had been doing; so on the seventh day he rested from all his work. And God blessed the seventh day and made it holy, because on it he rested from all the work of creating that he had done" (Gen. 2:2–3).

‖‖‖‖ Seismic Shift Suggestion ‖‖‖‖

Take Your Pulse. During a workout, it is helpful to occasionally stop to take your pulse. You stop running, doing aerobics, or whatever is making your heart race, and you check to be sure your heart is beating at a healthy rate. If your heart is beating too fast, you know you need to slow down.

Check your life-pulse by evaluating your schedule. Sit down with a calendar of the previous month's commitments and activities. When did you experience Sabbath? When did you allow time to meet with God? How often did you make space for rest and play? If your schedule says your pace is too fast, slow down your emotional pulse by making space for rest. Take a day of Sabbath in the coming week.

Why did God rest? Was he tired? Did he need a day off? Had he over-done it with all of his intense creating and hit a wall of fatigue? Was this downtime necessary for him to recharge his batteries for the next week of activity?

No!

God took a day off as an act of love. He rested so he could model a rhythm of life essential for the health and well being of his children. The very first Sabbath was not for God; it was for us. In Genesis chapter 2, we see one of the first teachable moments in the history of the world. Before the man and woman were even aware of their need, their Father was set-ting an example.

God knew the only way our souls could find true refreshment would be through learning the secret of Sabbath. As the Creator of life, God under-stood what it would take to sustain the health and vitality of his people, so he showed us the way. Then with open arms he invited us to discover the life-giving rhythm of six days of labor and one day of Sabbath rest.

Ever since that first Sabbath, God's children resisted this amazing gift. Like a moth to the flame, we are drawn to a hurried lifestyle. We run from the rest God offers. We resist the refreshment we claim our hearts desire. The prophet Isaiah captures this ongoing battle when he writes, "This is what the Sovereign Lord, the Holy One of Israel, says: 'In repentance and rest is your salvation, in quietness and trust is your strength, but you would have none of it' " (Isa. 30:15).

God offers rest and quietness, and we politely say, "No thank you. I'm not interested." Isaiah goes on to paint a picture of how God's children run away from the peace he offers: "You said, 'No, we will flee on horses.' Therefore you will flee! You said, 'We will ride off on swift horses.' There-fore your pursuers will be swift!" (Isa. 30:16).

Our Creator knows we were made for more than endless days of labor. Because he designed and sculpted us, he understands we need time to love him, connect with each other, and enjoy the blessings of this beautiful world. Yet he also knows that we run from the very things that give life and joy. Sometimes a busy schedule and the refusal to take a Sabbath are signs that we are running from God and avoiding intimacy with him and oth-ers. As Isaiah says, we flee; we ride off on the fastest horse we can find. But God is even faster. He can always catch us. Isaiah goes on to say, "Yet the Lord longs to be gracious to you; he rises to show you compassion. For the Lord is a God of justice. Blessed are all who wait for him!" (Isa. 30:18).

When we feel God close on our heels and try to run even faster to escape him, we prove that we have no idea who we are dealing with. We can't outrun God. We should never try to escape from him. He wants us to stop running, turn around, and face him. When we do this, we discover that the things our hearts long for will never be found in a frenzied pace, a seven-day work week, or a schedule that leaves no room for rest. God knows our only hope to experience lasting peace in our souls will come when we find our life and rest in him.

Sabbath Is Not about Legalism and Limitations

Many people avoid keeping a Sabbath because they have never experienced the joy and peace God intends us to find in this day. Many people have a limited or inaccurate understanding of why God calls us to experience Sabbath. And many of those who do observe a regular Sabbath have allowed it to deteriorate into a new list of "thou shalt nots" in an already legalistic and limited lifestyle.

The sad truth is that in the days of Jesus, the Sabbath had become an occasion for absurd legalism. But before we too quickly or severely judge the people in Jesus' day, it is important to understand how their Sabbath regulations evolved (or devolved). It all started with the Ten Commandments. When God gave the law, he said, "But the seventh day is a Sabbath to the LORD your God. On it you shall not do any work" (Exod. 20:10). From the very beginning, the people of God tried to take this command seriously. They knew there were consequences for those who broke the Sabbath. So the people asked the most natural question: what is work?

Over the centuries, the religious leaders identified no less than thirty-nine distinct categories of work. Some of the behaviors that were declared work were reaping, threshing, winnowing, preparing a meal, and lifting a burden. Within each of these categories, the leaders of the community developed clear explanations as to what was allowed and what was forbidden on the Sabbath.

For instance, one category of activity that was deemed work was lifting a burden. From this declaration, an obvious question emerges: how much is a burden? Again the religious leaders deliberated in an effort to decide exactly what could be lifted on the Sabbath day. Here was their conclusion: a burden is anything that weighs more than two dried figs. This is absolutely true. In the days of Jesus, the detailed explanation of what was allowed and not allowed on the Sabbath had devolved to this point.

This example of lifting a burden is one among hundreds of rules that had developed around the simple command not to work on the Sabbath. In some of the ancient literature, we discover that Sabbath rules became so restrictive that even thinking about work was labeled as a sin deserving punishment. In the fiftieth chapter of the Book of Jubilee, an ancient nonbiblical book, we find these words about the Sabbath: "Whoever lies with his wife, or *plans* to do anything on the Sabbath, or *plans* to set on a journey, or *plans* to buy or sell, or draws water, or lifts a burden on the Sabbath is condemned" (italics added). It was this excessive development of tradition that got Jesus and his followers into trouble in the first century. They did not break the biblical law, but they did step on the toes of the traditions developed by the religious community.

There was the day when Jesus and his followers were walking through a field and started a conflict about the Sabbath: "At that time Jesus went through the grainfields on the Sabbath. His disciples were hungry and began to pick some heads of grain and eat them. When the Pharisees saw this, they said to him, 'Look! Your disciples are doing what is unlawful on the Sabbath'" (Matt. 12:1–2). It is important to note that the law of Moses allowed travelers to pluck a handful of grain and eat it. Jesus' disciples were not stealing. As a matter of fact, those who owned fields in those days would leave the corners unharvested so travelers and the poor of the land could help themselves.

The religious leaders were not angry at Jesus' followers because they were plucking and eating grain. Their fury came because they believed the disciples were working on the Sabbath. The followers of Jesus had reached out and plucked off the heads of grain, rubbed the grain in their palms to separate the seed from the chaff, and let the wind blow the chaff out of their hands, and then they popped this fast-food snack into their mouths. In doing this, they had engaged in no less than four categories of work as defined by the religious leaders. They had reaped, threshed, winnowed, and prepared a meal. And for this they were condemned.

In this biblical account, as in many others, Jesus argued that these pious leaders had missed the whole point of Sabbath. The bottom line was that Jesus wanted these people to know that the Sabbath was given as a gift to be a delight to the people of God, not to be an occasion to tighten the noose of legalism. Somehow along the way they had never gotten the memo: "The Sabbath was made for people, not people for the Sabbath" (Mark 2:27 TNIV).

Sadly, this same legalistic view of the Sabbath endures to our day. Many people have forgotten that the heartbeat of Sabbath is rest, refreshment, and recalibration. It should be centered on intimacy with God and fellowship with his people. I have never met anyone who was told they could not lift a burden that weighed more than two figs on the Sabbath, but I have heard people say the following about their Sabbath observances as they were growing up:

- We could not raise our voices above a normal conversational volume.
- We could not run in the house or outside, but a brisk walk was allowed.
- We could go to a lake on Sunday afternoon, but we could not go in the water. Particularly, we were not allowed to put our feet in the water.
- We could not play any games that could get overly boisterous.
- We were forced to take a nap, even when we were well beyond an age when our bodies needed one.

Understanding Sabbath

It is difficult to describe Sabbath without stepping on toes or sounding legalistic. But in an effort to be clear, here is a working definition. Sabbath is the God-ordained discipline of setting aside one day out of seven for the sake of refreshing worship of the Lord, joyful community with his people, and rest-filled activity that is different from what we do on the other days of the week.

There are three elements in this description. First, Sabbath is a time to connect with our Maker and provide space for worship, praise, prayer, and growing in intimacy with the Lover of our souls. Second, it is a time to experience the blessings of community. On Sabbath we connect with those we love. This community is experienced in homes, in church buildings, at a lakeside, and anywhere the people of God might gather. Third, Sabbath is a day dramatically different from the rest of the week. On this day, we are free to move at a different pace. A soul-enhancing slowness is afforded us on the Sabbath.

What does it mean to say that this day should be different from the rest of the week? In Jesus' time, most people were occupied with agricultural pursuits and physical labor. They were shepherds, farmers, and tradespeople. But much of the culture centered on agriculture, the seasons, and harvest time. For someone who worked in the fields every day of the week, avoiding activities like reaping, threshing, and winnowing on the Sabbath would have been a good idea. But today, a person who spends six days a week sitting in an office might want to get out in their garden, pull some weeds, and enjoy the outdoors on their Sabbath day. Is this allowed?

‖‖‖ Seismic Shift Suggestion ‖‖‖

Ask Good Questions. If you are trying to decide if you can or should do something on your Sabbath day, you might want to use these questions to help you set a healthy direction:

- Will this connect me more closely with God?
- If I do this, will it enhance my relationship with God's people and develop authentic community?
- As I engage in this activity, do I find myself feeling rested, refreshed, and recharged?
- Is this activity a departure, a change from what I do the rest of the week?

The real question is, Are they working, or are they experiencing rest?

If someone says their time in the garden refreshes their soul and allows them to connect with God, it is not work. It could be quite appropriate for them on the Sabbath. But if they see this as a chore and if it is something they do all week long, it is work and should be avoided on the Sabbath. This might seem somewhat subjective, but this is the challenge we face. The Sabbath was not made to confine us but to set us free.

Many people ask if they must celebrate Sabbath on a Sunday. For most people, this is the most logical and practical day. But it is certainly not a requirement. If a person wants to be highly legalistic about the Sabbath, they should celebrate it from sundown on Friday evening to sundown on Saturday evening. Historically, the Sabbath was the final day of the week. But God's plan for Sabbath is a rhythm of one day out of seven. This rest-filled day is set aside to make space for God and people and to engage in activities that are different from those of the rest of the week.

As a pastor, I have developed the habit of celebrating my Sabbath on Tuesday. Saturday and Sunday are always work days for me. Weekends are not good days for most pastors to experience Sabbath rest. On Monday, I am back in the office for morning prayer with our pastors, lots of meetings, and debriefing. But by Tuesday, I am ready for a seismic shift! On Monday night, I am anticipating the glorious Sabbath that awaits me. I have grown fond of referring to Monday night as Friday night. Tuesday is not just a day off, it is a day set aside to meet God, connect with the people I love, and to live at a dramatically different pace.

Seek God's wisdom as you determine the best day for you to dive into the refreshing waters of Sabbath. But don't miss out. Choose not to repeat the folly of the people of Israel, who ran from the refreshment God offered. Embrace the Sabbath as a gift and discover the joy of God-given rest.

The Secret of Sabbath

God did not create the Sabbath to bury us under a mountain of legalistic minutia. He gave us this wonderful gift to show us the pathway to freedom and rest. We are the ones who turned the Sabbath into an occasion for bondage. God's desire is to help us rediscover the secret of Sabbath. If we let God's truth about Sabbath rest fill our hearts, we will begin to make the seismic shifts needed to find the enduring refreshment our hearts long to experience.

Observing Sabbath is a declaration that we trust God is capable of running the universe without us. Every time we take a Sabbath, we declare our confidence in God. When we unplug, stop working, enjoy the blessings of worship, engage in the joys of fellowship, and dive into the refreshment of God-led play, we walk in the spirit of Sabbath. Each time we step back from our labor and daily responsibilities for the sake of meeting God and finding rest, we make a statement to God, ourselves, and others. We declare that we are not in charge of the world or even of our own lives.

In Psalm 127, Solomon acknowledges the profound truth that unless God is in control, nothing of value will be accomplished. Solomon knew a great deal about busy schedules, massive building projects, and living in a complex relational world. He understood that only God can run the universe and manage our lives. This is how Solomon expresses this truth, as inspired by the Holy Spirit: "Unless the Lord builds the house, its builders labor in vain. Unless the Lord watches over the city, the watchmen stand guard in vain. In vain you rise early and stay up late, toiling for food to eat—for he grants sleep to those he loves" (Ps. 127:1–2).

If you read the story of Solomon's life recorded in the Bible, you quickly discover that few people could rival Solomon for being a type-A, highly motivated overachiever. Yet with his driven personality, Solomon was still gripped by this truth: he was not in charge of his own house, city, and certainly not the universe. Only God had the power and wisdom he needed. Solomon's words in this psalm reveal a heart surrendered to God.

Then after acknowledging that God is in charge of his life, Solomon comes back to the theme of rest. He speaks to those who are caught in the Robert Syndrome and who can't seem to slow down. For those who have spent their whole lives rising early and staying up late, spinning from place to place like a Tasmanian devil, he gives a stern warning: "In vain you rise early and stay up late, toiling for food to eat." God is speaking through his servant Solomon. This message cuts through centuries and cultures and deep into the hearts of those who toil in an endless cycle of a life that leaves no room for Sabbath. The closing words of this verse leave us longing for something that seems to elude so many in our fast-forward world: "for he [God] grants sleep to those he loves." God's love for his children assures us that rest can be ours. We don't have to get up early every day, stay up late every night, and live in a state of fatigue.

The lesson of Sabbath is that the Lord is the one who builds the house, watches over the city, and runs the universe. If we step back and rest for a day, the planets will stay in their places, the earth will turn on its axis, and the sun will rise and set without our help. No matter how hard we work, if God is not in our work, it can't succeed. And if God is watching over the city, no one can tear it down. Each time we observe Sabbath rest, we declare to the world and to heaven that we trust God to do what he has done so well since before time began. He can run the universe.

Observing the Sabbath shows that we are confident God can provide all we need in six days of labor. All through the Bible, we see that God wants his children to look to him for their daily bread. Jesus taught us to pray, "Give us today our daily bread" (Matt. 6:11). In the Old Testament, God provided manna from heaven to feed his people in the desert. Yet too many of us have a feeling deep in our gut that if we don't work seven days a week, we won't have our daily bread. We worry that if we fail to labor every day of our lives, our nest egg will never be big enough for the comfortable retirement we dream about. In short, we don't trust that God can provide what we need. Each time we observe Sabbath, we become signposts for the world. We declare by our actions that we trust God to meet our needs, provide our daily bread, and watch out for us. Why? Because we are his beloved children.

One of the greatest illustrations of this comes from an Old Testament truth I call "The Lesson of Manna and Maggots." In Exodus 16, we find the people of Israel wandering in the desert. God provided heavenly bread for them called manna, which literally means, "What is it?" Every day the people of God were to gather the amount of manna their family needed for one day. This action declared they trusted that God would provide one day at a time.

But some of the people did not trust God's promise to provide. They decided they needed a manna buffer, a little extra stock to create a sense of emotional well being, just one extra helping of "what is it" to guarantee their future. So they collected more than they needed. To their surprise, when they went to their storehouse of manna the next morning, it was full of maggots, and it reeked! They were forced to throw it out and develop the daily discipline of collecting what they needed, not what they wanted.

Then God surprised his people. This is what we read in the book of Exodus:

> Each morning everyone gathered as much as he needed, and when the sun grew hot, it melted away. On the sixth day, they gathered twice as much—two omers for each person—and the leaders of the community came and reported this to Moses. He said to them, "This is what the LORD commanded: 'Tomorrow is to be a day of rest, a holy Sabbath to the LORD. So bake what you want to bake and boil what you want to boil. Save whatever is left and keep it until morning.'"
>
> So they saved it until morning, as Moses commanded, and it did not stink or get maggots in it. "Eat it today," Moses said, "because today is a Sabbath to the LORD. You will not find any of it on the ground today. Six days you are to gather it, but on the seventh day, the Sabbath, there will not be any."
>
> **—Exodus 16:21–26**

When they kept the manna overnight, it spoiled and was useless the next morning. But on the Sabbath day, the extra manna was fresh and delicious. God taught his children a lesson we are still learning thousands of years later. When we take a day for Sabbath, God promises to take care of us. Each time we stop our usual activity, turn our eyes to heaven, and experience God's rest, we declare to a watching world that we know God can provide all we need in just six days of labor.

||||| **Seismic Shift Suggestion** |||||

Take a Sabbath. Identify a day in the coming week that would be good for Sabbath. Then plan to spend this day at a slow and refreshing pace. Make space for worship and deep connection with people, and engage in activities that are different from what you do all week long. As you enjoy this day of Sabbath rest, reflect on these three things:

- God is on the throne; he can take care of things without my help today.
- God has promised to provide my daily bread.
- Loving God and people matters more than anything else.

Observing a Sabbath shows our understanding that slowing down and meeting with God and his people is a priority in our lives. A weekly Sabbath day allows us to make space to connect with God and with people. It was Jesus who said that the greatest commandment is to "love the Lord your God with all your heart and with all your soul and with all your mind." A close second is, "Love your neighbor as yourself" (Matt. 22:37–39). When we observe Sabbath, we are able to make private and corporate worship a priority and connecting with people in unrushed moments a possibility. Sabbath is a gift that enhances the two most important things in life, loving God and loving people.

Choosing to Dive Deep

In a pathologically hurried culture, we can choose to slow down and go deep. The gift of Sabbath is God's way of reminding us weekly that if we move too fast, we can end up hydroplaning over God's best gifts. My wife and I learned this truth in an unforgettable way on our twentieth anniversary. Sherry and I had never been to Hawaii, so we made plans to spend a week on Maui. We discovered why people rave about this modern-day paradise. The plants, wildlife, and landscape are stunning. One day we went on a boat trip. As we skimmed across the water, the captain told us all about the beautiful sea life just a few feet below us. I looked over the side of the boat but could see nothing. I believed him, but the speed of the boat made it impossible to see below the surface of the water.

As we got near the dive site, a member of the crew began to tell us about snuba diving. I had heard of scuba diving, but never snuba diving. He told us that in just fifteen minutes, he could teach us how to dive twenty-five feet under the water. This seemed almost too good to be true. But we listened. Apparently scuba diving demands training and expertise because you carry the oxygen on your back. In snuba diving, on the other hand, the oxygen tank floats on a small raft on the surface of the water. Each diver is paired with another person and has a twenty-five-foot air hose that keeps them from going any deeper.

After brief training, Sherry and I decided to try snuba. It was amazing. The captain had told us about the colorful fish below the surface. He had promised we would see blues, yellows, and greens we had never imagined. He had even tempted us with the thought that we could swim alongside giant sea turtles. But all of this was just words as we skimmed over the surface of the water.

When we got to our dive site, we put on our gear and jumped in. It was all true. In the course of two dives, we saw fish that God had painted colors we had never seen before. We investigated coral formations that looked like moonscapes. We caught sight of a very shy octopus that flew through the water with the grace and ease of a ballerina. We even got to swim with a number of giant sea turtles.

When you are twenty-five feet underwater, everything moves in slow motion. Between breaths and the sound of the oxygen flowing is an eerie silence. In those slow, quiet moments under the surface of the ocean, a radical contrast unfolds. When we were in the boat and speeding over the surface, we saw none of the beauty that lay just feet below us. Only after we slowed down and chose to dive deep could we experience the staggering splendor of what God had made.

In the same way, when we rush through life, we miss much of what God has in store for us just under the surface. We skim over relationships with spouses, children, and friends. We fail to go deep with God. We hydroplane over intimacy, joy, and rest. God knows us better than we know ourselves, and he understands our propensity for hurry. He was so concerned about us that he gave us a pathway to an unhurried life. After six days of work, God rested. He calls us to learn from his example. It is time to slow down, take a deep breath, chew our food before swallowing, rediscover God's presence, reconnect with people, dive deep, and learn the secret of Sabbath.

FOR REFLECTION ● ● ● ● ● ● ● ● ● ● ● ● ● ● ● ● ● ●

- What would be the best day for me to experience Sabbath rest?
- What speeds up my emotional engine and drives me away from experiencing Sabbath rest?

FOR PRAYER ●

- Thank God for his example of rest and for offering you the amazing gift of Sabbath.
- Ask God to help you develop a consistent discipline of Sabbath rest, even when your life is very busy.

Chapter EIGHT

The Seismic Shift from Stuffed to Satisfied

Do you not know that your body is a temple of the Holy Spirit, who is in you, whom you have received from God? You are not your own; you were bought at a price. Therefore honor God with your body.

—1 Corinthians 6:19–20

Since we have these promises, dear friends, let us purify ourselves from everything that contaminates body and spirit, perfecting holiness out of reverence for God.

—2 Corinthians 7:1

On the refrigerator in our home is a magnet with one simple line: "Nothing tastes as good as being thin feels." I'm not sure if I always agree with this statement, but it makes a great point. The momentary pleasure of a huge bowl of ice cream or an extra helping of lasagna never outweighs the food hangover you have in the morning or the weight you gain over time.

I grew up in a family in which eating played an important part. Although we were not a "religious" family and did not go to church, we had our own family tradition on Sundays. We regularly went to Don Jose's for a Mexican feast. From the prelude of chips and salsa, to the celebration of the main course, all the way to the postlude of a sucker from a big plaster pot near the exit, this experience was the closest thing to worship I experienced in my childhood. I didn't know all the official religious terminology growing up, but I can say in retrospect that we would have been called "charismatic" by many people if they had watched us during our Sunday gathering. The moans, groans, and utterings conveyed more than words could say!

With time I discovered that food was an integral part of all of our family gatherings. We always had plenty for us and anyone else who might drop in. As the years went by, I learned that food was good for celebrating when things went great; feasting was part of the rejoicing process. I also discovered that food was a natural consolation when things did not go well. When our Little League baseball team lost a game, a trip to the snack bar always took the edge off the pain. From the highs of life to the low times, food always seemed to have a prominent place.

This pattern of eating my way through the joys and struggles of life seemed to work just fine, until I got out of college. This was when I stopped playing organized sports and hit that time in life when the metabolism slows down. All of a sudden, my lean physique began to spread, soften, and widen.

Now I was a pastor spending lots of hours sitting behind a desk. Or worse, I was having regular meetings over lunch with members of the congregation or other leaders. To top it off, it seemed every gathering in the church demanded freshly baked cookies and other tantalizing refreshments. It would be wrong to hurt the feelings of church members by refusing their generous offering of snickerdoodles or brownies. Above and beyond the normal sweets and snacks that accompany pastoral life, holidays would bring a tidal wave of cakes, pies, and cookies onto my desk.

What's a pastor to do? The answer was clear: eat! Doesn't the Bible say everything is a good gift from God and that all food should be received with thanksgiving? Over the next two decades, I went from being a fairly lean 170 to a soft and undisciplined two and a quarter! Now, you have to understand, I am six-foot, four-inches tall, give or take about six inches! This is not a sufficient height for storing and hiding two hundred and twenty-five pounds, and I was feeling it.

The Power of a Good Example

During this time, my wife consistently modeled a lifestyle of exercise, great eating habits, and disciplines that impressed, inspired, and occasionally depressed me. Her example often stirred my heart, but for a long time it did not impact me deeply enough to change my habits.

I can still remember the humorous but poignant words of the host of the Academy Awards one year. He looked at the amazing physiques and firm bodies of all the stars that had paraded across the stage that night and he shook his head. Then he looked at the camera and said, "I would do anything to look like those people, except exercise or diet!" I laughed, but the comment also cut like a knife.

I knew the only way I would be able to make progress in my health and in truly glorifying God with my body was to make some seismic shifts in my habits. The problem was, the task seemed so big and my self-control so small.

‖‖‖ Seismic Shift Suggestion ‖‖‖

Watch and Learn. Besides my wife, Sherry, I have another person I watch and learn from. A fellow pastor named Don Porter is a constant example of good eating and health. He regularly gets up and works out at 5:00 a.m. Whenever we meet for lunch, I am always impressed with the way he orders reasonable portions and stops eating while others keep packing it in. He even asks the server strange questions like, "Do you have a low calorie dressing?" and, "Do you have a menu with healthy options?" All of us can identify one or two people we can look to as a positive example of good health habits. Identify one or two people who can play this role in your life. Next, become a student of their patterns and habits. Watch, learn, and follow their example.

I did not change my habits right away, but I did learn from my wife. I watched her behavior, studied her habits, and listened to her talk about health in a way I had never heard before. I knew she had studied the topic over many years, so I gleaned all I could from her. Through her example, I identified some seismic shifts I could implement in my life.

I am not claiming to be an expert in health or eating habits. I still face the daily battle of choosing to make the seismic shifts needed to honor God with my body. If the truth be known, I have failed far more than succeeded in this area of my life. Even during the first two decades of my life when I was thin, I had terrible health habits. My life included too much fast food, late-night eating, and sweets, coupled with not enough fruits, vegetables, sit-down meals, and healthy foods. Though I looked healthy on the outside, my habits were horrible, and I was on a collision course with becoming overweight and putting my health at risk. I was not honoring God with my body!

A Living Sacrifice or Sacrificing Life?

God made our bodies, and he makes it clear that he is concerned about how we care for them. He does not dwell in buildings made of bricks, stone, and wood. He lives in the hearts, lives, and—dare I say?—the bodies of those who love him. The Bible is emphatic about this. The apostle Paul says, "Do you not know that your body is a temple of the Holy Spirit, who is in you, whom you have received from God? You are not your own; you were bought at a price. Therefore honor God with your body" (1 Cor. 6:19–20). In context, the primary focus of this passage is on how we use our bodies sexually; however, the broader application of taking care of our bodies in all respects makes perfect sense. The Holy Spirit of God takes up residence in all who follow Jesus. God cares about how we treat our bodies, and so should we! We are his temple, his dwelling place.

The vision that should consume the heart and mind of every follower of Jesus is to offer their whole life, including their body, fully to God. The apostle Paul also writes, "Therefore, I urge you, brothers and sisters, in view of God's mercy, to offer your bodies as a living sacrifice, holy and pleasing to God—this is true worship. Do not conform to the pattern of this world, but be transformed by the renewing of your mind. Then you will be able to test and approve what God's will is—his good, pleasing and perfect will" (Rom. 12:1–2 TNIV). The pattern of this world includes overconsumption, gluttony, and pleasure at all costs. This should never describe our lives. We need to learn how to offer our bodies to God and submit our will to his. This means enjoying the good food God has given us but not compromising our health. Eating too much or too little can harm our bodies. And we need not only relaxation and rest but also appropriate activity that will keep us in shape.

Reality Check

Caring for our bodies in our fast-paced, pleasure-centered, drive-thru culture will always be a challenge. And if you have a lifetime of bad habits, it will be even harder. But it is not impossible. Jesus told his followers,

"With human beings this is impossible, but not with God; all things are possible with God" (Mark 10:27 TNIV). These words of hope should inspire us to take steps to honor God with our bodies, even if we have a long and challenging road ahead.

In the Old Testament, we discover that God was deeply concerned that his temple be built and maintained. At the time, it was a building made of stone and precious materials. The first temple was built in Solomon's day. It was restored and rebuilt in Nehemiah and Ezra's day. Throughout the history of Israel, God was concerned that his dwelling place, the temple, not be abused or run down. Today, God feels the same way about the temple of our bodies. Since he dwells in us, he wants us to keep his temple in good repair, a fit place for the King of Kings to make his throne.

Although a growing number of people struggle with eating disorders and eat too little, the vast majority of people today tend to eat too much. This will be our focus in the coming pages. For those who have tried every diet on the planet and still struggle to honor God with their bodies, it is time for a new approach. The seismic shifts described in this chapter are not a diet program. They are not magic or a three-step path to instant health. They are certainly not some easy, pain-free pill to suppress hunger, reduce fat cells, and melt away unwanted pounds while you sleep! The seismic shifts in this chapter are commonsense steps we can take to help us treat our bodies like the temples they truly are—dwelling places of God. As you adopt these simple practices, your body will take on a size and shape that will honor God and bring you joy.

Seismic Shifts That Build and Maintain God's Temple

From Stuffed to Satisfied

A basic seismic shift concerning food is this: you don't have to eat until you are stuffed. Learn to eat until you are merely satisfied. For many people, it feels natural to keep eating until their body says stop! When they feel stuffed, they push back from the table. In some cases, people eat until they are beyond stuffed. They will pack it in until they feel uncomfortable or even sick. They push back from the table only after stretching the capacity of their stomachs and pants. Once the belt has been let out a notch or two, it might be time to slow down! This is not God's plan for our bodies.

If we learn to tune in to our bodies, we will notice that we often feel satisfied long before our plates are empty, that there's a point during a meal when our bodies tell us, "That's the right amount of food." But in a supersize culture, we tend to keep eating well beyond this point.

Imagine this scenario. You go out to a nice Italian restaurant for dinner with friends. The server brings a beautiful basket of various kinds of bread and crackers. You nibble on them as you chat with those around the table. Then someone orders an appetizer plate with four different Italian treats that everyone at the table can share, so you try a little of each. Very tasty! Next the server brings your salad and a new basket of bread; somehow the first basket has disappeared. As you finish your salad and put down your fork, a strange feeling comes over you. A radical thought goes through your mind. You feel satisfied. You think to yourself, *I could stop eating right now and feel great.* But the pasta has not even come to the table yet, and this restaurant is famous for its cheesecake and other desserts. What will you do? You feel satisfied before the main dish has arrived. But you also know you could eat a lot more before feeling stuffed.

Most of us face some version of this dilemma pretty regularly. We might not be in a fancy restaurant, but the same situation repeats itself. A junior high student finishes her sandwich and apple and feels satisfied. But she still has a bag of chips and a Twinkie. What will she do? A family goes to the church potluck and everyone gets a modest plate of food the first time around. They want to be sure everyone else gets dinner. But after a while, someone announces, "Everyone has been through the line. Please feel free to come up and get seconds." Most of those who have had a plate of dinner are sitting back feeling pretty satisfied, but when they hear the announcement, something draws them up for another plate. In many cases, they feel good after the first plate and bad after the second. But they keep doing the same thing at church potlucks year after year. There are many other examples, but the point is clear. Too often we eat until we feel stuffed.

Here is the first seismic shift when it comes to your eating and honoring God with your body. Learn to identify when you feel satisfied, and then stop eating. Even if you are only halfway through the meal, even if there is still food on your plate, even if the dessert really looks good, even if you know you could pack away one more helping. When you feel satisfied, push back from the table and stop eating. You can still converse with others, but gently move your plate just out of your reach, place your napkin over the food, thank God for a meal that truly satisfied you, and enjoy the pleasurable feeling of not being stuffed.

From Gulping to Tasting

In our hurried culture, we can be tempted to gulp down our food and never really taste and enjoy it. God has given us food to be enjoyed. Too often we shovel our meals into our mouths, chomp them down, and don't savor the flavors. Some people reach the end of a day and realize they can hardly remember what they ate. The issue is not that they failed to eat. The problem is that they rushed through their meals and did not take time to enjoy the food.

There are a number of things we can do to help us slow down and taste our food. First, we can commit to stop to thank God for the food he has given us. Like Jesus, we need to learn to express our appreciation. Once, when Jesus was going to feed a large group, "Jesus said, 'Have the people sit down.' There was plenty of grass in that place, and the men sat down, about five thousand of them. Jesus then took the loaves, gave thanks, and distributed to those who were seated as much as they wanted. He did the same with the fish" (John 6:10–11). The process of slowing down and expressing appreciation to God helps us move into the meal at a less rapid pace. If you are moving too fast to thank God for your meal, there is a good chance you will inhale your food and not taste or enjoy it.

Second, let your meal become an experience and not a race. Try this sometime. Look at the food you are about to eat, and enjoy the colors, the sight of this gift from God. Smell your food, really soak in the wonder of the experience. Eat slowly. Feel your teeth sinking into each bite, and force yourself to slow down. Chew each bite and taste your food. As you do this, the slower pace allows your body and mind to work in sync. When we eat too rapidly, we don't give our bodies time to register how much food we have consumed. By slowing down, we come to a place of feeling satisfied with a lower food intake. Another value of this process is that we remember our meals more vividly when we make them enjoyable experiences.

Third, we can slow down our pace by doing a few little practical things. If you are eating a burger or a sandwich, put it down between bites. If you are eating a salad or a steak, put down your fork after every bite. Take a deep breath. No one is going to take your food away! Sip some water between bites. Then just for fun, watch the way other people eat. Are they enjoying their food or are they just racing through the meal? Learn from the examples, both good and bad, of others. If you are eating with someone else, engage them in conversation between bites of food. And remember, if you find yourself feeling satisfied, then push your plate back and enjoy the victorious feeling of not being stuffed.

From Guilty to Thankful

If you look at what you plan to eat and feel guilty, there is a chance you need to adjust your menu. If you can't honestly thank God for the meal or the food you are planning to put into your body, then you should pause and ask God for wisdom. The key is that these decisions need to be made between you and God. No person can tell you exactly what to eat at each moment. You need to learn to tune in to God's gentle and small voice as he speaks to you and guides your decision-making process.

|||||| Seismic Shift Suggestion ||||||

Write a Prayer and Use It Often. Write your own prayer to use before meals and snacks. Customize it to fit your thoughts on this topic. Write it on a 3 x 5 card, in your day planner, or somewhere you will see it regularly. You might also want to write 1 Corinthians 6:19 – 20 under the prayer. Read this prayer before meals, and let the Lord speak to you if you need to change your eating plans.

I have written a short prayer I keep in my PDA and read before I eat anything. If I can say this prayer with joy, I dig in and enjoy the food. If I feel uncomfortable as I say this prayer, or if I can't pray it with authentic thankfulness, or if I find myself trying to avoid saying it, I will often refrain from eating or change my menu. I share this prayer with you only as an example that has been helpful for me. Feel free to use it, or write your own. Here is my prayer:

> Lord, I eat this food with thankfulness to you
> and with the awareness that it is a gift from your hand.
> I eat it so that my body might be healthy,
> an acceptable temple for you.
> Let this food strengthen my body that I might serve you
> and live each moment for you. Amen!

It is important to remember that a growing number of people are dealing with serious eating disorders such as anorexia and bulimia. These people deal with deep pain that causes them to refrain from eating or to overeat and then purge. In these cases, it is best to talk with a counselor or doctor.

From Random to Planned

Most people eat in a random manner. We don't plan. We simply eat at mealtimes and snack a little, or a lot, between meals. When the day is done, many people would have a hard time remembering what they ate in the past twenty-four hours.

This is why programs that help people plan their meals are so helpful. One of the disciplines they teach is how to thoughtfully plan eating for a day. Although formal programs are helpful, we can also learn to plan our own meals. I want to suggest two approaches to planned eating. Both are simple, and each can cause a seismic shift in our dietary patterns and health.

The first approach is to sit down in the morning, pray for God's wisdom, and write out exactly what you will eat for the day. It is helpful to have some basic knowledge of meal planning, and there are dozens of books that can help with this. But even if you don't have a formal program to follow, simply listing exactly what you will eat during the day is valuable. Write down snacks as well as meals. Look at your schedule for the day and be sure you know when you will be eating at home and when you will be eating out.

For some people, planning a whole day of meals is impractical. In these cases, there is another easy option. Simply write down, right *before* each meal or snack, exactly what you are going to eat. This might seem perfunctory or silly. But seismic shifts are little changes that make a big difference. You will be amazed at what will happen if you write down exactly what you plan to eat just before you partake. This habit raises your level of consciousness and awareness of what you are eating.

Most people who go out for a Mexican meal don't plan on eating two baskets of chips. But if the food takes a long time to come and the server keeps refilling the basket, they can end up eating far more than their brain registers. But if you write down, "I will eat fifteen chips, two tacos, and a side of rice; I will drink water," there is a good chance you will slow down, enjoy each chip, and stop after you hit your limit. If you eat in a random manner, you could munch on thirty or forty chips and not even realize it.

Some may decide to keep a notebook to record planned eating. Others may want to keep track of this in a PDA or on notecards. Your system is not the big issue. But planning your meals, for the day or one meal at a time, and writing them down, creates the potential for a seismic shift.

Few people will sit down before they go to the movies and write down, "During the movie, I will consume a forty-four-ounce soft drink, a massive bucket of popcorn, and some Junior Mints. And on the way out, I will get free refills on my popcorn and soft drink for the road." In most cases, if they plan, really thinking it through, they will scale way back. And if they develop the discipline of writing down what they plan to eat, wisdom will often prevail. By simply taking the time to think it through, say a prayer, and write it down, most people will decide on something more reasonable like, "I will share a medium bucket of popcorn and have a small soft drink."

|||||| **Seismic Shift Suggestion** ||||||

Make a Plan. Try planning your meals for one or two weeks and see what impact this has on your eating patterns and health. Use either of the plans suggested in this chapter: writing down all of your eating for the whole day, or writing down what you will eat before each meal or snack. If you discover that this discipline is helpful, extend it for a month and evaluate again at the end of that time frame. You may use the Daily Health Sheet in appendix 3 of this book to guide your eating plans for a week.

Those who really want to take a big step forward in developing eating discipline might want to invite a good friend to occasionally review their eating record. This accountability really raises the bar and encourages responsibility.

From Fast Food to Sit-Down Meals

A huge shift in our culture over the past few decades has been the trend toward eating more meals away from home, whether it's in fast-food restaurants, in the car, or on the sideline of a sports field. Meals on the run have become the norm for many adults and, sadly, for too many children. It is time to recapture the joy and fellowship of meals shared with our loved ones. Randy Frazee has written a challenging book called *Making Room for Life*. In this book, he challenges people to rediscover the lost value of the *convivium*. This is an old Latin word that means "feast." The idea is that the evening meal becomes a gathering place for feasting on great food, rich conversation, and satisfying community. Sadly, this has been all but discarded in our culture.

On a trip to Dallas, I had a chance to share three consecutive convivium meals with Randy, his family, and friends. I was struck by the slow pace, deep fellowship, and rich sharing of life that grew out of these meals shared together. The food and drink were important. But they were only a part of the whole experience.

From Many Drink Options to Water

Another seismic shift is to drink more water. Water is one of God's great gifts, but many avoid it. Some doctors recommend drinking eight glasses of water a day. Even if we don't drink that much, it would be good for all of us to think about the various beverages we consume and to replace some of them with a glass of water.

One particular warning our culture needs to hear is the danger of overconsuming caffeinated drinks. Too many people are addicted to caffeine and consume more than they realize through soft drinks, coffee, and other beverages that try to mask the presence of this addictive stimulant. I raise this concern as a person who openly admits that I am a recovering addict. A Pepsi addict, that is!

I needed to make a difficult shift back in 2000 when I realized my addiction to the caffeine in Pepsi was affecting my health. If you can believe it, I was drinking up to two liters of Pepsi a day! I would drink it at meals and at my desk during the day. Then I would sit down to write in the evening and sip Pepsi for hours. I would get a big clear glass, fill it with ice, and slowly pour in the Pepsi. I loved the sound of the cracking ice and the quiet popping of the little bubbles. I savored the first cold, refreshing gulp. I still miss it.

But I also knew the intake of sugar and caffeine was harming my body. So I decided to make a seismic shift. I cut caffeinated soft drinks out of my diet for one year. I was just getting ready to travel to Israel, so it seemed like the perfect time. I fasted from caffeinated, carbonated, sugary drinks and began to drink only water.

|||||| **Seismic Shift Suggestion** ||||||

H_2O **Challenge.** For two weeks, try drinking five or more glasses of water a day. Note how this impacts your hunger level. If a beverage you really love is not healthy for you, you might want to replace a glass or two of this beverage with water and note how this shift affects you. As a bonus, if you cut back on a beverage like coffee or soft drinks, keep track of how much money you save over the two weeks.

I wish I could say that I loved the taste of water instantly and that the shift was easy, but there were challenges. First of all, I began to have headaches as my body went through withdrawal from my drug of choice. I have never been a coffee drinker, so cutting out the Pepsi was cutting virtually all caffeine out of my system. The headaches persisted for about a week, but I took some aspirin and stuck with my commitment. After the headaches went away, I stopped taking the aspirin. I felt great! After about a month, I started to love the taste and feeling of drinking a big glass of water. I still do.

What was really interesting for me was the effect this shift had on my energy. Everyone who knows me knows that I am very active. If I were a little boy, people would call me hyperactive. When I made the shift and stopped drinking caffeinated soft drinks, my energy went down, for a time. But after a few weeks, my energy level actually went up! One of the side benefits of shifting from Pepsi to water was a higher energy level. To my surprise, this seismic shift also led to a ten-pound weight loss.

I am still developing some of the other habits described in this chapter, but this change has become a lifestyle change for me and has made a huge difference in my health and energy.

Whatever beverage you love, if it is taking the place of water, you might want to make a shift. If I wanted to go after a sacred cow, I could bring up coffee consumption, but that might be going too far. Or would it? The point is that each of us should look at our lifestyle and make sure we are giving our body what it needs. And all of us need plenty of water. You will be amazed at how refreshing water can be. And in most places, water is free—a bonus!

From Anytime Eating to Planned Times

There are two very helpful shifts you can make in the times you eat. First, it is wise to determine in advance what snacks you will eat in the course of a day and when you will eat them. People who snack freely and graze throughout the day can't register how much they are eating. Making the shift from unlimited snacking to eating set foods at set times will have a seismic impact on your health. This might seem confining at first, but in the long run, it brings freedom.

Second, another huge shift is to actually set a time in the evening when you will be done eating. My wife has modeled this for me. She stops eating at 8:00 p.m. In rare situations, she is forced to adjust this, and she is free to do so. But it is not the norm. She has chosen a time that is a healthy cutoff point, which removes the late-night temptations most of us face. When we stop eating at a responsible time, we tend to sleep better and wake up feeling more energetic, and we enjoy breakfast more.

From Passive to Active Lives

One of the most popular chair companies in America makes a recliner called the La-Z-Boy. That says it all! We live in a culture that spins us in two directions. On the one hand, we are often too busy and need to learn the secret of Sabbath. One the other hand, inactivity marks too many lives. Being busy does not necessarily mean we are active and fit. With the advent of the internet, cable TV packages that offer hundreds of channels, and myriad video-games systems, passivity is becoming a national pastime.

||||| Seismic Shift Suggestion |||||

Move It. Pick one small way you can become more active. Maybe you can hide your remote control for a week and actually get up each time you want to change the channel. Or you might decide to do ten minutes of stretching each morning. Allow this activity to be an expression of your desire to offer to God a body with higher levels of fitness and energy so you can serve him more fully.

We need to make some seismic shifts in our activity level. I want to suggest three shifts we can make that will have a big impact on our health. First, we need to weave more physical action into our lives. We have too many remote controls and conveniences. We need to get off our backsides and become more active in the normal course of the day. For example, suppose you work on the fifth floor of an office building. Use the stairs and not the elevator and see how this impacts both your heart rate and your mental outlook.

Again, my wife has been an example to me in this kind of creative commitment. We were on vacation and ended up on the eighth floor of a hotel. As we were heading up to our room, Sherry said, "Hey, come take the stairs with me!" If you had been there to see the look I gave her, you would have known how I felt about her overly cheerful suggestion. For crying out loud, there was a perfectly good elevator right in front of us.

But I thought about it and said, "Okay." From that point on, I used the stairs (except when carrying luggage). One of the times, I had two of my sons with me, and we ended up racing! Good health became a game.

This is just one example, but you can be creative with this seismic shift. Start doing leg lifts every time you watch sports on TV. Walk instead of driving when you are going a short distance. If you are a golfer, boycott carts and use the two legs God gave you. Do some stretching exercises each time you get stuck at a red light. Create opportunities for activity instead of avoiding them.

A second shift is to set a time for exercise every day. You don't have to join a gym and drive miles to do a formal program (though there is nothing wrong with this). The key is to start somewhere. There are plenty of DVDs you can pop in at home and use to guide you through a good cardiovascular program. Walk or run for fifteen minutes each morning. Jump rope. Get a treadmill. Do jumping jacks. There are all sorts of options. The key is to do some exercise every day. If you make a shift and begin doing just ten to fifteen minutes of exercise early in your day, it will impact how you feel physically, emotionally, and even spiritually.

A third idea is to incorporate play into your week. For me, exercise is hard, but play is easy. After almost two decades off from soccer, I joined an adult winter indoor league and a summer outdoor league. My motivation to get into shape, knowing I would be competing with people half my age, was huge. I might miss a scheduled time to go jogging, but I would never intentionally miss a soccer game. Do you get the idea? Find some kind of activity that is fun for you. It could be lawn bowling (this actually works your back and legs), playing in a forty-and-over basketball league, joining a rowing club, cycling, or any activity you enjoy. If you check the internet or the yellow pages, or call your local community center, you will be amazed at how many options are available in your community.

Finally, it is always good to get someone to partner with you as you seek to be more active. If you know someone is waiting to walk with you in the mornings, you will be much more likely to pop out of bed and get ready. If you are riding with someone to your shuffleboard club, you are less apt to skip. Knowing that someone else is counting on you is a great motivator.

Like it or not, God has chosen to make our bodies his dwelling place. He didn't ask our opinion; he just let us know that he was moving in. So let's make the shifts needed to give him the best accommodations possible. If the president were coming to our homes, we would clean up! If the queen were dropping by, we would make sure everything was ready for Her Majesty's visit. Since the King of Kings has declared that his address will be your body, it is definitely worth making the shifts necessary to give him a fit dwelling place.

FOR REFLECTION

- What roadblocks stand in the way of my making a commitment to care for my body? What can I do to remove them?
- Most of us have had times when we took better care of our bodies and paid closer attention to our health. Or we know people who set a great example in this area. Think about the benefits of caring for your body. Let these motivate you to enter a season of better health.

FOR PRAYER

- Thank God for the physical abilities and strength you have. Acknowledge that every breath and each ounce of strength are gifts from him.
- Ask God to give you the discipline to implement a seismic shift in your health.

━━━⁓⁓⁓⁓⁓⁓⁓///⁄╱║||||||||||||| Chapter NINE

The Seismic Shift from Anxiety to Peace

Do not be anxious about anything, but in everything, by prayer and petition, with thanksgiving, present your requests to God. And the peace of God, which transcends all understanding, will guard your hearts and your minds in Christ Jesus.

—**Philippians 4:6–7**

Therefore I tell you, do not worry about your life, what you will eat or drink; or about your body, what you will wear. Is not life more important than food, and the body more important than clothes? Look at the birds of the air; they do not sow or reap or store away in barns, and yet your heavenly Father feeds them. Are you not much more valuable than they? Who of you by worrying can add a single hour to his life?

—**Matthew 6:25–27**

Peace I leave with you; my peace I give you. I do not give to you as the world gives. Do not let your hearts be troubled and do not be afraid.

—**John 14:27**

God wants his children to experience deep and lasting rest in every nook and cranny of our being. For our souls, he has modeled the secret of Sabbath. For our bodies, he invites us to make seismic shifts that reflect our understanding that the Holy Sprit dwells in us. But where do we find rest for our minds? How do we deal with the onslaught of stress, anxiety, and worry that can paralyze us? In a world filled with suffering, pain, and loss, is there really any way we can live with enduring peace of mind?

I saw the answer to this question lived out in a way that is more powerful and profound than I could explain with mere words. I was working in my office one evening when the phone rang. It was my wife, and she had bad news. Laura had taken a turn for the worse. This wonderful Christian girl had been in a serious car accident a few days before. She had a closed-head injury that had sent her into a coma. On this evening, the news from the doctors was sobering. All brain activity had ceased, and short of a miracle, Laura was beyond the help of the medical community.

I left my office immediately, drove by my house to pick up Sherry, and we headed straight for Spectrum Medical Center. When we arrived, we were greeted with hugs and tears. The Van Noord and Patmos families were waiting to hear from the doctors. This amazing group of Christians was no stranger to suffering. Laura's mother had battled cancer and passed away four years earlier. One of her uncles had fallen in a work-related accident and was still recovering. Now they had to face the prospect of losing Laura.

We decided to move from the lobby to gather in Laura's room for prayer. The rules limited the number of visitors, but this did not seem like one of those moments when the rules applied. About twenty of us gathered in the room. Ken, Laura's dad, stood at the end of the bed, gently caressing his little girl's foot. Joel, her big brother, held her right hand, and his wife, Jen, held her left. Laura lay in the middle, surrounded by a host of family members and friends who loved her dearly and desperately wanted her to be healed.

Tears flowed, monitors and machines beeped, and prayers ascended to the throne of God. For the next twenty minutes, that sterile hospital room was a holy place of worship. I don't know any other way to put it but to say that God showed up. A peace beyond description descended quietly and gently on each person. Ken prayed for the life of his only daughter. He asked God to spare her and to do a miracle. He also released her to God. "You made her, you gave her to me, I give her back to you." Her brother, Joel, prayed for his only sibling, and he too was filled with a staggering level of assurance. He told God that he wanted his little sister to live, but he agreed with Jesus, "Not my will, but yours be done." Grandpa and Grandma Patmos prayed. They had already lost their daughter, Beverly, to cancer, and now their granddaughter's life hung in the balance. Yet with a peace beyond explanation, they pled with God for Laura to live but also placed her in Jesus' arms.

When the amen was said, a holy hush hung in the air. In a moment that could have been anxious and without serenity, God was present, and he had brought his peace with him.

Three days later, Laura died. The Good Shepherd came and picked her up like a little lamb and laid her across his shoulders. He took her to a place of green pastures, to the home he had prepared long ago. Her eternity with the Savior she loved so passionately had begun a new chapter.

IIIIII **Seismic Shift Suggestion** IIIIII

Let Wisdom Speak. Identify a Christian you know who has walked through times of loss or turmoil with an extraordinary measure of peace. Ask this person how they experienced God's presence in their time of struggle. Ask what role honest prayers played in bringing peace to their heart. You might even want to tell them about a situation you are facing and ask for their wisdom on Bible passages you could read and how you can pray.

The faith and peace Laura's family exhibited in that hospital room have remained unwavering. One reason is that they do not just call out for God's help when things get hard. They walk with Jesus in the good and bad times of life. They have come to discover that the Lord is their Shepherd and that "even though I walk through the valley of the shadow of death, I will fear no evil, for you are with me" (Ps. 23:4). This lesson can be learned by all who follow Jesus. We do not have to live with worry-filled minds and anxiety-driven hearts. Peace can be ours no matter what we face, if we walk hand in hand with the Savior.

The God of All Peace ● ● ● ● ● ● ● ● ● ● ● ● ● ● ● ● ● ● ●

As much as you want to experience peace in your life, God desires it even more. He knows our propensity for feeling anxiety and shows us seismic shifts that will crush worry and replace it with peace. God takes this so seriously that he sent the Holy Spirit to be with us and in us. His

Spirit does many things, but near the top of the list is bringing peace to those who follow Jesus. This is why the Savior said, "All this I have spoken while still with you. But the Counselor, the Holy Spirit, whom the Father will send in my name, will teach you all things and will remind you of everything I have said to you. Peace I leave with you; my peace I give you. I do not give to you as the world gives. Do not let your hearts be troubled and do not be afraid" (John 14:25–27).

Australians have some colorful colloquialisms. One of my favorites is, "No worries, mate!" Jesus wants us to know that we can live with a mindset that says, "I don't have to be troubled in my heart, and I will not be ruled by fear." In Jesus Christ, we can have a "no worries" attitude.

This is not a flippant denial of the real challenges and struggles this life brings. It is a bold confidence that the presence and power of God's Holy Spirit in our lives can act as a counterweight to the pain each of us will face as we walk in this world. Jesus is teaching that our minds do not have to be playgrounds where anxiety, worry, and fear dominate like the neighborhood bully. There is a new kid in town, and his name is Jesus. He promises to give his peace to us. He assures us that what he offers is radically different than what the world gives. He wants to take up residence in our minds in such a way that his peace will rule. If need be, he will punch anxiety in the nose and send it home crying. God takes this so seriously that he comes to live inside us through the presence of his Holy Spirit, the Spirit of peace.

Anxiety Busters

Some people get nervous every time they pick up their mail. "Will there be a bill I can't afford to pay, a letter bearing bad news, or perhaps a cover story on a magazine that reminds me of the turmoil in the world?" In the movie *Roxanne*, a modern-day comedic retelling of the classic French story *Cyrano de Bergerac*, we see a picture of postal paranoia. C. D., the warmhearted, long-nosed fire chief, opens his mailbox, takes out a stack of letters, looks at them briefly, screams, jams them back in the box, and gets away as fast as he can. An action as simple as getting the mail can send some people into an emotional tailspin.

For others, going to work is so stressful that the very thought of it causes a knot to form in their gut. People can become anxious when they think about their past, present, or future. The national economy, the cost of crude oil, unrest in the Middle East, moral decay, the conflicting messages of the mainstream media, global warming, the loss of the rain forests, the plight of the spotted owl, hair loss, weight loss, and losses of any and every kind can give birth to stress. There is plenty to be worried about. Maybe just reading this litany of anxiety-producing things is causing you to get a little wound up.

Here is the good news. God is the great anxiety buster. He does not want us to live in the prison of worry, and he holds the keys that will set us free.

From Worry to Prayer

The first and greatest anxiety buster is the power of prayer. The apostle Paul had plenty of stress in his life. He gave a partial list of what he faced when he wrote to the church of Corinth. After telling about all of the physical abuse and pain he had suffered, he listed some of the mental and emotional turmoil he faced. Paul said, "I have been constantly on the move. I have been in danger from rivers, in danger from bandits, in danger from my own countrymen, in danger from Gentiles; in danger in the city, in danger in the country, in danger at sea; and in danger from false brothers. I have labored and toiled and have often gone without sleep; I have known hunger and thirst and have often gone without food; I have been cold and naked. Besides everything else, I face daily the pressure of my concern for all the churches" (2 Cor. 11:26–28).

If anyone had the right to live an anxious life, it was the apostle Paul. But with all of the legitimate reasons he had to camp under a cloud of worry, Paul refused. Instead, he battled back with prayer. Paul summarized his theology of worry with some of the most revolutionary words ever penned: "Do not be anxious about anything, but in everything, by prayer and petition, with thanksgiving, present your requests to God. And the peace of God, which transcends all understanding, will guard your hearts and your minds in Christ Jesus" (Phil. 4:6–7).

The answer to the stress, worry, and anxiety of this world is not to develop an escapist attitude. We are not called to run away or even to avoid the tension-producing challenges of life; we are called to answer with prayer.

When my wife, Sherry, was in college, she had an ongoing battle with a specific worry. It was an anxiety that many young women face. Her pressing question was, "Will I ever meet the right man, fall in love, and get married?" By her senior year, Sherry was not in love with a wonderful man, but four of her roommates were engaged and planning weddings. Though she was happy for each of them, the constant joy in the apartment and talks about wedding details felt like salt in her emotional wounds. There were times when she would lie in bed, facing the wall, and the tears would flow. She never let her roommates know, because in her heart, she truly was happy for each of her friends. What plagued her was the thought, the nagging worry, that love would pass her by.

||||| Seismic Shift Suggestion |||||

Trade It In. The apostle Paul teaches that God offers a trade. We can stop worrying and start praying. This might sound a little simplistic, but making this trade can change your life. Identify an area in which you tend to worry or deal with anxiety. Commit to pray every time you feel worry rising like a tide. Drive it back with prayer. If you worry about a lack of finances, pray for God's provision. If you feel anxiety about the welfare of loved ones, ask for God's protection. If you worry about your future, ask the Lord to go before you to prepare the way. As peace fills your heart, give thanks and praise to God.

When she shared her heartache with her mentor, Maria, she received wise and biblical council. Maria advised Sherry to use her time and energy to pray for her husband to be, even though she had not yet met him. So whenever worry about not being married someday began to creep in, she would pray for her future husband. Two decades later, she still testifies to the peace and hope God brought to her heart during those months. Rather than being anxious, Sherry committed to pray for the man she would someday marry, and I'm glad she did. It was only weeks after her college graduation that God led Sherry to work in California for the summer, and that is where we met.

This is just one simple example of how prayer can overcome worry. When we find our minds and emotional worlds becoming battlegrounds, it is time to pray. In the process, we petition God for help and strength. We thank him for the many ways we see his grace at work in our lives. Then we rejoice as God's peace replaces our anxious feelings.

Sherry found peace in one of the hardest times in her life when she replaced worry with prayer. Now, over two decades later, we practice this same principle with our three teenage boys. Sometimes we feel anxious about their future. In particular, we long for our boys to meet and fall in love with godly Christian women. Will we worry and stew over this, or will we pray? Most of the time we choose prayer, and rejoice as we see anxiety retreat and peace take over.

From My Plans to God's Will

Another seismic shift that breaks the back of anxiety is learning to seek God's will for our lives. Too often we feel it is up to us to set the goals, make the plan, work the program, and arrive at the right place in our lives. Although God invites us into the process, for those who say they are followers of Jesus, we need to do a little more following.

|||||| Seismic Shift Suggestion ||||||

Hit Your Knees. Prayer is truly the greatest weapon against anxiety. For the next week, when you roll out of bed, don't hit your feet. Instead, go directly to your knees. Spend the first few minutes of your day thinking through any points of worry or concern. Then offer them to God. Ask for his help, strength, and wisdom to help you through the day. At the end of your prayer, before you stand up and get rolling, confidently invite the peace of God to fill your heart and mind.

When Jesus called his disciples, he said, "Follow me" (Matt. 4:19; 9:9). He made it clear that his people were like sheep with a shepherd and that they should recognize his voice (John 10:1–6). Jesus himself followed the will of his Father. This is why he could say, "I tell you the truth, the Son can do nothing by himself; he can do only what he sees his Father doing, because whatever the Father does the Son also does" (John 5:19). This was not a sign of weakness; Jesus was God in human flesh. It was his declaration that doing the will of the Father was the passion of his heart. Jesus also said, "When you have lifted up the Son of Man, then you will know that I am the one I claim to be and that I do nothing on my own but speak just what the Father has taught me" (John 8:28). Though Jesus was the greatest leader to walk on this earth, he was also a humble follower. As he faced the reality of going to the cross, he expressed the ultimate yielded spirit when he said to his heavenly Father, "Not my will, but yours be done" (Luke 22:42).

All through the Bible, we are called to seek and to follow God's will. We are also warned of the folly of trying to live only by our plans. In the book of James, we read, "Now listen, you who say, 'Today or tomorrow we will go to this or that city, spend a year there, carry on business and make money.' Why, you do not even know what will happen tomorrow. What is your life? You are a mist that appears for a little while and then vanishes. Instead, you ought to say, 'If it is the Lord's will, we will live and do this or that'" (James 4:13–15).

In the book of Proverbs, we hear this same wisdom: "In his heart a man plans his course, but the Lord determines his steps" (Prov. 16:9). When we decide to seek and follow God's will instead of making our own plans, peace is a by-product. This is not to say that God's will is always easy. But when we know we are following God's plan for our lives, we experience a peace that overcomes all circumstances.

The best way to discover God's will for your life is to dig deep into his Word. Many of our questions are answered with clarity. Here is a sample of questions that the Bible answers definitively:

- Should I enter into a business deal that is a little shady?
- Is it God's will for a Christian to marry a nonbeliever?
- Is there anything wrong with gossiping about someone who has hurt me?
- Should I share my resources with the poor and oppressed in this world?
- Is sex outside of marriage God's plan for human intimacy?
- If I'm a Christian, is it my responsibility to tell others about Jesus?

These and many other questions find direct answers in the Bible. The best way to discover God's will for your life is by reading his Word and following what it says.

It would be wonderful if the Bible answered every question, but it is not that simple. There are hosts of other question that don't find a direct yes or no in the pages of God's Word. Here are some examples:

- Is this the right time for me to change careers?
- Should I move from one community to another?
- Should I buy the Ford or the Honda?
- Am I best suited to be a school teacher or to go into sales?
- Would it be better for me to go out for the soccer team or the tennis team?
- Is this the right person for me to date and maybe marry someday?

These are the kinds of questions that are not answered explicitly in the Bible. They demand prayer, wisdom, counsel, and discernment. We all have times when we wish God would spell out his will with the clarity that would guide us through the complex decisions in life. Wouldn't it be great if each of us could turn to a page in the Bible and discover a passage written just for us? Imagine Bill opening his Bible and reading this:

Dear Bill,

All right, here's the deal. When you turn eleven, you will meet a cute little girl named Susie. She is the girl you will marry, even though all you can think of now is that she has cooties. Just play it cool and take your time. By the time you are twenty-one, you will be engaged, and a year later, you'll be happily married. Your career will be working for a hospital, providing technical support for their computer and communications systems. This will be a bonus, because Sue will give birth to all three of your kids at that hospital, and you will have great insurance coverage. Just as a heads-up: your first child will be a boy. Then get ready for identical twin girls.

You will be attending Riverview Community Church for the first ten years of your married life, but then you will switch over to Second Baptist on the other side of town. Now, as for hobbies, don't worry, it's all planned out. You will play tennis and golf, and bridge on Friday nights.

Have a great life,

God

This might seem attractive, but the truth is, the Bible does not answer many of the questions we ask. We won't find a portion of the Bible that gives the fine print and details for every decision we will make. In the moments we have these questions, we must learn to listen for the still, small voice of the Holy Spirit. If we face a worrisome situation and need direction not overtly given in the Bible, we can ask God to speak to our hearts and show us his will. This might sound superspiritual, but it is a simple concept. When Jesus says, "The sheep listen to his voice. He calls his own sheep by name and leads them out" (John 10:3), he is speaking about how his followers are to listen and respond to his leading. Jesus expects us to learn to recognize his voice and follow where he leads.

This takes time and dedication. Followers of Jesus can ask God for promptings, leadings, and direction for specific situations. We can wait on the Lord and invite him to orchestrate situations that help indicate where he is leading. In the book of James, we are assured, "If any of you lacks wisdom, he should ask God, who gives generously to all without finding fault, and it will be given to him" (James 1:5). We can also seek council from Christians we respect and invite the Lord to give direction through them. In all of these situations, we still need to exercise discernment. We must also remember that God's leading will never be inconsistent with what the Bible teaches.

▪ From Alone to Hand in Hand with Jesus

One more anxiety buster is living with the assurance that we are never alone. God has promised he will never leave us nor forsake us (Josh. 1:5). The Father watches over us, the Spirit dwells within us, and Jesus intercedes for us. If we see ourselves through the eyes of God, our worries melt away.

One powerful biblical example of this is when Elisha and his servant were surrounded by a powerful enemy army. Elisha's servant was terrified, and with good reason. This mighty force had come with one goal in mind, the destruction of Elisha, the servant of God. All the servant could see were horses, chariots, and soldiers surrounding them; there was no way out. He was overcome with fear. Elisha, on the other hand, did not seem worried, anxious, or even concerned. Elisha simply said to him, "Those who are with us are more than those who are with them." But his servant did not get the whole picture. That was the moment Elisha prayed, "O LORD, open his eyes so he may see," and this is what we read: "Then the LORD opened the servant's eyes, and he looked and saw the hills full of horses and chariots of fire all around Elisha" (2 Kings 6:15–17).

Can you imagine what this servant felt when he saw the army of God surrounding the enemies that had come to attack them? Courage must have surged in his heart. God wants us to know we are never alone. When anxiety surges through our veins, it is time to remember that Jesus is with us, always.

Ken Davis, a Christian speaker and comedian, came up with an idea for a T-shirt that captures the heartbeat of the seismic shift from anxiety to peace. On the shirt is a scrawny little lamb walking through a valley. All around him are wolves with glowing eyes, sharp teeth, and drool dripping down their faces. It is clear they have one thought on their minds as they look at the little sheep: dinner.

But walking next to this lone sheep and holding his little hoof is Jesus. There is a little dialogue bubble coming up from the sheep's mouth with three words that say it all: "I'm with him!" When we walk with Jesus, we can walk in peace because we are never alone.

FOR REFLECTION

- What situations tend to generate the highest levels of anxiety for me? How can prayer and the confidence that God is with me help replace worry with peace?
- How can knowing and believing God's Word help lower my stress level? What is one example of how I grew in peace as I reflected on the truth of God's Word?

FOR PRAYER

- Thank God for the times you have experienced his presence and peace in the midst of difficulty or uncertainty. In particular, thank Jesus for sending his Holy Spirit to be with you and in you.
- Ask God to develop your hearing, your spiritual ears. Pray for the ability to recognize when God is speaking to you. Tell God that you want to be a sheep that recognizes his voice, and commit yourself to follow as you hear him speak and lead.

Part 4

Shifts That Build Dynamic and
Lasting Relationships

In a complex world with lots of moving parts, checkups are not merely helpful, they are essential for health and safety. Anyone who wants a car to last many miles and years brings it to a mechanic for regular tune-ups. The mechanic changes the oil, rotates the tires, tops off fluids, and gives the engine a thorough review. If the mechanic spots any problems, they are fixed.

Likewise, we are all familiar with the importance of medical check-ups. Those who are wise visit their physician regularly. The complexity of the human body demands careful medical examinations to maintain health and identify potential problems.

As our world grows more and more dependent on computers and the integration of communications systems, most companies run regular diagnostic checks on their computer networks. The church I serve has a seven-member volunteer technical team that maintains the church's communications systems. This maintenance includes computers, phones, audio-visual equipment, the integration of PDAs, and other technical support. The team's faithfulness keeps the church from having to deal with the frustration and cost of lost information and systems crashes.

Regular checkups on our cars, bodies, and computer systems make sense to most people. No one thinks it's a waste of time, energy, or resources to invest in routine maintenance. Rather, most agree it costs more in the long run if we fail to conduct regular checkups in any of these complex areas of life. We have all heard the saying, "Pay me now or pay me later." Wise people have the foresight to invest in regular tune-ups, checkups, and upgrades so they don't have to pay a huge price in the future because of neglect in the present.

Since we all agree regular checkups are helpful when dealing with complex things like cars, bodies, and computers, it shouldn't be hard to see the need for a similar approach to our relationships. The moving parts in a car are child's play compared with the infinite complexities of the human psyche. If ever there was a complicated system in need of regular checkups, it is our relationships. Nothing is more complex, and few things seem to break down more often. The problem is, most of us don't know where to begin when it comes to relational checkups.

The next three chapters lay out a three-point relational checkup strategy. This includes seismic shifts we can make to bring new levels of health and vitality to our families, friendships, and churches, and to all of our relationships. Although the chapters can't cover every dynamic, they focus on areas that can have a big impact.

First, learning to encourage and bless others is a great investment in any relationship. Affirmation is essential. Second, committing to serve others develops the heartbeat of Jesus in our interactions with the people in our lives. When we are devoted to Christlike servanthood, we discover new levels of relational health. Third, if we want our connections with other people to thrive, we will to learn to speak the truth in love. Flattery kills; truth-telling infuses life into a relationship.

Cars, bodies, and computer systems all crash without routine checkups. Relationships that go unchecked are also in danger of breaking down. If we fail to invest in routine maintenance, our relationships will never thrive. In too many cases, they break down and are tossed into the relational junkyard of our lives. The good news is, if we commit to making a few seismic shifts and conduct regular checkups, we can avoid unnecessary pain and discover greater depths of health and vitality in all of our relationships.

Chapter TEN

The Seismic Shift from Burning to Building

The tongue has the power of life and death,
and those who love it will eat its fruit.

—**Proverbs 18:21**

Reckless words pierce like a sword,
but the tongue of the wise brings healing.

—**Proverbs 12:18**

Do not let any unwholesome talk come out of your mouths, but only what is helpful for building others up according to their needs, that it may benefit those who listen.

—**Ephesians 4:29**

I should have listened to my parents. But I was a third-grader, and their warnings about playing with fire fell on deaf ears. Rather than heeding their words, I was just extra careful never to let my parents know that I liked playing with matches.

One day my grade-school buddy Chuckie and I decided to drop lit matches through a plastic pipe to see if they stayed lit when they came out the other side. When I think back, I wonder why we did not perform our little science experiment over pavement. Instead, we did this in the privacy of my tinder-dry, weed-infested, tumbleweed-ridden back yard.

What we learned is that matches, at least some of them, do pop out the other side of a plastic pipe very much on fire. We also learned that an overgrown back yard in the middle of a Southern California summer was a fire waiting to happen. The flames spread so fast we could not contain them. They leaped so high that they were over our heads in seconds. So we ran across the street and hid in Chuckie's room until the fire engines arrived.

I learned a valuable lesson that day. My parents were right. Some things are not to be played with! Fire is fine when it is in a fireplace, in a fire ring, or on the stove. But when the flames hit the kitchen curtain or jump out of the fire ring and climb up a tree or spread through a back yard, they can be dangerous and downright deadly.

There is a reason the Bible compares the tongue to a fire. When it is under control, it can be a blessing. But when the tongue is out of control, the potential for a devastating forest fire is great.

A Force to Be Reckoned With

One of the most startling passages in the Bible was written by Jesus' younger brother, James. Describing the power of our words, he writes, "The tongue is a small part of the body, but it makes great boasts. Consider what a great forest is set on fire by a small spark. The tongue also is a fire, a world of evil among the parts of the body. It corrupts the whole person, sets the whole course of his life on fire, and is itself set on fire by hell" (James 3:5–6). James seems to be going a little over the top. He thinks the tongue is like a fire, that a whole world of evil lives in this tiny pink organ, that it can corrupt us through and through, that it ignites the very fabric of our lives with flames that must be quenched, and that all of this fiery mess has been ignited by hell itself. Wow! James, please tell us how you really feel about the tongue.

It is easy to wonder if James might be overstating his case a bit. Is the tongue really as dangerous as he thinks? Do our words have the potential for the kind of destruction James seems to be worried about?

His counsel about the power of our words makes sense when we take an inventory of our emotional battle scars. We don't have to walk long on this earth before we discover that some of our deepest wounds are the result of careless or hurtful words. It is also true that when people speak words of love, affirmation, and blessing, we experience some of the most precious memories in this life.

|||||| **Seismic Shift Suggestion** ||||||

Fire-Prevention Program. Do you remember Smokey the Bear? He was the spokesman for the forest service. His big line was, "Only you can prevent forest fires." If Smokey could give advice on preventing relational fires, I think he would recommend memorizing these three short verses:

- Proverbs 18:21
- Proverbs 12:18
- James 3:6

Commit these to memory and see if the truth of these passages impacts how you use your words.

It is no surprise that God gives all kinds of warnings about how we use our words. Thousands of years ago, God inspired Solomon to speak on this topic. Slowly read these truths out loud and let the message sink into your mind and heart:

The tongue has the power of life and death,
    and those who love it will eat its fruit.
        — Proverbs 18:21

Reckless words pierce like a sword,
    but the tongue of the wise brings healing.
        — Proverbs 12:18

Solomon was the wisest man of his generation. He understood that words have the potential to burn or to build. They can pierce or heal. They can bring death or life. The truth of the matter is that if we are not careful, our words tend toward the negative. If we push the default button, we tend to use words in ways that destroy relationships and fracture community.

God has something very different in mind. He longs to see us build healthy and lasting relationships. But to do this, we must learn to control our speech.

The Sweet and the Sour

My third-grade teacher was Mrs. Sour. Ironically, she was the sweetest teacher I ever had. She routinely encouraged, affirmed, and praised all of us kids. I can still remember finishing a big project for her. I made a picture book of the story "This Is the House That Jack Built." To the untrained eye, it looked like a poor-to-average job of copying a story and drawing pictures. But I had poured my heart into this assignment. It was an offering of love to the sweet Mrs. Sour. As always, she said just the right words to lift my self-esteem and inspire me to greater heights of accomplishment. Although I can't remember exactly what Mrs. Sour looked like, I do remember that she was beautiful. I also remember that I loved school.

The next year, I asked my parents if I could stay in third grade. Unfortunately, fourth grade was my fate, and my new teacher was anything but sweet. She had a sharp tongue and a critical spirit, and she had me in the sights of her rifle of disapproval. When I look back, I realize I was a very hard kid to manage, but the way she tried to tame me was anything but a self-esteem building experience.

One day she asked the class to turn to page 57 of our reading book. She announced there was a picture of Kevin Harney on that page. I was shocked and excited as I began rustling through the pages to find my picture. What an amazing treat for a fourth-grade boy to get his picture in a school book.

Some of the other kids turned to page 57 faster than I did, and the laughter began. When I reached the page, I was confused. The only picture was of a monkey in a cage. I sat in shock as the truth set in. Her words, accompanied by the laughter of the students, cut deep into my heart. Before I knew what I was doing, I threw my book at her with all the force I could muster. Then I made a mad dash for the door. I did not stop running until I reached home. As I ran, my mind raced faster than my feet. I vowed that I would never attend school again.

My parents "had a talk" with my teacher. They also had a talk with me and explained that dropping out of fourth grade was not an option. My teacher and I coexisted in the classroom for the rest of the year, but I knew how she felt about me, and she had little question about how I viewed her. Through this experience, I discovered just how deeply reckless words can wound. My teacher did not hit me or steal my bike. All she did was make "a harmless little joke." And in the process, she drove a knife into my heart. More than three decades later, I still have a visceral response when I think about that moment.

My third- and fourth-grade teachers taught me that words have great power. With them we can bless or we can curse. We can burn to the ground or build up to heaven. The choice is ours. And if we want to have healthy and growing relationships, each of us must learn to use our tongues as instruments of healing and encouragement.

Guard Your Mouth •

Virtually every person who makes it through grade school can testify to the fact that words can be a fire. We have all been burned at one time or another. And if we are honest, we are also guilty of using our words to hurt others. I have to admit that there are plenty of times when words I spoke burned like fire. Too many people could write a story about how my words have pierced their hearts. Sadly, some of these people are the very ones I love the most and never want to hurt. James warns us that no one can tame the tongue (James 3:8). This declaration is not meant to discourage us. Rather, it is a warning we need to heed. Even when we feel we have our tongues under control, we need to beware.

|||||| **Seismic Shift Suggestion** ||||||

Fire Hazards. We all have fire hazards in our lives: people who can ignite our tongues just by walking into the room; situations that just seem to invite us to lash out with words. Make a list of the fire hazards in your life. When and where are you most prone to let your words become negative? Once you have your list, do two things. First, try to avoid these hazards. Second, if you can't avoid them, be ready before fire season comes. Be prepared to replace burning with building. Foresight can make a big difference.

Every so often, we get a vivid reminder that some creatures will never be fully tamed. Just ask anyone who was in the crowd on October 3, 2003, for Siegfried and Roy's famous magic show featuring rare tigers. These massive felines were tamed, domesticated, and nothing more than big pussycats. Then one of them attacked, mauled, and almost killed Roy. The crowd was horrified. But should we really be surprised? They were playing with *tigers*!

In the same way, we should not be shocked that the Bible warns us to beware of the tongue. We are told it will never be fully tamed. We need to be on our guard at all times. If we are, we can learn to use our words to bless and not to burn. If we are not mindful, our words will do more damage than we can imagine. Although the tongue will always be a fire hazard, we can learn how to handle our words carefully and also what we should do when a fire ignites. As we make this seismic shift and submit our speech to God, we experience changes that lead us from burning to building.

The Danger of Grumbling • • • • • • • • • • • • • • • •

It would be helpful if people came with warning labels. Just as cigarette packages have a message of caution from the surgeon general, and music CDs with explicit lyrics have warning labels, people who grumble and complain should have stickers on their foreheads that say, "Poison."

Does this sound too harsh? It shouldn't. When we grumble, we cause a massive amount of damage. The sad fact is that it's far too easy to fall into this pattern. When we grumble, we adopt a negative attitude about almost everything. We can always find something bad to say. We have the uncanny ability to see the dark cloud in the middle of every silver lining.

In the city of Corinth, about two thousand years ago, there was a problem with church members grumbling and complaining. People felt it was their God-given right to gripe and moan about anything they did not like or understand. Sound familiar? So God, in an effort to bring about a seismic shift for the future of the church, reminded them of their sins.

What is fascinating about Paul's warning to the church at Corinth is the way he reviewed the history of Israel and pointed out some of its lowest moments. One by one, Paul projects a Technicolor picture as he warns the Corinthians not to repeat the mistakes of their ancestors. Paul writes, "Now these things occurred as examples to keep us from setting our hearts on evil things as they did. Do not be idolaters, as some of them were; as it is written: 'The people sat down to eat and drink and got up to indulge in pagan revelry.' We should not commit sexual immorality, as some of them did—and in one day twenty-three thousand of them died. We should not test the Lord, as some of them did—and were killed by snakes. And do not grumble, as some of them did—and were killed by the destroying angel" (1 Cor. 10:6–10).

The forty years Israel spent wandering in the desert was a time they would have preferred to forget. They had highlights they loved to remember, such as the exodus from Egypt, crossing the Red Sea, and entering the Promised Land. But the forty years of wandering was something they wanted to leave in the past. When Paul brought this up, it would have been as comfortable as asking someone to talk about their hemorrhoid surgery during the second course of a dinner party. Some things are better left unsaid.

Paul brings up this awkward topic and lists four sins the people of Israel committed while they wandered in the wilderness. Here are the first three:

- idolatry
- sexual immorality
- testing the Lord

Each sin had serious consequences. They were behaviors unfit for God's people in the days of Moses and in the days of Paul, and they are unfit for us today as well. Imagine someone setting up an idol-filled shrine in the foyer of your church on a Sunday morning. As people walk in, they see a church member bowing down and worshiping idols made of stone, wood, and metal. Do you think anyone in the church might express concern about this? Would a pastor or church-board member make the person stop? Of course they would! Do you think people in your church might feel some discomfort if people committed sexually immoral acts in the church building in full view of the members? You had better believe someone would make sure this behavior would cease and desist! What if someone opened their mouth and challenged God right in front of everyone? Would this send a chill down a few spines and raise a few eyebrows?

Here is the reality. All three of these behaviors would be seen as sin and dealt with immediately. It would be hard to imagine any congregation, leadership team, or pastor ignoring them.

The question then becomes, Why do Christians practically ignore the fourth sin Paul addresses in this passage? Why don't we take this one as seriously as the other three? Paul points out Israel's sins of idolatry, immorality, testing God, and finally, their grumbling.

Grumbling? What place does grumbling have among such huge and obvious sins? Why would Paul include grumbling in the same list as idolatry and sexual immorality?

Paul is simply communicating God's heart on this topic. If you read about what happened when God's people were stuck in the wilderness for forty years, it becomes clear why Paul emphasizes this sin. Grumbling was one of their most consistent and damaging behaviors. This sin plagued the people of Israel all through their history, it was damaging the church in Paul's day, and it still runs rampant in the lives of too many Christians and churches today.

In my twenty-five years as a pastor, grumbling is the one sinful practice I have seen more often than any other. Some people grumble and complain constantly, but no one ever tells them it is wrong. No one declares, "This is sin. It grieves the heart of God, breaks the unity of the church, and becomes a foothold for Satan to enter and destroy the church."

Not only do few church members, church boards, or pastors deal with this sin, it is often dressed up, perfumed, and given the name Annual Congregational Meeting. In some churches, coffee hour is a breeding ground for grumblers. This is when they pick apart the sermon, complain about the music, gripe about all the changes in the church, and generally spout off about anything and everything they don't like. Their poison spreads quickly; it breeds discouragement, breaks unity, and dishonors God.

It is time for the church to call grumbling by its true name, "Sin!"

Zero Tolerance Zone

Grumbling is a poison in our relationships. From homes to schools to the workplace to the church, destructive fires burn when grumbling goes unchecked. To keep our relationships from being damaged by grumbling, we need to declare our lives Zero Tolerance Zones. We must take grumbling as seriously as the other sins Paul deals with in 1 Corinthians.

||||| Seismic Shift Suggestion |||||

Establish ZTZs. Have a conversation with the people in your family, small group, neighborhood, or any other group with which you gather regularly. Discuss establishing this cluster of people as a Zero Tolerance Zone for grumbling. Do it lovingly but firmly. Agree that if someone starts grumbling, you will throw some water on the fire; you won't join in. This is a ZTZ for grumbling.

To do this, we must first look at our hearts and attitudes. We must ask the question, Am I a grumbler? If you have gotten into the habit of complaining constantly at work, pointing out everything that is wrong in the church, or incessantly criticizing your spouse, children, or friends, you just might be a grumbler. If negative people are attracted to you like moths to a flame because you quickly reinforce their complaining spirit, you just might be a card-carrying member of the Grumbler's Club. If you have a natural ability to see what is wrong with everyone you meet and you feel compelled to share your insights with others, hold onto your hat, you just might be the president of the local chapter of Grumblers-R-Us.

If you are a grumbler, it is time for a seismic shift. God calls grumbling a sin, and so should you. In Moses' day, if you had fallen into idol worship, you would need to throw away your pagan idols and turn your heart back to worshiping the one true God. If you have become a grumbler, you need to close your mouth and invite God to change your heart. Silence is the best antidote for a complaining spirit. Commit to bite your tongue and grumble no more. Confess this sin to God and ask for the conviction of the Holy Spirit to fall on you each time you even think about grumbling. Then give one or two close friends permission to point out when you start grumbling. Maybe you can make a few bright-red warning stickers that say, "Beware the Grumbler." Give them to your friends and tell them to slap one on your forehead each time you start complaining. Or maybe a gentler approach would work for you. Have your friends say, "You are starting to do it again," anytime you start grumbling. Whatever it takes, get some accountability and extinguish this sin if it is burning in you.

If you are not a grumbler but you know people who are, commit to help them stop their destructive patterns. If we want to extinguish the fire of grumbling, we must turn a deaf ear to those who engage in grumbling like it's a recreational activity. Fire spreads only when there is fuel to burn. For a grumbler, the fuel is listening ears. If no one listens, the flames die. In our homes, in our communities, and particularly in our churches, we must refuse to listen to grumbling.

The easiest way to help stop the spread of grumbling is to avoid those who grumble. When you must interact with a grumbler, show no interest in their litany of complaints. Don't fuel them. Make it clear you feel that what they are saying is not appropriate. If they ask, "Is something wrong?" let them know you don't feel comfortable with the content of the conversation and tell them why. You might even want to open your Bible to 1 Corinthians 10:10. If they continue to do their best to use you as fuel for their grumbling, you might even have to say, "I can't listen to you complain about other people. This is inappropriate, and I won't be part of this conversation." I have discovered this rarely has to be done more than once with a grumbler.

As a pastor, I occasionally interact with people from other congregations who visit our church. On a few different occasions, these guests have been grumblers who complain to me about their churches and even their pastors. Sometimes they try to disguise their grumbling by leading with a compliment. "Pastor, what a wonderful sermon. I wish our pastor actually preached the Bible. His sermons are boring and no more than ..." At this point, I typically cut in and say, "I'm glad you enjoyed our service and the message, but I don't think it is appropriate for you to share your concerns about your pastor with me." On one occasion, the pastor being slandered was a personal friend, and I told the couple maligning him how much I respect him. I let them know that he was the only person who should hear their concerns. They looked a little hurt and offended, but they stopped grumbling.

I tend to be blunt, so I deal with these situations head on. My wife is tenderhearted, so when she bumps into a grumbler, she typically says something like, "I'm sorry, but I don't think I should be hearing this." Even gentle correction makes a big difference in the life of a grumbler. However we communicate our concerns, we need to make it clear that grumbling is wrong and it won't be tolerated.

The bottom line is this: grumbling is a sin. It destroys relationships, and it must be stopped. At least once a year, I preach a sermon on this topic and announce that our church functions with zero tolerance for grumbling and complaining. The result has been a level of unity and peace in the church that honors God and enhances relationships. In our home, we don't allow grumbling. If our boys have an authentic concern about someone, we have them work it out with that person, not vent it at the dinner table. On the cul-de-sac where we live, there is not a single grumbler. Or if there is, they never complain in public. We have all agreed that if we have a relational concern, it won't be handled by grumbling but by lovingly talking with the right person.

The Delight of Blessing

Grumbling burns, consumes, and destroys relationships; speaking words of blessing can heal, strengthen, and rebuild them. If we want to experience dynamic and lasting relationships, we can begin by committing to use our words as a source of blessing and encouragement. God wants us to celebrate the good we see in others. We can speak uplifting words face to face, we can write encouraging notes, and we can even become ambassadors of "good gossip."

The apostle Paul wrote many letters to churches in the first century. When he mentioned other believers, he often celebrated their character, strengths, and spiritual progress. In the letter to the Colossian church, Paul singled out some people and praised them. When Paul wrote about Tychicus, he blessed him by referring to him as "a dear brother, a faithful minister and fellow servant in the Lord" (Col. 4:7). When he mentioned Epaphras, he labeled him "our dear fellow servant, who is a faithful minister of Christ on our behalf" (Col. 1:7). Paul's affection for these brothers comes through strongly. He was committed to bless and build up people with his words.

In the book of Ephesians, Paul writes, "Do not let any unwholesome talk come out of your mouths, but only what is helpful for building others up according to their needs, that it may benefit those who listen" (Eph. 4:29). According to Paul, our words should do three things: build people up, be spoken according to their needs, and benefit them. If we took this single verse seriously, it would revolutionize our relationships. We would become prayerful and careful whenever we speak.

When we develop the habit of affirming others, a seismic shift occurs. In a world where the tongue is often used to burn, we create a culture of blessing. A home where parents and siblings encourage each other is a gift greater than most people dream. A church where affirmation and blessing flow freely and grumbling is a relic of the past is a jewel in God's crown. And this kind of church will naturally overflow with joy and become a gift to the community. Neighborhoods where people look for reasons to encourage each other will be lights of God's grace in a dark world.

We can begin with little steps to see how God transforms our relationships. Speaking words of blessing is a lot like taking that first bite of popcorn at the movie theater. One little piece of popcorn and we just can't stop. Before we know it, the whole gigantic bucket is empty. When we begin expressing blessing to others and see the impact it makes, we become addicted. We just have to do it more and more. And that's a good thing!

A Note a Week

If you want to build others up, consider making a commitment to write one note of blessing each week. Put this on your schedule and make it a habit. As you go through the week, try to notice people who could use a word of encouragement. Maybe you will see someone who does an unsolicited act of service or a young person who shows kindness to others. You might bump into someone who is discouraged or hurting. When it comes time to write your weekly note, sit down, say a prayer, and do your best to extend God's care and grace as you build this person up with words. One note a week might not seem like it will make a big difference, but at this reasonable pace, you will still write over fifty notes a year. And you will begin to reflect the heart of Jesus through this commitment to regularly express affirmation.

|||||| Seismic Shift Suggestion ||||||

My First Note. Seismic shifts begin with a little decision, a small action. Write your first encouraging note today. Don't wait until tomorrow. You don't even need to have a fancy card. A lined or blank sheet of paper will do. E-mail is also fine. It is not the card that people will remember but the words that come from your heart. Choose the recipient prayerfully and write the note. Look at this as a sacred moment. Ten years from now, you might look back and realize you have written over five hundred notes to build others up. God will use each of them to bless people more than you dream.

Why is writing a note so important? Because we live in a world where people are burned by harsh words every day and need affirmation. When we write a short note, the recipient will be blessed when they get it, but they can also hold onto the note and read it again when they are feeling discouraged. I can still remember a man pulling me aside one Sunday after church. He told me that over the years, I had written him four letters. This tough, self-assured man got a little teary as he told me that he kept these notes in a drawer and took them out to read when he was feeling discouraged. I had no idea they meant so much to him.

Writing notes is also a great way to build people up because you can choose your words carefully and express exactly what is on your heart. For those who might be nervous about speaking words of affirmation, writing a note is a safe way to go. And you don't have to write a book or an essay. A few sentences expressing what is on your heart are all that is needed. It might even be helpful to keep a few cards in your purse, your glove compartment, or at work so you can write a note when a person comes to mind.

One year I spent time intensively digging into the book of Colossians. As I mentioned earlier, I was struck by how the apostle Paul went out of his way to bless and encourage people. I felt prompted to write letters to a handful of people who have made a big impact on my spiritual life. I wanted to let them know how God has used their lives to sharpen mine and to help me love Jesus in fresh and life-changing ways.

Most of these people were friends and leaders whom I see regularly. But a couple of them were people I know only from a distance. In particular, I sent a letter to Philip Yancey, a Christian author whose writing has touched my life on many occasions. I wanted him to know that his passionate writing and faithfulness in his ministry were impacting many lives, including mine.

To my surprise, I received a letter back from him. This is a portion of what he wrote:

Dear Kevin,

We writers work in isolation, with little idea of the impact of our work. Responses like yours keep me going, and I thank you for taking the time and effort to write me.

I am thankful for and humbled by your kind, affirming words for me, and haven't felt so appreciated and "graced" in a long time. What a great application of something you learned from Colossians! Thank you again, and may the grace and love of God keep flowing out from you to others.

Yours,

Philip Yancey

When I read his letter, something struck me. Even a man whose books are widely published and read by many people needs to receive words of blessing.

A Blessing a Day

Some relationships merit a blessing a day. If you are married, commit to speak at least one word of affirmation to your spouse each day. "I love you." "You're beautiful." "You're a stud." "You're my best friend." Say what is on your heart. Don't assume your partner always knows how you feel. Put it into words every day. If this does not come naturally to you, you will find that practice really does help. After a few weeks of making an effort to give a blessing, it will feel more natural.

|||||| **Seismic Shift Suggestion** ||||||

Daily Blessing List. Prayerfully make a list of the people in your life you feel should receive a blessing a day from you. Then after their name, write down two or three ways you can affirm them with your words. Keep this list in your purse, wallet, or somewhere you can see it each day. Use it as a reminder to develop a lifestyle of blessing.

If you have children, a blessing a day is a great habit. Parents should regularly speak words of affirmation to each child, even if they are grown. This can be as informal as telling her "You are a great daughter" as she walks out the door, or letting him know "I am so proud of you." It can also take the shape of a more formal and consistent pattern of expressing a blessing. A man I know sits by the bedsides of each of his children every night and blesses them. He places his hand on their forehead and repeats Aaron's Blessing. These words from the book of Numbers have been imprinted on the hearts of his children: "The Lord bless you and keep you; the Lord make his face shine upon you and be gracious to you; the Lord turn his face toward you and give you peace" (Num. 6:24–26).

He would tell you that there are times when his kids have rolled their eyes or looked at him like he was a little goofy. But this is the way he daily speaks God's blessing into their lives. And as his children move toward adulthood, they begin to understand how much their father's blessing has meant in their lives.

Aside from the people who should receive a blessing from us each day, we can also find one other person who needs a word of encouragement, affirmation, or healing. We can make it our mission to be ambassadors of blessing wherever we go. If we open our eyes, notice people, and listen for the Holy Spirit, we will discover countless opportunities to build people up with our words, and we will experience a seismic shift that will change our relationships forever.

Just in case you are wondering, my childhood home on Santa Barbara Street did not burn to the ground when Chuckie and I lit the back yard on fire. Thankfully, the fire trucks got there in time to quench the inferno. I learned my lesson and, with courage and humility, willingly admitted to my parents that I was responsible for the fire ... about two decades later when the statute of limitations had run out.

FOR REFLECTION

- How have the words of others hurt me? How have people used words to bless and build me up? How have my words caused pain for others? How have my words blessed and built people up?
- Identify one or two people whom you cross paths with regularly who are grumblers. Think about how you will respond the next time they corner you and start their whole grumbling routine. Pray for the wisdom, strength, and grace to be able to stay away from them and not to fuel their grumbling by listening.

FOR PRAYER

- Ask God to forgive you for the ways you have used your words to hurt others.
- Thank God for the people he has placed in your life who have consistently blessed and supported you with their words.
- Pray for the Holy Spirit to convict you when your words are becoming a fire. Also, pray for the courage to open your mouth and build others up with your words.

Chapter ELEVEN

The Seismic Shift from Served to Serving

Jesus knew that the Father had put all things under his power, and that he had come from God and was returning to God; so he got up from the meal, took off his outer clothing, and wrapped a towel around his waist. After that, he poured water into a basin and began to wash his disciples' feet, drying them with the towel that was wrapped around him.

—John 13:3–5

For even the Son of Man did not come to be served, but to serve, and to give his life as a ransom for many.

—Mark 10:45

Do nothing out of selfish ambition or vain conceit, but in humility consider others better than yourselves. Each of you should look not only to your own interests, but also to the interests of others. Your attitude should be the same as that of Christ Jesus:

Who, being in very nature God,
  did not consider equality with God something to be grasped,
but made himself nothing,
  taking the very nature of a servant,
  being made in human likeness.
And being found in appearance as a man,
  he humbled himself
  and became obedient to death—even death on a cross!

—Philippians 2:3–8

The pastor made two massive mistakes and everyone noticed. There was no way to miss them. During a wedding service, even a little slipup stands out, and this was no little slipup.

The bride had walked the aisle with grace and adorned the whole room with her beauty. The groom had taken her arm, and they had moved forward and stood before the pastor. The music was excellent, the moment was sweet, everything was going according to plan. Then the pastor opened his mouth.

"On behalf of Bill and Nancy, I welcome you to the joyous union of their hearts in the bonds of holy matrimony. Let us pray." As the pastor prayed, no one heard a word he said. You could feel the tension in the air. The bride's name was Susan, not Nancy.

Through the entire service, the pastor called the bride Nancy. For some reason, no one corrected him. Nancy, Nancy, Nancy. With each use of the name, the guests felt the tension rise. Then when it seemed the situation couldn't get any more awkward, the pastor began to preach.

He didn't read the usual "love passage" from 1 Corinthians. He took a slightly different route. He turned to the Song of Songs and read a particularly steamy and sensual passage. For fifteen very long, very uncomfortable minutes, he talked about the joys of erotic, romantic, sexual love. While he preached his NC17 message to a G audience, he continued to refer to Susan as Nancy.

It would not take an etiquette expert to point out this pastor's mistakes. Everyone knew he had committed a faux pas, a blunder in etiquette of gargantuan proportions.

Each culture has its mostly unspoken but well-known rules of etiquette. Mealtimes seem to have a particularly high number of etiquette rules. Don't put your elbows on the table. Pull out the chair for a woman. Use the correct fork or spoon for each course. Place your napkin on your lap. Serve guests first. Chew with your mouth closed. When it comes to meals, certain behaviors are deemed appropriate, and others fall outside the boundaries of good manners.

Imagine dining at a nice restaurant when all of a sudden a man at the next table lets out a burp so loud it can be heard all the way in the kitchen. You would expect the whole restaurant to fall silent as heads turn to identify who released this massive belch. The glares and hushed conversations that would follow would be evidence that this is an epic breech of etiquette. Unless, of course, you are in a part of the world where a burp after the meal is understood to be a compliment. In this case, no one would be offended, and the cooks in the kitchen would smile with satisfaction.

The rules of etiquette change based on location and culture. On his website, the Sideroad, Neil Payne gives guidelines for avoiding dining faux pas in different parts of the world. If you are having dinner in Germany, cut your food with your fork and not your knife; this will tell the cook that the food is tender. In Japan, it is good manners to try a little of everything. In Turkey, asking for more food is taken as a compliment to the chef. Diners in the Middle East cut their meat by holding it against the dish and tearing off bite-size pieces with their forefingers and thumbs. In that part of the world, making a mess while eating is not considered bad manners.

The Servant Heart of Jesus • • • • • • • • • • • • • • • •

The rules of etiquette of Jesus' day might seem strange to us today. For instance, in the first century, it was common practice to have a servant greet guests at the door and offer to wash their feet. There was always a water pot and a towel by the door. Because most people wore sandals and the roads were often dusty or muddy, it made sense to wash guests' feet before they entered a home, especially if they were gathering for a meal. If there was no servant available to perform this task, the host would often do it. If the host was occupied or unable to wash feet, it was not uncommon for one of the guests to wash the feet of the others.

When the disciples arrived for the Last Supper, there was no one at the door to wash their feet. The basin and towel were by the door, but no servant was present. Sadly, not one of them offered to wash each other's feet, or the feet of Jesus. This unwillingness to offer a simple act of service would have been noticed by all. Their refusal to serve may have been spawned by the same prideful attitude that led to a conversation about which of them was the greatest (Luke 22:24–27). While they reclined at the table and debated, they still had dirty feet. So right in the middle of the meal, Jesus solved the problem. He got up, wrapped a towel around his waist (just like a servant would have done), and washed the disciples' feet.

It is likely that when Jesus got up to wash their feet, the disciples realized their mistake and were ashamed by it. Any one of them could have and should have offered this service. Now Jesus, their leader, mentor, and rabbi, knelt before them to wash the grime from their feet. Jesus even washed the feet of Judas, knowing that this man was going to betray him.

When their feet were clean, Jesus said, "You call me 'Teacher' and 'Lord,' and rightly so, for that is what I am. Now that I, your Lord and Teacher, have washed your feet, you also should wash one another's feet. I have set you an example that you should do as I have done for you. I tell you the truth, no servant is greater than his master, nor is a messenger greater than the one who sent him. Now that you know these things, you will be blessed if you do them" (John 13:13–17).

Jesus made a declaration to every human being on earth and every angel in heaven. Can you imagine the angels looking on and shaking their heads as the Creator of the universe bent down to clean the dirt off the feet of common men? The Lord of glory, God in human flesh, served his children by doing a humble act of service that his own followers had refused to do.

Jesus modeled the heart of a servant on many levels besides washing feet. When he left the glory of heaven and came to earth as a baby boy, he was serving us. In the Bible, we read that Jesus, "being in very nature God, did not consider equality with God something to be grasped, but made himself nothing, taking the very nature of a servant, being made in human likeness" (Phil. 2:6–7). Even his birth was an act of sacrificial service. The manger and our yearly celebration of Christmas stand as reminders that God served us long before he asked us to serve each other.

All through his life, Jesus loved people, healed them, offered them deliverance, and cared for their needs. His life was a constant example of humble service. Jesus' ultimate act of service was offering his life on the cross as the payment for our sins. His willing sacrifice on Calvary makes every other act of service in human history pale in comparison. When Jesus uttered what could be considered his mission statement, he said, "The Son of Man did not come to be served, but to serve, and to give his life as a ransom for many" (Matt. 20:28). From the manger to the cross, Jesus' life declared that service is the pathway each of his followers must walk.

To Serve or Be Served, That Is the Question ● ● ● ● ● ● ●

Jesus set an example for how we are to live. It was not just a subtle message he hoped we would pick up all on our own. He made it explicit, because he knew that serving is not the natural behavior of human beings. He said, "You call me 'Teacher' and 'Lord,' and rightly so, for that is what

I am. Now that I, your Lord and Teacher, have washed your feet, you also should wash one another's feet." Jesus picked one of the humblest acts of service to send a clear message to all who follow him. There is no act of service below a Christian. And those who want relationships that reflect the heart of Jesus must learn to serve each other.

The dilemma is that our world sends a dramatically different message. When we "arrive" in life, when we have finally "made it," we are supposed to find ourselves pampered and served by others. When we go to a restaurant and tell the server what we want, we expect that person to take care of us. We might even reach a place of success where we can afford a chauffeur or a personal masseuse. Some people even have private shoppers who run their errands for them. The higher we climb the ladder of this world, the more entitled we feel and the more we expect others to serve us.

Then Jesus comes along and turns our whole understanding of success upside-down. He says, "You know that the rulers of the Gentiles lord it over them, and their high officials exercise authority over them. Not so with you. Instead, whoever wants to become great among you must be your servant, and whoever wants to be first must be your slave" (Matt. 20:25–27). He reinforces this truth when he says, "The greatest among you will be your servant" (Matt. 23:11). Jesus modeled this so clearly and taught it so emphatically because he knew that everything inside of us, and everything in our culture, would push in the opposite direction. But he also knew that true joy and healthy relationships are just two of the benefits of being a person who serves others.

If you long for your relationships to be healthy and thriving, you will decide to serve others. Acts of service can erupt in the workplace when a supervisor offers to help someone under their authority. Service can happen in the home when a spouse decides to meet the needs of their husband or wife. Service can appear in surprising ways when a self-centered sibling offers to help a brother or sister. Another natural place where each of us can serve is in our churches, where we can discover ways to care for fellow Christians. Wherever and whenever they happen, acts of service become a force that strengthens our relationships and blesses the lives of others.

The writer of the book of Hebrews gives us a vision of how Jesus found joy in the most extreme moments of service. These words say it all: "Let us fix our eyes on Jesus, the author and perfecter of our faith, who for the joy set before him endured the cross, scorning its shame, and sat down at the right hand of the throne of God" (Heb. 12:2).

|||||| **Seismic Shift Suggestion** ||||||

Homework Project. Choose one person in your home and perform an act of service for that person. If you are not sure what you can do that will mean a lot to them, you can use an idea from the list presented later in this chapter, or simply ask them. If you discover that serving this person strengthens your relationship, look for another opportunity.

There is no act in all of human history more sacrificial than Jesus' death on the cross. Yet we read that Jesus endured the pain and anguish for the "joy set before him." How can making the shift from being served to serving bring joy? Because when we grow in our commitment to serve others, it strengthens and fortifies every relationship. When Jesus served, he honored his Father and blessed the lives of people. When we follow his example, we do the same.

Serving in Our Homes

"Home is where the heart is."

I suppose.

"There is no place like home."

Sure, Dorothy, but that can be a good or bad thing depending on your home. Not everyone lives on a cozy farm with Auntie Em and Uncle Henry.

We can echo all sorts of cliches about home, but when push comes to shove, it is the place most of us can be ourselves. When we are out in the world with many sets of eyes watching us, we have to be on our best behavior. We are not as prone to grab the last piece of pizza and jam it in our mouths before someone else gets it. We don't stretch out on the couch and look on apathetically as others sit on the floor because we don't want to sit up and share the space. We are not as quick to demand our own way and pout if we don't get it. When we are in the workplace, at school, in social settings, and at church, we put on a good show and muster the strength to serve others, at least while someone is watching. But at home, we think about ourselves. Out in the world, we give and give; when we get home, it is time to focus on me.

One of the most challenging places in the entire world to serve is in our homes and among our family members. But Jesus' example of washing feet applies to the home as well. We must always remember that when God is above us, no act of service is below us. And we need to commit to serve the people who live in our homes.

When a couple decides to serve rather than be served, relationships become fun. Imagine a newlywed couple is going to rent a movie for a date night. She says, "Let's rent an action-adventure movie in which lots of things blow up and there are plenty of car chases."

He responds, "But honey, you don't like action movies. Can't we get a romantic movie with endless dialogue about feelings and human relationships? Maybe something set in Europe in which all the characters have really neat accents and everyone wears wonderful clothes."

"No, no, I insist," she presses. "We must get an action movie. Something with Arnold Schwarzenegger, Keanu Reeves, or Will Smith would be perfect."

In exasperation, he finally says, "My love, my darling, I want to see a movie you would enjoy. It's Renee Zellweger, Emma Thompson, Kate Winslet, or no one at all!"

And this freshly married couple has their first fight. They are both tenaciously committed to serving the other. Of course, this is a fictional conversation, but wouldn't it be wonderful if couples served each other by insisting on what the other wanted?

Serving siblings has its challenges. I can still remember the first time I tried to serve my sister, Gretchen. I was a new Christian and had heard a message about how Jesus washed the disciples' feet. So when I got home, I went up to Gretch's room and cleaned it for her. She was mad at me, at first. In the past, I had been quite mean to her. We fought a lot, and she was suspicious anytime I came near her stuff. Now I had invaded the sanctuary of her room and, inexplicably, vacuumed and straightened up her things. Something was very wrong.

When she asked me why I had cleaned her room, I told her I did it because I loved her. This act of service, and the resulting conversation, was a seismic shift in our relationship. Today, we love each other and would do anything to help and serve one another.

There are all kinds of ways we can learn to serve in our homes. Here are just a few ideas to get the wheels turning. The truth is, the options for serving are plentiful if we just look around, listen, and take action when opportunities present themselves. Try one of these mini service projects and see what happens:

- Offer to do another family member's chores for a day.
- Surprise everyone by offering to cook dinner and do the dishes.
- Clean the bathroom and scrub the toilets. This can have a humbling, foot-washing feeling to it.
- When someone else sits down to watch TV, offer them the remote control and watch whatever they want to watch.
- Identify a certain task that a family member is responsible for but you know they don't enjoy. Once a week, step in and do this chore for them.
- Offer to loan an outfit or a pair of shoes to a family member who would love to borrow them.
- Instead of calling, "Shotgun!" and fighting for the front seat, call, "Back seat!" and give someone else the front. You can have fun watching people stare at you each time you do this.

The primary issue is not the act itself. It is about creating a culture of serving in your home. As you do this, watch the seismic shifts that begin to occur in your relationships with family members or roommates.

Serving in the Church

Picture a church in which everyone wants to be served. Each person believes the church exists to meet their needs, to make them happy, and to cater to their whims and tastes. Imagine a congregation in which everyone has a "take care of me" attitude and is quick to complain whenever things are not just the way they feel they should be. Sadly, some people don't have to use their imagination to picture such a church.

This kind of church will never have a positive impact on the world. It will grow small, inward, and unhealthy. This kind of church does not honor Jesus and bring glory to God. This is not a church ruled by a servant spirit.

Now imagine a church in which every single person has a passion to serve others. Think about what God could do through a group of people who are committed to sacrificial ministry to each other. These people know that the Holy Spirit has given each of them unique abilities (spiritual gifts) that are to be used for building up people and bringing glory to God. So they are purposeful about discovering their gifts and developing and using them. What could God do through such a church?

We are either on the stretcher or helping to carry it. There are times we need to be served. But most of the time, we are called to serve others. The bottom line is that God wants each of us to help carry people through their times of need. The church was never meant to be a bunch of people watching as a few exhausted workers strain to carry the burdens of a whole congregation. The old saying, "Many hands make light labor," is true. A church filled with people who serve will change the world.

When we are hurting and are in a time of need, we can be thankful that God's people will help carry us through. But once we are strong and healthy, we need to get off the stretcher and help support others. Sometimes those who are strong in Christ hit a time of deep pain, loss, and sorrow. They can be thankful that there are others ready and willing to serve them. But those who are making the seismic shift from being served to serving discover that God wants to use them to help, support, teach, encourage, and bless others. As we become more like Jesus, we learn we are called to serve others, not just to have them meet our needs.

|||||| **Seismic Shift Suggestion** ||||||

Serving Like Jesus. We are invited to be like Jesus in many ways. Right near the top of the list is the call to serve. Identify one person you know who is on the stretcher right now. They might have a physical need, but it could also be any kind of need: emotional, financial, relational, or spiritual. Think of one way you could help carry them during their time of struggle. How can you serve them? Send a note of encouragement, help alleviate a financial burden, bring a meal, or do some act of service that shows the love of Jesus.

We can follow a three-step process if we want to find our place of service in the church. First, take a class that helps you discover your spiritual gifts. Different churches will offer various curriculums or courses, but most will have some kind of training in this area. Don't just jump into a ministry in your church because there is a need. Make sure your passions, temperament, and gifting fit the ministry area. Once you have taken a class or read a book and have a sense of areas of service that fit the unique way God has made you, it is time to get involved.

Next, explore options for ministry in your area of giftedness. You might have the spiritual gift of teaching, but it could take some experimenting to discover whether you are best suited to teach second-grade Sunday school, the junior high group, or an adult class. If you have gifts in administration, you could help in almost any area of the church ministry. Those who have compassionate gifts can find numerous ways to serve. Have fun visiting different ministries, talking with leaders and participants, and praying about where you will best fit. Through this process, you will find the right place to serve.

||||| Seismic Shift Suggestion |||||

Part of the Family. We will never feel like a full-fledged member of God's family until we help with some of the household chores. Every church has a multitude of opportunities for service. Take a class in your church to discover your spiritual gifts. If your church does not offer this kind of a class, you might want to meet with the pastor or a church leader and ask them to help you discover how you can serve others in your church. Or you might want to review the *Network* curriculum and help start a spiritual gifts class in your church.

Third, commit to be a lifelong worker in the church. Don't give just a year or two; make service a lifestyle. As you do this, it is helpful to remember that there will be different seasons in your life and in your service in the church. The right ministry for you might be different when you are in your early twenties than ten years later when you are married and have two kids. Be committed to serve, but be flexible about what, where, and when. New times in your life might lead you to new expressions of your spiritual gifts.

Serving Those outside of the Church   • • • • • • • • • •

One realm of service that often gets missed by followers of Christ is the powerful ministry of service in the community or among those in your life who are not yet followers of Jesus. Sometimes Christians get so heavily invested in their own families and congregations that there is little time left for serving those outside the church. This is a sad oversight.

One of the most influential people in my early spiritual formation was a man by the name of Doug Drainville. Doug was only a few years older than me, but he showed me Jesus more than anyone else I knew at that time in my life. Doug was a passionate follower of Jesus, and he loved to serve. I was a punk kid and very self-centered. I can still remember Doug offering to drive me places if I needed a ride. He lived about twenty minutes away, but if I called him, he would jump in his brown VW Beetle, drive over and give me a ride, and then head home. When I look back, it breaks my heart to realize that I never offered him gas money, and I think there were times I even failed to thank him. But he just kept serving and showing the love of God to me.

If I had to point to one person who had the greatest impact on my becoming a Christian, it would be Doug. He became a reflection of Jesus in my life. He never washed my feet, but his willingness to drive me all over town was a living example of a servant's heart I will never forget.

In the same way, entire congregations also can develop service ministries to care for those who are not part of their church. Many churches are good at serving their members. For example, there are people who bring meals to those who have had surgery or who are facing a prolonged illness. Or there are ministry teams that help needy church members with work around the house or yard. But any church that is already serving their members could make a great impact on their community by expanding this care to those outside of the congregation.

Just imagine what could happen if an unchurched single mother who just had her first child received a call from your church asking if people from your congregation could bring over a meal every day for a week after she gets home from the hospital. She might ask, "Why are you offering this?" The answer might be, "Your friend down the street goes to our church, and she mentioned that you just had a baby. We just wanted to help you through this time." Not only would this new mother receive some great meals, she would make some new friends and experience the love of Jesus in a life-changing way. Who knows how God might use this service to extend his love and open the door for this woman to learn about Jesus?

. . . .

Jesus' followers committed a faux pas when they missed the chance to wash each other's feet. Our Savior set them back on the path of service by his shocking example. It is helpful for each of us to realize that if we had been sitting at that table, Jesus would have washed our feet too. Every day there are people around us with dirty feet, broken hearts, heavy burdens, and needs we can help meet. It is time to get a basin and a towel and start serving like Jesus.

FOR REFLECTION • • • • • • • • • • • • • • • • • •

- If I had been sitting at the table and Jesus knelt down at my feet and washed them, how might I have responded? How would this experience have shaped my view of serving others?
- When is it most difficult for me to serve? Who in my life is hard for me to serve?

FOR PRAYER • • • • • • • • • • • • • • • • • • •

- Thank Jesus for the many ways he has served you and been an example of how you are to serve others.
- Praise God for the people he has placed in your life who have modeled the servant heart of Jesus. Reflect on the lives and examples of these people, and thank God for giving them to you.
- Ask Jesus to grow a servant's heart in you. Confess where you are resistant, and ask for a renewed passion for service.

Chapter TWELVE

The Seismic Shift from Flattery to Truth-Telling

"These are the things you are to do: Speak the truth to each other, and render true and sound judgment in your courts; do not plot evil against your neighbor, and do not love to swear falsely. I hate all this," declares the LORD.

—Zechariah 8:16–17

Instead, speaking the truth in love, we will in all things grow up into him who is the Head, that is, Christ.

—Ephesians 4:15

Truthful lips endure forever,
    but a lying tongue lasts only a moment.
The LORD detests lying lips,
    but he delights in men who are truthful.

—Proverbs 12:19, 22

On April 21, 1980, Rosie Ruiz won the Boston Marathon with the third fastest time ever recorded for a female runner. She finished the twenty-six-mile race in just two hours, thirty-one minutes, and fifty-six seconds. Two Boston police officers supported her after she crossed the finish line and concluded one of the most grueling races of her life. The crowd watched as this previously unknown runner accepted the victory laurels and raised her arms toward heaven in a sign of triumph. Surprisingly, Rosie looked fresh and energized as she climbed the winner's podium.

In a matter of minutes, questions began to rise about Rosie and her right to the title of this prestigious race. Authorities reviewed checkpoint monitors along the course and found no video evidence of Rosie actually running the Boston Marathon. None of the competitors remembered her passing them or running ahead of them during the race. Not one person in the crowd could produce a photograph that supported Ruiz's claim that she had run the entire marathon. Eventually, some spectators reported they had seen her jump into the race in the final half mile. Every indication was that Rosie had simply cut in before the finish line, sprinted a short distance, and accepted the prize.

After further investigation, race officials discovered that this young woman had qualified for the Boston Marathon by cheating in the New York Marathon. She had started the race but then hopped on a subway train that dropped her near the finish line. In light of the overwhelming proof that she had not actually run the marathon, Rosie Ruiz was stripped of her victory and the laurels were given to Jackie Gareau, the true winner.

Against all evidence to the contrary, Rosie Ruiz continued to insist she ran the entire Boston Marathon and won. She never admitted any wrongdoing.

The Challenge of Truth-Telling

Before we come down too hard on Rosie, each one of us should look long and hard at our own heart. We are all tempted to fudge the truth, to tell a little white lie, to bend the truth. We might not try to convince the world that we won the Boston Marathon, but all of us are enticed to deceive ourselves and others with words that are simply not true.

If you are not convinced that sinful human nature keeps us away from speaking the truth, just watch any court TV show. One person presents their case, and what they say seems to make sense. Their argument is compelling. Then the other person gets their turn. They argue their side of the issue, and they seem to be telling the truth. But as you listen, you realize that there is no way both of them are recounting things as they really happened. One of them has to be stretching, bending, and breaking the truth. By the time most of these shows end, the audience has a fairly good sense that both sides have failed to tell the truth. The book of Proverbs says,

"The first to present his case seems right, till another comes forward and questions him" (Prov. 18:17). Apparently, some things in human nature do not change with time.

Some questions we need to ask in our postmodern, relativistic, anything-goes world are, Does it really matter if we tell the truth? And can we even know truth in such a way that we can claim someone is speaking it? These questions are nothing new. They have been with us since the dawn of time. There are no easy answers to these questions, but we had better acknowledge that if we want relationships that are healthy and lasting, speaking the truth is essential. Jesus taught, "Simply let your 'Yes' be 'Yes,' and your 'No,' 'No'; anything beyond this comes from the evil one" (Matt. 5:37). Jesus implies that we can speak the truth and stand on it. Truth-telling may not be easy or popular, but it is a cornerstone of healthy relationships.

Telling the Truth to Ourselves

There is a wonderful little cartoon, just two frames long. The text is simple: "What he sees, and what she sees." On one side is an overweight man looking at himself in the mirror. He has a sagging potbelly and clearly has mastered the Baby Huey physique with a steady regimen of Doritos, fast food, and extended time on a couch with a remote control in hand. But as he looks in the mirror, he sees Mr. Olympia. In the second frame is a woman who has a lean and shapely figure. When she looks in the mirror, she sees only a frumpy, overweight woman. In both cases, deceit has set in. Neither of these people has an honest perception of themselves. Neither sees the truth.

Too often we are like the figures in this cartoon. Our selective vision tailors our reality to suit us. Or we perceive things much more severely than they really are. If we are going to make the seismic shift to becoming truth-tellers, we need to see the world as God sees it.

Entering the Tunnel of Chaos, Willingly

It is easy to say that speaking the truth in our relationships is important. The challenge is actually doing it. Making the commitment to communicate honestly with each other means choosing a measure of messiness. Moving beneath pleasantries to a deeper level of communication is worth the investment, but it is expensive. One of the costs is an end to the surface-level peace we seek to maintain in our relationships by not rocking the boat, asking hard questions, or speaking the truth, hoping we will all just live happily ever after.

In his book *The Different Drum*, Scott Peck questions the assumption that avoiding truth-telling will keep the peace in our relationships. Peck argues that relationships that shy away from the hard work of telling the truth only establish what he calls "pseudocommunity"—a false sense of peace based on avoiding honesty and constantly sidestepping confrontation. But pseudocommunity does not lead to deep and healthy relationships. Instead, it eventually gives birth to bitterness, resentment, anger, and doubt. It takes love by the throat and slowly squeezes the life out of it.

What Peck suggests as the antidote to pseudocommunity is chaos. He means we have to risk letting our relationships get messy through truth-telling in order for them to become healthy. In a Bible study on authentic relationships, Bill Hybels coins the term "the tunnel of chaos" for this process of choosing to tell the truth in our relationships, because it breaks our false sense of peace and leads us to a place of chaos. But if we push through this tunnel, we will come out the other side with authentic community and healthy relationships.

Everyone who has traveled through the tunnel of chaos understands that this process is necessary for a deeper level of relational health. I discovered this after seven and a half months of marriage. I was the perfect husband for almost eight months after I said "I do." I knew this because my wife said so. When I asked her how I was doing at the whole marriage thing, she said, "Great!" Though we had radically different family backgrounds, we did not seem to have any big problems getting along. When my brother called and asked me to meet him at the beach for some early morning bodysurfing and I asked Sherry if she minded, she smiled and said, "No problem." When my friends asked if I could hang out and do something with them at night, she never seemed to mind that either. Things were going great. Or so it seemed.

Then on our first Valentine's Day, I crossed a line. Sherry expected a certain level of celebration on this particular day. I did not. So we entered the tunnel of chaos. My beautiful, gentle, sensitive wife told me what she really thought of my busy schedule, early morning trips to the beach, late nights with my friends, and general insensitivity to her. When she finally finished saying everything that was on her mind, we were two hours into the tunnel of chaos. Apparently, I was not the model husband I had been led to believe I was.

When Sherry finished with her first truth-telling session in our married life, she said, "From now on, I'm not going to hold these things in for seven months!" I said, "Good." When I asked why she had not shared these feelings along the way, she talked about wanting to be a good wife, to make me happy, and to keep peace in our home. What we both realized was that her keeping these feelings inside accomplished none of these things. So we made an agreement. We would tell the truth to each other. We would go through the tunnel of chaos instead of living with a false sense of peace in pseudocommunity.

Sometimes the trip through this tunnel is quick. At other times, it takes a little longer. But every time we speak the truth, and do it in love, our relationship is strengthened.

If You Love Me, You'll Tell Me When I Have ● ● ● ● ● ● Something between My Teeth

This is how you know someone is a real friend: if you have something between your teeth, a real friend tells you. It is the loving thing to do. A real friend looks at you, shows you her teeth, and makes that strange sucking noise as she presses her teeth together. This is code for, "Check your teeth." Or he rubs his teeth with his tongue as he looks at you and does a little head nod thing as if to say, "There is a funny green thing right about *there* on your teeth." Some friends skip the whole mime routine and just blurt out, "Hey, check your teeth."

> ||||| **Seismic Shift Suggestion** |||||
>
> **Is There Something between My Teeth?** Go to one or two people you trust and invite them to be a truth-teller in your life. You might want to have them read this chapter so they understand what you are asking. Let them know you want their input not only on your teeth but also on your character, choices, and anything else they see in you.

What is amazing is when we go for hours after lunch with a chunk of food the size of Delaware stuck between our teeth and no one mentions it. Then we go to the bathroom, and as we are washing our hands, we look into the mirror and smile to check our pearly whites. There it is, an entire head of broccoli poking out of our two front teeth. We do a quick mental rewind of the last two hours and realize we have been with lots of people. We have laughed, smiled, chatted, and no one reached over and pulled the thing out with both hands for us. They just let us go on like they didn't even notice.

If we love people, we will tell them when they have leftovers stuck to their teeth. It might be embarrassing for a moment, but it is better than finding out at the end of the day. This same principle should apply to all areas of life. Early on in our marriage, I told Sherry I was not very good at flattery. If she asks me how an outfit looks, I feel the need to be honest. What I have learned is that we can be both honest and diplomatic at the same time. My wife is a beautiful woman, but not every outfit works on her. If she tries on an outfit that does not look great and asks my opinion, I don't have to say, "I don't like it." I can ask a clarifying question, such as, "Well, what look are you going for?" She has learned that this question is code for, "You might want to try another option."

Over the years, my wife has occasionally pulled out of the closet some outfit she wore many years ago. She can still fit into the same clothes she wore when we met over two decades ago. Whenever she pulls out an outfit that looks a little dated and asks me what I think, I don't answer. I simply break into song. I sing an old Archies song: "Sugar, sugar, ah, honey, honey. You are my candy girl, and you got me wanting you." This is code for, "That outfit might be just a little out of style! Maybe someday it will be hip and retro, but not yet! For now, leave it in the closet!"

Some people might see this kind of honesty as unkind and hurtful. Maybe it would be better for me just to smile and say, "What a beautiful outfit, and it looks great on you!" But this is not speaking the truth in love. Sherry has come to appreciate the fact that when she asks me if an outfit looks good, she will always get an honest answer. By the way, she is just as honest with me about clothes and lots of other things that are far more important.

These might seem like little things, but honesty on this level is very important. We all want a few people in our lives who we know will shoot straight with us. If we are wise, we will invite the people closest to us to speak the truth when they see broccoli between our teeth, when they notice our blouse is way out of style, when they see a flaw in our character, when we make a poor moral choice, or whenever they have a concern about our well being.

If you love me, you will tell me when I have food between my teeth. And I will do the same for you.

Speaking the Truth When We Have Been Hurt ● ● ● ● ●

One of the hardest times to speak the truth is when someone has wronged us. Jesus understood the complexity of this, so he gave us a process to follow. Jesus says, "If your brother sins against you, go and show him his fault, just between the two of you. If he listens to you, you have won your brother over. But if he will not listen, take one or two others along, so that 'every matter may be established by the testimony of two or three witnesses.' If he refuses to listen to them, tell it to the church; and if he refuses to listen even to the church, treat him as you would a pagan or a tax collector" (Matt. 18:15–17).

|||||| Seismic Shift Suggestion ||||||

Open My Ears and Heart. Ask God to prepare you to hear the truth from others and to accept it with a humble heart. Here is the reality: if you become a truth-teller, others will begin speaking the truth to you. They just might invite you into the tunnel of chaos. Prepare for this by praying for a heart that is ready to receive what others want to say to you.

The process laid out by Jesus is not complex or difficult to understand. It is clear and straightforward. What is surprising is how many of Jesus' followers don't use the guidelines he set out for us. If we would, a seismic shift would occur that would lead to relationships that are deeper and healthier than most of us dream they could be.

Here is how the process works. First, if someone has hurt you, say nothing to anyone about it until you talk with the person. If you speak with others about how you feel, even in the guise of a prayer request, you sin against this person and against God. You need to meet with this person one on one and share your heart honestly and humbly. Don't attack or blame; just share how you feel about what they did or said. Enter this process prayerfully and humbly. Then be ready to listen and to reconcile. If this issue is resolved and the relationship is healed, you are done. If not, move to step 2.

Second, if you talk with this person but are not reconciled, invite one or two people to come with you to meet with the person again. Choose people that both of you respect. These should be godly people who can bring wisdom, perspective, and balance to the conversation. Meet, pray for God's help, and share your heart honestly, gently, and with humility.

Again, if there is healing in the relationship, the process is complete. If not, move to step 3.

Third, if the person still won't respond, invite someone from your church leadership to enter into the process with you. This person represents the church body and can be a pastor, elder, or some key leader. The goal is a restored relationship, not blaming or fault-finding. If you are reconciled, the process is finished. If not, go to step 4.

Fourth, when a person who has wronged you still refuses to communicate or to reconcile, Jesus says to treat the person like they are a pagan or a tax collector. Many people have taken this to mean that we should reject this person. But I don't believe this is an accurate reading of the text. Jesus loved pagans and tax collectors. He reached out to them. He knew they were in deep need of his grace. When Jesus says to treat a person like a tax collector or a pagan, he is inviting us to reach out to them as if they were lost. He is calling us to double our efforts to extend the love of God to them! This means we remain in relationship with these people, we pray for them, and we seek to show them the love of Jesus.

If we follow this four-step process, the seismic shifts we experience will redefine the landscape of our homes, neighborhoods, schools, workplaces, churches, and everywhere we go.

There is no place in this process where we are permitted to gossip and speak ill of someone who has wronged us. Too many followers of Christ are quick to tell others about how they have been hurt and who has hurt them. This is ungodly gossip and is never part of God's plan. We are called to speak face to face with the one who has sinned against us. We are not to broadcast their sin to the world.

||||| Seismic Shift Suggestion |||||

A Risk Worth Taking. Identify one person in your life who has hurt you, but you have never talked with them about it. Think through why you have resisted addressing this issue with them, and also reflect on how this choice has impacted your relationship. Then set a time to talk with this person and share the hurt you feel. Do it with a gentle heart and careful words. Make sure you proceed prayerfully. You might even want to tell them what you learned in this chapter and help them understand that the reason you want to work through this point of hurt is that you love them and do not want to compromise your relationship with them.

If we follow Jesus' teaching on this topic, we will avoid countless relational pitfalls. Sadly, we see too many examples of Christians who want to deal with their hurt by holding onto it and talking to all the wrong people.

On my first day at my new church, I received a phone call from a church member who just had to talk with me. I agreed, and she came in that very day. After brief introductions and pleasantries, this woman launched into a diatribe against one of the other pastors. She got about a minute of her complaint out before I realized what she was doing. She had an issue with someone else, but she was bringing it to me instead of him. She was violating the teaching of Matthew 18:15–17.

I cut her off in midsentence when I realized what she was doing. I asked her, "Have you talked with him about this?"

"No!" she replied. "I'm sure he won't listen to me."

She then launched back into her story. I stopped her again and said, "I can't hear this. If you have not talked face to face with this person, I can't listen to your story!"

She looked at me with amazement, as if she had never heard such words. She paused and then slowly explained that she was sure he was at fault and would not listen to her concerns. She wanted to tell me. And she began to tell her story one more time.

|||||| Seismic Shift Suggestion ||||||

Cleanup Project. Many of us have failed to follow Jesus' guidelines for dealing with brokenness in a relationship. Instead of going to the person who has wronged us, we gossip to others. Then eventually we talk with the person who has hurt us, and the relationship is restored. In the process, we often discover that what we told others about this person was untrue. If this is the case, we are compelled to clean up the mess we made. God wants us to go back to those we gossiped to and apologize for our gossip and also correct any misinformation we might have passed on. Forcing ourselves to do this is a great deterrent against future gossip.

As gently and firmly as I could, I asked her to stop telling me her story. I told her that I would help her set up a meeting with this person, and I explained that she needed to simply share her hurt feelings with him and that they needed to try to work it out on their own. I assured her that if they could not figure things out as a brother and sister in Christ, I was more than willing to sit down with them and give it a try. And if that did not work, we could bring in a few elders from the church, and we would figure things out prayerfully, lovingly, and biblically.

She seemed skeptical at best but realized, after we had spent a little time looking at Matthew 18:15–17, that this was God's model for dealing with conflict. I assured her I would set up a meeting as soon as I could. I assured her God really would bless her and this other person in the process. We prayed together, and she left my office.

Later that same day, the woman called me and said, "I have thought and prayed about it, and I don't think I want to meet with him after all. I think I am okay with things now." I told her I had already set a time for her to meet with him. So, reluctantly, she agreed.

What followed was a pattern I have seen more times than I can remember. When these two people met, they expressed the truth, they extended grace, and they were reconciled. In their conversation, the woman expressed what she had heard about this man and why she had become so angry with him. Here is the amazing thing. Once they talked, she found that her feelings and frustrations were based on misinformation. After a short conversation, she discovered that she had no reason to be angry. They prayed together and have gotten along great ever since.

Here is the sad thing: she had carried around hurt feelings and anger for more than four years because she had never gone to speak with this man. During those years, she had told her story many times to many people who most likely formed negative impressions about someone who had done nothing wrong. Gossip is a poison that can spread through a church, a community, an entire city.

God calls us to guard our mouths when we are angry and hurt. There is a right way to deal with our pain. Jesus made this clear. We need to establish a lifestyle of telling the truth in the right way. Might this force us to travel through the tunnel of chaos in our relationships? It certainly will. But when we come out on the other side, we will discover that a seismic shift has occurred. We will no longer be satisfied with pseudo-community and false peace. We will experience better communication and deeper intimacy because we have learned to do the hard work of truth-telling.

FOR REFLECTION

- When am I most prone to stretch the truth? How can I deepen my commitment to speak honest words in these situations?
- Think through some of your key relationships. Are you living in pseudocommunity because you are failing to speak the truth? If so, what step can you take toward entering the tunnel of chaos and learning to speak the truth?

FOR PRAYER

- Ask God to forgive you for settling for pseudocommunity and false peace in your relationships. Pray for the courage to begin speaking the truth. Also, pray for strength as you enter the tunnel of chaos and move toward authentic community.
- Think about the people who would tell you that you have food between your teeth, and praise God for placing them in your life.
- Pray that your relationships will be based on honesty and consistent truth-telling.

Part 5

Shifts That Open the
Floodgates of True Riches

When I was a little boy, in the dark of the night, I would stand on my bed with my back against the wall, then run the length of my bed and launch myself through the air toward the door of my bedroom. This was not an indication of some deep desire to be an Olympic long jumper. It was not part of some aerobic exercise program. It was an act of raw fear.

I was certain there was a monster living under my bed. I never saw it, but I was positive it was there. Sometimes, in the quiet of the night, I could hear creaks and rustlings below me that confirmed my fear. Though I had no evidence to prove it, I knew this malicious creature had very long arms. It was waiting to grab me by the ankles and drag me under the bed when I got up in the middle of the night. The presence of this malevolent creature made getting to the bathroom at midnight a risky enterprise.

I still can't pinpoint the origin of my deep-seated childhood fear. Maybe it was the fact that I did not have a night light in my room, and it got pitch black when the door was closed. Possibly it had something to do with my overactive imagination. Maybe it was the pictures I carried in my mind from the colorful pages of *Where the Wild Things Are*. It might have been because my dad said that if I got up at night, the monster that lived under my bed would grab my legs. I'm no psychologist, so I may never know the genesis of my fear. But as a little boy, it seemed logical and well founded.

As I grew up, I left my childish fear behind. There came a day when I could just step out of bed like a normal kid. With years and maturity, I learned that there were no creatures in the closet or monsters under my bed.

This confidence brought great comfort that lasted for many years. But as I started reading the Bible and entering the world of grownups, I learned about another kind of monster. This creature is always on the prowl, it is evil and powerful, and it has very long arms. It is called the money monster, and it is dreadfully real.

This monster wants to steal your joy and distract you from experiencing the true riches God offers. This creature is not looking to grab your ankles. But it will never rest until it has your heart. Jesus gives us lots of warnings about this sinister creature. He says, "Do not store up for yourselves treasures on earth, where moth and rust destroy, and where thieves break in and steal. But store up for yourselves treasures in heaven, where moth and rust do not destroy, and where thieves do not break in and steal. For where your treasure is, there your heart will be also.... No one can serve two masters. Either you will hate the one and love the other, or you will be devoted to the one and despise the other. You cannot serve both God and Money" (Matt. 6:19–21, 24 TNIV).

The apostle Paul also warns about the money monster: "For the love of money is a root of all kinds of evil. Some people, eager for money, have wandered from the faith and pierced themselves with many griefs" (1 Tim. 6:10).

God wants to fill our hearts and lives with riches beyond compare. The problem is, we hold so tightly to the toys and trinkets of this world that we miss the treasures God offers. The money monster is alive and well. It does not sleep or rest but is always looking for a way to get a grip on our hearts.

God has the power to break this creature's influence. Like a loving parent, God desires to give good gifts that bring joy and contentment to his children. It is time to receive the riches of heaven. The question is, Are we ready to trade the fakes, forgeries, and counterfeit treasures for the riches God offers us?

Chapter THIRTEEN

The Seismic Shift from Mine to God's

Every good and perfect gift is from above, coming down from the Father of the heavenly lights, who does not change like shifting shadows.

—James 1:17

"Bring the whole tithe into the storehouse, that there may be food in my house. Test me in this," says the LORD Almighty, "and see if I will not throw open the floodgates of heaven and pour out so much blessing that you will not have room enough for it."

—Malachi 3:10

As a pastor, I interact with lots of people each week. One thing I love to do is to get to know the children of the church. I don't agree with the adage, "Children are the church of tomorrow." I believe they are the church of today. If the younger generation does not believe they are an important part of today's church, they will be gone tomorrow.

So I interact with kids in the church. I ask questions, listen to their thoughts, and learn from them. I also try to teach biblical truths in language they can understand. One of the ways I get to know the kids is by asking them to share their candy with me. At first glance, this might seem selfish and wrong, a pastor taking candy from the little kids in the church.

But when I see a little boy or girl with a pack of candy or a roll of Smarties, I will often ask, "Can I have one?"

I get all kinds of responses. Sometimes a child will look at me with a frightened stare and hide behind a parent. Sometimes a child will reluctantly share as Mom or Dad coaxes them to "give a piece of candy to the pastor." And sometimes a little one will smile and offer to share their candy.

Years ago, a little boy named Dustin entered the Smarties stage of life. It might not be in the psychological journals, but there is a time in the development of every child when they are ready to receive their first pack of Smarties. You remember Smarties, a row of multicolored, chalklike, bite-size candies wrapped in clear plastic, about ten to twelve pieces in a pack. They are perfect for sharing.

I am not a huge fan of Smarties, but when I saw Dustin come into church with a fresh roll, I just had to ask him if I could have one.

Dustin immediately became my Smarties hero.

He peeled out a piece with a smile and handed it over gladly. This was surprising enough, but at that moment, something happened in this little boy's heart. From that day on, for the next two years, every time Dustin got a pack of Smarties, he took out the first one and set it aside for me. Every Sunday, Dustin would track me down at church and generously offer me one or more Smarties. He did it gladly, with a smile, as if he enjoyed it.

Sometimes Dustin would open a pack of Smarties during the week, but he would still save me the first round, sugary, chalky tablet in his pocket. By the time Sunday came, the Smarty was a little mangy and would have lint and other pocket paraphernalia stuck to it, but he never forgot to bring it for me. In those cases, I thanked him and put it in my pocket so I could "enjoy it later."

Dustin loved Smarties. He also loved his pastor. Every week before the worship service began, Dustin and I shared a time of communion. Jesus was present as we shared a few moments of conversation and partook of Smarties together.

Somewhere along the way, Dustin's mother pointed out that the packs of Smarties she bought for him had ten pieces, and she saw this weekly ritual as Dustin's introduction to tithing. What I saw was a little boy who loved to share and who understood the power of generosity.

Since that time, I have asked myself many times, How am I doing with my Smarties? This is a question each of us could ask regularly. How is your heart when it comes to generosity? Are you a person who is learning to share freely with others? How are you doing with your Smarties?

It All Belongs to God • • • • • • • • • • • • • • • • • •

God longs for his children to live with freedom and joy. He does not want us caught in the clutches of the money monster. In the next three chapters, we will look at three stakes we can drive into this monster's heart. This creature can't be domesticated or trained. It must be killed. To do this, we need to drive a stake through its heart.

The first stake is living with the conviction that all we have belongs to God. James, the brother of Jesus, put it this way: "Every good and perfect gift is from above, coming down from the Father of the heavenly lights" (James 1:17). All we have, every gift, each moment, every ability, is given by the hand of a loving God. Ultimately these things are not ours. They never were, and they never will be.

This thinking is radically countercultural. Most of us believe that what we have belongs to us, that somehow we earned it by the sweat of our brow, by our intellectual prowess, or by using our abilities. But who gives us strength to work, a mind to think, and abilities to use? These are all from God. If we are going to be set free from the clutches of the money monster, we must see things the way God does. Everything in our care belongs to God, not to us. We are stewards, caretakers of his resources. When this truth sinks in, the foundation of our lives begins to shake and a seismic shift takes place.

Living with Open Hands • • • • • • • • • • • • • • • • •

The appropriate posture of a follower of Jesus is to live with our hands turned upward, imagining that everything we have is resting in our palms. Here are my talents, my material resources, my intellect, my spiritual gifts, the people I love, everything. We need to see ourselves holding these things in open hands. Then we lift them as high as we can. Like a child offering a gift to a loving parent, we offer back to God all that he has placed in our care.

This posture of living with open hands helps us battle the temptation to fall in love with things. It helps us keep an appropriate perspective. All is from God; all goes back to God, including our own lives. Jesus gave us this sobering warning: "No one can serve two masters. Either you will hate the one and love the other, or you will be devoted to the one and despise the other. You cannot serve both God and Money" (Matt. 6:24 TNIV). These words should shake us and wake us. In a world that says life is really about the accumulation of things and that our value is wrapped up in the amassing of earthly toys, Jesus' words call us to a dramatically new way of thinking.

> |||||| **Seismic Shift Suggestion** ||||||
>
> **God's Stuff.** Take a walk through your house, apartment, dorm room, or wherever you live. Slowly look over all the material things God has placed in your care. As you look at each item, tell God, "This is yours; use it as you will." In your mind, take a label that says "God's Stuff" and put it on each item of clothing, each piece of furniture, every toy, and all that you have. Then think about all the resources you have that are outside of your home. Label these also. Finally, live as if it is true. Treat all that is in your care as if it belongs to God, because it does.

A Test for God and for Us • • • • • • • • • • • • • • • • •

God rarely asks people to put him to the test. When Jesus was tempted in the wilderness, the Devil dared him to jump off the pinnacle of the temple to see if God would send angels to catch him before he hit the ground (Matt. 4:5–7). Jesus replied by quoting from the Old Testament: "Do not put the Lord your God to the test" (Matt. 4:7). These words tell us that it should never be our practice to test God. In general, it is ill-advised and to be avoided.

But in the book of Malachi, God actually invites his people to put him to the test:

> "Will a mere mortal rob God? Yet you rob me.
> "But you ask, 'How are we robbing you?'
> "In tithes and offerings. You are under a curse—your whole nation—because you are robbing me. Bring the whole tithe into the storehouse, that there may be food in my house. Test me in this," says the LORD Almighty, "and see if I will not throw open the floodgates of heaven and pour out so much blessing that there will not be room enough to store it. I will prevent pests from

devouring your crops, and the vines in your fields will not drop their fruit before it is ripe," says the Lord Almighty. "Then all the nations will call you blessed, for yours will be a delightful land," says the Lord Almighty.

—Malachi 3:8–12

God is testing the people by calling them to put him to the test. It is a test within a test. God is reminding his people that everything they have belongs to him, but that the first 10 percent, the tithe, is non-negotiable. Our giving of this first 10 percent should be on autopilot. God goes so far as to say that keeping this first portion of our resources for ourselves is like robbing from him.

He also extends a promise. If we give the tithe, he will open the gates of heaven and pour out more blessings than we could possibly imagine. A blessing flood will hit our lives. This promise should move each of us to take God at his word and put him to the test by making tithing a personal spiritual discipline.

A Journey to Tithing

For many people, the very idea of giving the first 10 percent of their income to God seems unthinkable. They might love the Lord and be very thankful for all they have, but 10 percent is a lot of money! Living in a world with so many financial demands and nice things to buy, and with so much instability, we might feel that the idea of God's wanting such a big chunk of our resources is a little presumptuous.

For many years, this is exactly how I felt. I had a hard time understanding why God would want me to give him the first 10 percent of all I earned. If the rumor I heard was true, that God owns the cattle on a thousand hills (Ps. 50:10), why did this big-time rancher need the modest contribution of my 10 percent? I would say to myself, "I'll do even better; I'll give everything to God. In my heart, I will live as if everything I have belongs to him." This kind of thinking is great, in theory. But I lived as if it were all mine, and I put very little in the offering plate. I was a committed Christian working toward my seminary degree, but I was not a generous giver.

Then I met my wife-to-be. She was the one who taught me how to tithe. I had not grown up in the church and had never seen an example of someone who joyfully tithed and gave offerings beyond the tithe. I was walking with Jesus but did not have a biblical perspective on finances and personal resources. I still lived with the outlook that what I earned was mine.

Sherry, on the other hand, had grown up with parents who had modeled faithful tithing her whole life. Every week, when her father cashed his paycheck, he would sit down at the kitchen table and put money in envelopes to pay the bills and cover the living costs for the family. The first envelope he filled was for the tithe. He would take the first 10 percent and set it aside for the offering that Sunday. This was as regular as clockwork, as natural as breathing. There was no debate over tithing in her home. Using that money for recreation or even to pay bills was not an option. It was God's money, and that was the end of the discussion.

When Sherry and I got married, our financial worlds collided. Even though I was working in the church, I still did not understand God's call to make tithing a normal part of my life. Sherry made it all very clear. She opened the Bible, read from the book of Malachi, and said, "The tithe is God's." We lived on a very modest income: her teacher's salary and a small amount I received from the church. But as we looked at God's Word, it became clear how we should live. At the start of our married life, we decided that the first step in keeping our finances in order would be tithing.

|||||| Seismic Shift Suggestion ||||||

Become a Reporter. Find a person you know and respect who has developed a lifestyle of tithing and giving generously. Ask them if you can spend half an hour talking to them about giving. When you meet or talk on the phone, interview them using these questions and whatever else you want to ask:

1. How has tithing impacted your perspective on material things?
2. How have you experienced God's blessing and provision?
3. If you could go back to living without tithing, would you do it? Why or why not?

At first, I felt it was irresponsible and risky to give this first 10 percent of our income to God. Then something happened in my heart; I gained a new perspective. I began to understand that everything is God's. We are not giving God 10 percent of our money. He is allowing us to use 90 percent of what he puts in our care. And as strange as it might seem, we began to look for ways to give away some of the 90 percent that God allowed us to manage. This was, and continues to be, a seismic shift in my life. It has been freeing and faith-building. And after more than two decades of tithing, we have never regretted it! We have seen God open the windows of heaven and pour out his blessing on us over and over again.

Even when Sherry stopped teaching to go to seminary and we were living on four hundred dollars a month, we knew tithing would be part of our lifestyle. And when we had three little boys and it seemed impossible to make ends meet because we were living on one income—and the income of a young pastor at that—the first 10 percent always went to the Lord.

Here is the strange thing: we never missed the money. We knew it wasn't ours to start with, so it never really factored into the equation. After twenty years of marriage and raising a family, we could write a whole book on the many ways God has opened the floodgates of heaven and poured out more blessings than we could have ever dreamed of. We could also tell countless stories about other Christians who have experienced the same thing. Sometimes those blessings have been financial. Sometimes they have taken other forms: a sense of God's peace and nearness, the support of a loving person, priceless spiritual blessings, a front-row seat for the miracles God still does in our lives, and so much more. We have learned that though the blessings are not always material, faithfulness in tithing has always yielded blessings.

A Rude Awakening

Once I understood the joy and blessing of tithing, I thought it would be right to share what I learned with others. I wanted them to experience the peace, security, and freedom that comes with understanding that all we have belongs to God.

What I discovered was that people have strong feelings about their finances and material stuff. Many followers of Jesus have not yet experienced the seismic shift from mine to God's. Some people get very prickly, defensive, and even angry when the topic of giving comes up. I thought I was bearing good news about the joy of tithing, but there were people who responded like God was trying to take away their money, security, and joy.

One older gentleman had a line he would use every time the topic of giving and tithing would come up in church. He would approach me after the service and say, "Well, Pastor, the battery in my hearing aid ran out about halfway through the service today." This was his way of saying, "When you started talking about my finances, I stopped listening." This made me sad because I realized this man was missing an amazing chance to make a seismic shift that would change his life. As long as the battery in his hearing aid kept dying, he would never know the life-giving joy and freedom of a biblical view of finances.

|||||| Seismic Shift Suggestion ||||||

Open Mind, Heart, and Ears. After reading this chapter, you might decide you still are not ready to take God's test and begin tithing. If this is the case, God does not love you any less! But keep your mind, heart, and ears open on this topic. Tell God, "I am not ready to take this step now, but I am open for you to help me discover more about tithing." Maybe you can begin by giving a small amount. Just like a muscle gets stronger with use, giving gets easier the more we do it. And remember, when you hear a sermon about this topic, make sure you have a fresh battery for your hearing aid.

I debated leaving this chapter out of the book because it can be such a touchy subject. But I had to include it because my heart's desire is for those who follow Jesus to experience the outpouring of God's heavenly blessings. One of the keys that unlocks the storehouse of these blessings is tithing. So I'm taking the risk and extending God's invitation to "'bring the whole tithe into the storehouse, that there may be food in my house. Test me in this,' says the LORD Almighty, 'and see if I will not throw open the floodgates of heaven and pour out so much blessing that you will not have room enough for it'" (Mal. 3:10).

I occasionally have to remind people that when I preach about tithing, it is not because I get a raise if the offerings increase. I don't get year-end bonuses, perks, or commissions. When a pastor opens the Bible and helps God's people focus on this topic, it really is for the good of each person in the church. Every person who makes this seismic shift will enter a new level of joy and blessing. This is one of the ways we discover true riches in this life.

Tithing Q & A •

Over my years as a pastor, I have had many conversations with people about the seismic shift from mine to God's. I have identified the recurring questions people ask when it comes to tithing and growing in generosity.

Since this is such a personal topic, I thought it would be helpful to address some of the most common questions, giving the best biblical and pastoral answers I have. I know not everyone will agree with my responses. But maybe these answers will stir the pot and get you thinking about how God wants you to see and use the resources he has placed in your hands.

What Is a Tithe or Tithing?

Tithing is the biblical model of giving the first 10 percent of our income to God. In Genesis, we read, "Then Abram gave him a tenth of everything" (Gen. 14:20). In Leviticus, we learn that "a tithe of everything from the land, whether grain from the soil or fruit from the trees, belongs to the Lord; it is holy to the Lord" (Gen. 27:30). And as we have already seen, in the book of Malachi, God invites us to put him to the test by bringing "the whole tithe into the storehouse." Tithing is a commitment to follow the biblical example by giving the first 10 percent of all of our resources to God.

One Sunday, a man came up to me after a worship service and said, "I think I know the answer already, but should I be tithing before or after taxes?" I could see that he truly wanted to honor God with his resources. He did not want to hold back anything that belonged to God. I said, "My best and quickest answer is, 'Before.'" I explained that my understanding is that God gets the *first* 10 percent. This means we don't itemize or take off a bunch of personal deductions before giving the tithe. We remember that it all belongs to God, and we joyfully give the first 10 percent to his work.

Another time, I had someone corner me and say, "I don't believe tithing is biblical. The Bible does not talk about it very much." I responded by asking him, "Do you believe Jesus Christ was born of a virgin?" He seemed a little confused by the question but gave a heartfelt "Yes!" I asked him why he believed this, and he explained that it is in the Bible. Then I pointed out that the Bible talks more about tithing than it does about the virgin birth of Jesus. This came as a surprise to him, but I sensed it put things in perspective.

The beauty of tithing is that it is the same for everyone: 10 percent. If a person earns five hundred dollars in the course of a year, their tithe is fifty dollars. If another person earns five million dollars, their tithe is five hundred thousand dollars. Both have tithed, and both have given the same proportion of their income.

▪ Is Tithing the Maximum or the Minimum?

Tithing is just a starting point. The first tenth belongs to God. After this, we are invited to give offerings. An offering is any gift we give above our tithe. This means that we can never give an offering until we have first given our tithe. Followers of Jesus should seek to develop a lifestyle of tithing, and then learn to make the other 90 percent available for God's use. As the Holy Spirit stirs our hearts, we can give offerings to meet special needs and help causes.

I remember a conversation with a wealthy businessman who said, "If I were to tithe, I would be living in rebellion against God." I knew that he and his wife were generous people, so his words surprised me. Then he said, "With all that God has given me, if I give less than 50 percent to God, I am being a selfish pig!" I got the point and laughed. He was not saying tithing is wrong. For him, if all he gave was a tithe, he would have been out of God's will for his life.

▪ Why Does God Want Us to Tithe?

I believe there are three reasons we are called to tithe. First, the discipline of tithing is a gift to us. It helps us remember, regularly, that everything we have is from God. Each time we give God his tithe, we remind ourselves that he has been good and that we are responding out of love and gratitude. Tithing helps recalibrate our thinking about material things, because we acknowledge that everything we have has been given to us by God.

Second, tithing is for God. It is a declaration that we love God and appreciate all he has given us. Have you ever seen a parent take a child out for dinner and watch as the child refuses to share a French fry or a bite of dessert with the parent, who is paying the bill? It is not very attractive. But when a little girl tells her mommy, "Help yourself to anything on my plate," it is a declaration that she understands who provided the whole meal. When we tithe, we declare to God that he is welcome to anything on our plate.

Third, tithing is a blessing to the church. In Malachi, we read, "Bring the whole tithe into the storehouse, that there may be food in my house" (Mal. 3:10). The tithe provides for the ongoing ministry of the church. This food in God's house should be plentiful. God's desire is to build a church that is healthy and vibrant. If everyone in a congregation were committed to tithing, needs would be met, the poor would be fed, creative outreach would be underwritten, and resources would flow freely. Sadly, many churches struggle because the people who attend have high expectations of what they will receive and a low commitment to giving. One reason God calls for a tithe is to make sure churches have the resources to help believers grow and to reach out to those who are not yet part of God's family.

Is Tithing a Form of Legalism?

Absolutely not! It is an act of freedom. Jesus taught that falling in love with material things brings bondage. When we are set free from the clutches of the money monster, we discover liberty. God does not love us more if we tithe and less if we don't. He wants us to experience the best life possible. Tithing helps to set us free from the oppressive power of money and to enter a better life. Some people will say, "If I give God 10 percent, I will have that much less." Those who have discovered the freedom of tithing say, "Every time I give God the first 10 percent, I discover that I have what I need and more than I ever dreamed."

Must I Give My Tithe to My Church?

I have discussed this question with other leaders and discovered there are varying views. I have heard some pastors say, "The tithe must go to the church you attend. Then you can give offerings outside the church." I have heard others say, "It does not matter. Give wherever you want as long as it is for God's work." I don't believe there is an emphatic yes or no to this question. But I think it is important for every person who is part of a church to generously support the ministry of that congregation.

It is important to remember that most churches are supported by the tithes and offerings of those who attend. Very few churches have other sources of income. When church members give generously outside the church and don't support their own congregation, it creates undue stress on the work of the church. It is good to give toward national and international ministries, but most of these are supported by a large base of people from churches all over the country or the world. The only source of ongoing support for most churches are the gifts given by those who attend weekly. It is important to give generously to your church.

What If I Want to Tithe but Am Struggling Financially?

There are those who will say, "I can't afford to tithe." This may seem true from where they are standing, but the truth is, it costs more not to tithe. For those who have become so financially leveraged that they feel tithing is impossible, there are a couple of options to help you move toward becoming a tither.

First, increase the amount you give every month. Graduate your giving until you reach a tithe. You might want to raise it by a percent or half a percent each month. This way you can ease your way into a tithing lifestyle.

This is what Dan and Dawn did. Over the years, Dan had been an elder in his church and also a deacon, but Dan and Dawn had never reached the point where they were giving a full 10 percent. They were raising three girls and had all the expenses of a young family. It just seemed impractical and even impossible to make this step. Then they felt God was calling them to raise the bar in their giving and to move toward a full 10 percent. They sat down and made a plan. Dawn, who handled the family checkbook, would keep giving a little more, when they could, until they reached 10 percent of their income. They agreed they would keep working at it until they hit this biblical benchmark. One day, Dan felt it was time to make the final step. He sat down with Dawn and told her he felt they were ready to take a risk and bump their giving up whatever amount was needed to begin tithing. She looked at him with a smile and said, "We have been tithing for the past three months!" Dan was stunned and overjoyed! And so was God.

‖‖‖‖ Seismic Shift Suggestion ‖‖‖‖

Graduation Time. If you have not yet developed a lifestyle of tithing, consider regularly graduating your giving amount until you hit a tithe. Determine a specific amount to increase each month or quarter. Then follow through. You might even want to keep a personal journal or notes on how God moves in your heart and life as you are learning to tithe.

This moment began a seismic shift in their lives that continues to this day. Not only do they find deep joy in giving their tithe, they also have begun to give offerings above the tithe. As God has blessed their business and family, they have continued incrementally increasing their giving, and they are watching as God opens the floodgates of heaven and pours out an overflowing blessing. The seismic shift started with a commitment to small but regular increases in giving until they reached a tithe. Now their perspective on life has been transformed. They are a testimony that little changes can make a big difference.

Second, some people need to simplify their lives so they can begin tithing. If a person can't tithe because they are paying for a nice new car or a summer cottage, something is out of balance. If the monthly bill for all five of the family cell phones is being paid but God is not receiving a tithe, things might need to be adjusted. It might just be that twelve-year-olds don't all need a personal cell phone with a thousand-anytime-minutes plan. If our habits or hobbies are so expensive that we can't give God the first 10 percent, it might be time to break a habit or scale back on a hobby. Sometimes living a life that honors God means making sacrifices. When Jesus called people to follow him, he said, "Whoever wants to be my disciple must deny themselves and take up their cross daily and follow me" (Luke 9:23 TNIV). We were never promised that following Jesus would be painless. Learning to tithe will often mean growing in the willingness to sacrifice.

Should I Wait to Begin Tithing until I Am out of Debt?

If only debt-free people tithed and gave offerings to God's work, virtually every church would close. Most people have a mortgage or a car payment, or carry some kind of debt. If you are in severe debt, it might be time to take a class on personal finances, read a good book on the topic, or meet with someone who can help you plan a budget and learn to live on it. But if the tithe is the first 10 percent, it should be given before anything else.

If I Tithe, Am I Guaranteed to Get Back Ten Times What I Give?

Over the years, I have had people ask this question. They have listened to a TV preacher promise that if they sow a seed of faith (and the seed always seems to be money sent directly to that minister or ministry), God will reward them with four times or even ten times as much as they give.

I believe that those who promise a specific financial return on money given to a ministry are misrepresenting what the Bible teaches about giving. The Bible does teach that "whoever sows generously will also reap generously" (2 Cor. 9:6), and that when we tithe, God will "throw open the floodgates of heaven and pour out so much blessing that you will not have room enough for it" (Mal. 3:10). But there is never a guarantee that the blessing will be monetary, and the Bible never sets out a heavenly investment plan that says we will get back ten times what we give.

The Bottom Line

Tithing is a challenge for all of us. Even those with massive resources can struggle with keeping this discipline. But the bottom line is, tithing is biblical, and those who know and love Jesus can discover the freedom and joy of giving.

D. James Kennedy tells a story of a man who came to Peter Marshall, a famous former chaplain of the United States Senate, with a concern about tithing. He said, "I have a problem. I have been tithing for some time. It wasn't too bad when I was making twenty thousand dollars a year. I could afford to give the two thousand. But you see, now I am making five hundred thousand dollars a year, and there is just no way I can afford to give away fifty thousand dollars a year."

Dr. Marshall reflected on this wealthy man's dilemma but gave no advice. He simply said, "Yes, sir. I see that you do have a problem. I think we ought to pray about it. Is that alright?" The man agreed, so Dr. Marshall bowed his head and prayed with boldness and authority. "Dear Lord, this man has a problem, and I pray that you will help him. Lord, reduce his salary back to the place where he can afford to tithe."

Right in the middle of the prayer the man jumped as if someone had poked him in the ribs with a cattle prod and he let out a yelp. He stopped Peter Marshall in mid-prayer and said, "No, Dr. Marshall, that's not what I meant!" He realized that his perspective had become warped. He was ready to take a new look at how he should understand the resources God had placed in his care.

What about Your Smarties?

There are many responses to the question, Can I have some of your Smarties? Some kids recoil and protect their candy; there is no way anyone is getting a single piece. Other children will share, but it is obvious they are not happy about it. Then there are kids like my Smarties hero, Dustin. They share freely, gladly, and generously. We can choose how we will respond to God's request that we share our Smarties with him. It helps to remember that he gave us the whole pack to start with.

How are you doing with your Smarties?

FOR REFLECTION • • • • • • • • • • • • • • • • • • •

- How has making the seismic shift from mine to God's impacted the way you manage your resources? If you have not yet made this shift, what is standing in the way?
- Close your eyes and turn your hands upward. Imagine all of your resources sitting in the palms of your hands. Then ask yourself, Are my hands open and free to share with God and others? Are my hands closed tightly around "my" things? What can I do to live with open and generous hands?

FOR PRAYER •

- Think about all God has placed in your care, and thank him for trusting you with these resources.
- If you are not yet tithing, pray for the wisdom and courage to move in this direction. Ask God to help you learn to be a joyful and generous giver.

Chapter FOURTEEN

The Seismic Shift from Hamsters to Sharers

Remember this: Whoever sows sparingly will also reap sparingly, and whoever sows generously will also reap generously. Each man should give what he has decided in his heart to give, not reluctantly or under compulsion, for God loves a cheerful giver. And God is able to make all grace abound to you, so that in all things at all times, having all that you need, you will abound in every good work.

—2 Corinthians 9:6–8

I was young and now I am old,
   yet I have never seen the righteous forsaken
   or their children begging bread.
They are always generous and lend freely;
   their children will be blessed.

—Psalm 37:25–26

And do not forget to do good and to share with others, for with such sacrifices God is pleased.

—Hebrews 13:16

Some years ago, our family made our first foray into the world of pet ownership. Our three little boys had been barraging Sherry and me with appeals for dogs, cats, lizards, monkeys, and a variety of exotic animals. We settled on hamsters, which we figured was sort of like getting a pet with training wheels. We purchased a starter kit complete with two hamsters, an exercise ball, a habitat, a bag of wood shavings, food, and a water bottle. What could be easier? The pet store even threw in a little book with a brief history of hamsters and instructions for their care.

Since Sniffy and Goldie were becoming part of our family, I thought I should become the resident expert on hamsters. I learned quite a bit about *Mesocricetus auratus*. The word *hamster* means "to hoard." Hamsters were first found and domesticated in the Middle East. Hamsters in Germany are quite a bit larger than the fluffy little golden hamsters that come from Syria. These hamster relatives are the size of large rats. In our hamster book, I learned that hamsters by nature hoard their food. They can't help themselves. They gather as much as they can and hide it. Then they find more and hide it too. I read about one hamster that had stolen over three hundred pounds of grain from a farmer. There was no way this little critter needed such a massive storehouse, but it seemed he just kept collecting anyway.

Exorcising the Hamster Spirit

We live in a hamster-like world! There is something innate in the human spirit that makes us want to hoard far more than we need. If left unchecked, most of us will spend a good deal of our lives accumulating as much as we can. Hamsters have elastic facial skin that can stretch over an inch away from their bodies without discomfort. If our lives go unguarded, we too can stretch to grotesque proportions as we accumulate to a degree that rivals many hamsters.

In our family experiment, one of our hamsters, appropriately named Goldie, was a golden hamster. The other one, Sniffy, must have been a hybrid of a hamster and a pit bull. Anytime one of us reached into the cage, he tried to take a chunk out of our fingers with his razor-sharp teeth. On more than one occasion, he was successful. He was afraid we were trying to steal his hoard of food. It got to the point that we could not reach into the cage without wearing gloves. When Goldie and Sniffy hid all of their food, we would have to reach in, uncover it, and put it back in the bowl. When we did this, they were not happy.

If we want to slay the money monster, we have to learn to identify the hamster spirit that rules our culture and fight against it. We have to admit that we are prone to hoard far more than we really need. Sometimes we even try to bite those who get too close to our stuff.

The second stake we must drive into the heart of the money monster is generosity. When we make the shift from being hamsters to being sharers, we discover a whole new kind of wealth and prosperity.

|||||| **Seismic Shift Suggestion** ||||||

Enough Is Enough. Identify an area in your life in which you have enough. It might be the clothes in your closet, the technological toys you use for work, jewelry, or tools you keep hanging in the garage. If it's clear that you have enough, declare it! Decide that you won't shop for another outfit, upgrade your computer's memory, order another bracelet from a TV shopping channel, or visit the home improvement superstore this weekend. Just say, "I have enough," and declare a moratorium on collecting more.

Generosity moves us to a lifestyle of looking for, even praying for, opportunities to share what we have with God and with others. When the hamster spirit is driven out and a generous spirit moves in, our resources take on a whole new purpose. We begin investing them in eternal things.

The Generosity of God

The greatest example of generosity in human history is God's sending his only Son as a gift to pay the price for our sins and to set us free. Jesus, God in human flesh, modeled generosity on a level infinitely greater than we can comprehend. He left the glory, majesty, and splendor of heaven to be born in the squalor of a stable. In the book of Philippians, the apostle Paul writes that our attitude should be the same as that of Christ Jesus, "who, being in very nature God, did not consider equality with God something to be grasped, but made himself nothing, taking the very nature of a servant, being made in human likeness. And being found in appearance as a man, he humbled himself and became obedient to death—even death on a cross!" (Phil. 2:5–8).

Our minds can't begin to embrace the magnitude of what Jesus did when he left heaven to enter human history. But his generosity did not end there. Jesus offered the greatest sacrifice imaginable—his own life. He showed the depth of his love by dying on the cross, laying down his life as the payment for our sins. It was Jesus who said, "Greater love has no one than this, that he lay down his life for his friends" (John 15:13).

Jesus did not give 10 percent for us; he gave 100 percent. He invites us to follow his example.

God has a dream that his people will live with aggressively generous hearts. No more hamster-like hoarding of resources. An end to self-centered pursuits and constant upgrades. It is time we offer everything we have back to God with a joyful heart.

As we become intentionally, consistently, and joyfully generous, we will see the hamster spirit run for the door, and we can be confident that another stake has been driven into the money monster's heart.

Is *Cheerful Giver* an Oxymoron?

Have you ever run across one of those humorous lists of oxymorons? An oxymoron is a phrase made up of words that we often use together but when examined don't quite seem to belong with each other. One definition calls an oxymoron "a rhetorical figure in which an epigrammatic effect is created by the conjunction of incongruous or contradictory terms." Some examples are:

act naturally

cafeteria food

clearly ambiguous

deafening silence

educational television

flexible ethics

friendly takeover

good grief

government organization

half-naked

jumbo shrimp

nonworking mother

open secret

plastic silverware

pretty ugly

seriously funny

unbiased opinion

Many people think *cheerful giver* should be added to the top of this list.

What in the world do joy and giving have to do with each other? How are generosity and cheer linked? The apostle Paul makes it clear that there is a close relationship between a joyful heart and sharing our resources. He writes, "Each of you should give what you have decided in your heart to give, not reluctantly or under compulsion, for God loves a cheerful giver" (2 Cor. 9:7 TNIV). If God loves those who give cheerfully, it must be possible to live this way. There seems to be an intrinsic connection between learning to be a person who freely shares resources and growing in cheer. The problem is, we don't see many examples of cheerful giving in our world. In many cases, we see just the opposite.

A parable of this principle once played itself out right before my eyes. A little boy sat on the floor of the church nursery with a red rubber ball in each arm and three Nerf balls clenched on the floor between his pudgy little knees. He was trying to protect all five from the other children in the nursery. The problem was he could not hold all five at once, and the ball nearest to his feet was particularly vulnerable to being stolen. So whenever another child showed an interest in playing with one of the balls, he snarled to make it clear these toys were not for sharing.

I suppose I should have stepped in and made the little guy give up one or two of the balls, but I was too wrapped up in the drama of it all. For about five minutes, this little guy growled, postured, and kept the other children away from the balls. Like a hyena hunched over the last scraps of a carcass, this snarling little canine was not in the mood for sharing. The other kids circled like vultures around the kill, looking for a way to jump in and snatch a ball without being attacked and bitten. I honestly did not know whether to laugh or cry as I watched.

Then it struck me. This little boy was not having any fun at all. There was no cheer within ten yards of this kid. Not only was he unhappy, but all the other kids seemed sad as well. His selfishness created a black hole that sucked all of the joy out of that nursery.

Here he was with five balls and he did not spend a single moment playing with them. Because of his commitment to hoarding, he never had time to enjoy his stockpile. It took every ounce of his energy just to keep the other kids away from toys that weren't even his; they belonged to the church nursery. When church was over and his parents came to pick him up, he left the balls behind. I guess the old saying is true, you can't take it with you.

As I thought about this little boy, I realized there is a hamster spirit in each of us. The Bible calls it sin. Our natural tendency toward selfishness does not bring joy and cheer. On the contrary, it brings fear, isolation, and mistrust.

> |||||| **Seismic Shift Suggestion** ||||||
>
> **Give It Away**. Identify one thing you have that you don't really need, that is just collecting dust or taking up space on a shelf. Then as a declaration of war on the money monster, give this thing away. Maybe you have an extra car and there is a single parent in your church who does not have one. Give it away. Possibly you have a lawnmower in the garage that you don't use. Give it to a neighbor who needs it. You might have lots of clothes you never wear. Give them to an organization that meets the needs of the poor. If after doing this you feel free and even cheerful, do it again.

As I replay the mental tape of that day in the church nursery, I see my own face and heart. I can be just as guilty of snarling, growling, and protecting "my stuff" and missing the joy of sharing with God and others. I can be prone to spend my time and energy protecting the gates of my storehouse and miss the chance to invite others over so we can enjoy life and God's goodness together.

That day in the nursery, I was reminded that unless you are a juggler, playing pool, or an amateur golfer, you don't really need more than one ball. And half a ball is usually even better. Why half a ball? Because when you share it with someone else, you both have more fun!

Cheerful giver is not an oxymoron. God says it is exactly what all of his children should be. In God's dictionary of oxymorons, here are some of the entries you might find: selfish Christian, reluctant giver, greedy disciple, and ball hog.

Lessons in Generosity

The world would be a much nicer place if generosity came naturally. It would be wonderful if little children said, "May I share with you?" instead of, "It's mine. Don't touch it." But most of us will battle selfishness our whole lives. Knowing this, it is important to learn some lessons that will help us on our journey toward generosity. If a generous lifestyle is one of the stakes that kills the money monster, we had better learn how to drive it in deep.

Giving Is Countercultural

Few things are more countercultural than generous giving. Committing to a lifestyle of sharing freely means swimming against the current of this world. If we don't keep swimming toward God's vision for sacrificial living, we will get swept downstream. When we exert our energy and learn to share our resources freely and cheerfully, the world will look on in amazement. Few things will raise more eyebrows and garner more attention than living generous lives.

|||||| **Seismic Shift Suggestion** ||||||

Surprise Someone. Let your light shine by giving a gift to someone who would never expect it. Identify a person or family in your community who does not have a church home and who is in a time of need. Then pray about what you could give them that would help them through their difficult time. Generosity is more art than science. There are no rules. But if you pray for the leading of the Spirit and make your resources available, God will show you what to give and how to give it. If this person is surprised by your generosity and curious as to why you care, let them know that God placed them on your heart and moved you to help them so that they could see and experience his love.

Our joy-filled acts of giving can reveal Jesus to a watching world. He is the one who said, "You are the light of the world. A city on a hill cannot be hidden. Neither do people light a lamp and put it under a bowl. Instead they put it on its stand, and it gives light to everyone in the house. In the same way, let your light shine before others, that they may see your good deeds and glorify your Father in heaven" (Matt. 5:14–17 TNIV). One way to show the presence and power of Jesus to this world is by doing good deeds that people can see. When they see them, we can point to God and give him the glory.

Anyone Can Be Generous

Sometimes we can be tricked into thinking that only the rich can be generous. But Jesus made it clear that generosity is dictated not by the size of our bank accounts but by the size of our hearts. In the gospel of Mark, we read about a teachable moment Jesus had with his followers. As we look over their shoulders and listen to what Jesus taught them about generosity, we discover that even the poorest of people can be rich toward God and others:

> Jesus sat down opposite the place where the offerings were put and watched the crowd putting their money into the temple treasury. Many rich people threw in large amounts. But a poor widow came and put in two very small copper coins, worth only a fraction of a penny.
>
> Calling his disciples to him, Jesus said, "I tell you the truth, this poor widow has put more into the treasury than all the others. They all gave out of their wealth; but she, out of her poverty, put in everything—all she had to live on."
>
> —Mark 12:41–44

Jesus celebrated this woman's staggering generosity. Out of her poverty, she gave freely, and God celebrated her actions and her heart. Wealthy people can give much and still be possessed by a hamster spirit. Those with modest means can give a small amount, and it can be an act of radical faith and love. More interested in sacrifice and generosity than in the bottom line, they are all about having a heart ready to give anything and everything as God directs.

Giving Has Rewards and Blessings

God would not have inspired Malachi to write "bring the whole tithe into the storehouse, that there may be food in my house. Test me in this ... and see if I will not throw open the floodgates of heaven and pour out so much blessing that you will not have room enough for it" (Mal. 3:10) unless there were rewards and blessings for giving. Every time we give a tithe or an offering, we will receive a blessing. First and foremost, we experience the joy of sharing in God's work in the church and in the world. Also, there is the blessing of being set free from the money monster. On top of this, there are often times when God will give material blessings. When God opens the heavenly windows and pours out financial resources, he does this as an act of trust. When we have been good stewards of his resources, God often entrusts us with more so we can invest it in his work.

It is dangerous to expect money back when giving of our resources. We looked at this in the last chapter, but I feel the need to emphasize this point.

God does not promise to give a specific dollar amount in return for our tithes and offerings. He is not some heavenly investment specialist who promises a percentage of return on what we give to him. Sometimes when we give our tithes and offerings, our bank account ledgers show that we have exactly that amount less at our disposal. But this does not mean God has failed to pour out an overflowing blessing. We have to realize that God's understanding of blessings is much bigger than ours. Often God will surprise us with something much greater than a few dollars in a bank account.

A good friend of mine tells of how his parents were led by the Lord to pay the costs another family incurred in the process of adopting a child. This family could not have children and could not afford the expense of adoption. This act of Christlike giving led to an overflow of blessing as my friend's parents watched this child grow up in a loving Christian home. If you asked them whether they received ten times the money they gave for the adoption, they would say no. If you asked whether they saw the windows of heaven open and God's blessings pour over their lives in response to their generosity, they would say yes.

Another couple I know decided to limit their lifestyle so they could give aggressively. They chose to live in a very modest home when they could have afforded a larger and more extravagant one. When I asked them if they ever thought of moving to a bigger house, they said, "We have talked about it off and on over the years. But if we did, we could not give as much to God's work." I felt a little embarrassed that I had asked, but I could see that their greatest joy was in discovering new ways to invest their resources in God's kingdom work.

Giving Indicates the Condition of Our Hearts   • • • • •

Jesus teaches that our treasures and our hearts are very closely linked. He says, "Do not store up for yourselves treasures on earth, where moth and rust destroy, and where thieves break in and steal. But store up for yourselves treasures in heaven, where moth and rust do not destroy, and where thieves do not break in and steal. For where your treasure is, there your heart will be also" (Matt. 6:19–21).

How do we know whether our hearts are surrendered to God? Jesus says that we can look at where we store our treasure. If massive portions of our resources are stored away in bank accounts, spent on toys, and tied up in earthy things, the money monster just might have a tighter grip on our hearts than we know. On the other hand, if we are investing in eternal things, living with open hands, and growing in generosity, our hearts are resting safely in Jesus' hands.

The system of this world invites us to hoard everything we have for a rainy day. Or to spend it selfishly today because there might not be a chance to enjoy it tomorrow. When we live this way, we expose a heart in love with the stuff of this world. But a person with a heart captured by Jesus' grace declares war on a culture that is all about me, mine, and more. This kind of person raises a banner that says, "Other people matter, the world is bigger than my needs and wants, and God's interests and concerns are worth investing in." A generous giver sends a message that says, "God and his people live with a whole different economy. Our hearts are not bound by the love of material things. There are investments that earn more than earthly dividends." When our hearts beat with the heart of Jesus, generosity can't be stopped.

The Church and Generosity

Over the past decade, I have visited churches throughout the United States and Europe. I have also talked with thousands of pastors and church leaders from around the world. What I have discovered is that the hamster spirit that lives in our hearts can also creep into the soul of a church. It is shockingly common for a church to hoard their resources and refuse to share with other Bible-believing congregations in their community. Instead of working together, blessing each other, and celebrating our common victories, we look at each other as competitors.

||||| **Seismic Shift Suggestion** |||||

Heart Check, Checkbook. Schedule about thirty minutes at the end of the month to have a meeting with God about the condition of your heart. Bring just two things to this meeting: your Bible and your checkbook. First, pray for a humble heart to hear what God has to say. Second, look over your checkbook ledger from the past month. What do you learn about the condition of your heart from your spending? If you are a credit-card user, you might want to bring along those records also. Third, prayerfully read the following passages:

1 Timothy 6:6 – 10
2 Corinthians 9:6 – 8
Mark 12:41 – 44
Matthew 6:19 – 21

Finally, ask God if you need to make some changes in the way you use your resources. If this is a helpful exercise, do it again next month.

To be sure, the church has competition, but it is not the Christians meeting three blocks away from us. The one we compete against is very real. The apostle Paul says, "For our struggle is not against flesh and blood, but against the rulers, against the authorities, against the powers of this dark world and against the spiritual forces of evil in the heavenly realms. Therefore put on the full armor of God, so that when the day of evil comes, you may be able to stand your ground, and after you have done everything, to stand" (Eph. 6:12–13). This enemy is so real that we need to work together with all who call on the name of Jesus. The work we are expected to do is far too important to be compromised by insecurities and selfishness.

It is time for congregations to start giving away their resources to those in the world who are needy and to the struggling church down the street. If your church has a great outreach program, tell other churches in your community about it. Give away your best ideas, tell your secrets, spill the beans, learn to share. When we do this, we invest our resources in eternity, not just in our little kingdoms here on earth.

FOR REFLECTION ● ● ● ● ● ● ● ● ● ● ● ● ● ● ● ● ● ●

- Use the following questions to assess the condition of your heart regarding material things:
    1. Is one of my goals to accumulate more and more for myself, or do I find joy in sharing with others?
    2. Do I see what I have as belonging to God, or to me?
    3. Am I fundamentally selfish, or generous?
    4. Do I live a me-centered or a God-centered life?
- What could God do if I live with a generous spirit and make all of my resources available to him?

FOR PRAYER ● ● ● ● ● ● ● ● ● ● ● ● ● ● ● ● ● ●

- Pray that the Holy Spirit will open your eyes to the needs around you and then give you the courage to generously meet those needs as you are able.
- Thank God for his generosity in sending Jesus into this world. Thank Jesus for his sacrifice and for giving 100 percent of himself for you. Thank the Holy Spirit for lavishing so many spiritual blessings on you.

Chapter FIFTEEN

The Seismic Shift from Fleeting Wealth to True Wealth

Do not store up for yourselves treasures on earth, where moth and rust destroy, and where thieves break in and steal. But store up for yourselves treasures in heaven, where moth and rust do not destroy, and where thieves do not break in and steal. For where your treasure is, there your heart will be also.

—Matthew 6:19–21

Command those who are rich in this present world not to be arrogant nor to put their hope in wealth, which is so uncertain, but to put their hope in God, who richly provides us with everything for our enjoyment. Command them to do good, to be rich in good deeds, and to be generous and willing to share. In this way they will lay up treasure for themselves as a firm foundation for the coming age, so that they may take hold of the life that is truly life.

—1 Timothy 6:17–19

Harold was near the end. He had lived a full life. A rich life. But now the clock was winding down. Hospice care had moved a bed into the living room, and a nurse visited regularly. Everyone knew it would be a matter of days, maybe hours.

The pastor came to visit, to read some Bible passages, and to say a prayer with the family. After the amen, Harold gestured for the preacher to come closer. The pastor bent over the ailing man to hear what might very well be his final words.

His voice was coarse and quiet, but the pastor caught the sense of what Harold was trying to say. With a quizzical look, the pastor asked, "Are you sure?" Harold gave him a look that answered his question. Harold wanted to be helped out of bed and carried to the front window. It was only a few feet away, and it seemed wrong to deny a dying man his final wish. So the pastor and a few family members helped Harold up, put his frail arms over their shoulders, and carried him to the window.

Harold's wife pulled the cord for the curtains. As they parted, Harold looked out the window with longing in his eyes. He winced in pain but strained his neck to see over the hedge, across the yard, and to the drive-way. There it was, just like he had remembered—his silver Lexus SUV. With a sigh of relief, he whispered, "Thank you. I just had to see it one more time. Now could you help me back to my bed?"

You can file this story under the heading "Things You Will Never See"! When we draw near the end of life, we discover what really matters. No one whispers, "Let me look at my car one more time." Dying people don't ask, "How much do I have in my savings account?" You will never hear someone in the CCU of a hospital say, "I wish I had closed one more deal or gotten another raise."

||||| Seismic Shift Suggestion |||||

Let Wisdom Speak. Meet with a Christian who has more life experience than you do. It could be a parent, a grandparent, or a friend. Ask for advice on how you could invest the rest of your life in things that will make an eternal impact. Invite them to share what they invested in that they feel will last when they are gone. And invite them to tell you what they wish they had not spent so much time on in their life.

In these moments, the trinkets and baubles of this world pale in significance compared with things of enduring worth. We're more likely to ask, "Can you bring over the grandkids so I can tell them 'I love you' one last time?" This is when we make sure we are right with God and with those who mean the most to us. Many of the things that seemed so urgent for most of our lives fade into the background, and the two things that Jesus said should matter the most come to the forefront: God and people.

An Eternal Perspective • • • • • • • • • • • • • • • • •

God knows what matters most in this life and in eternity. That is why the gospel of Matthew records these words: "Jesus replied: '"Love the Lord your God with all your heart and with all your soul and with all your mind." This is the first and greatest commandment. And the second is like it: "Love your neighbor as yourself"'" (Matt. 22:37–39).

Lots of things will pass away, but love is an investment that lasts forever. The apostle Paul points out that many valuable things will cease but certain things will endure. He writes, "And now these three remain: faith, hope and love. But the greatest of these is love" (1 Cor. 13:13). We need to identify what treasures and riches are temporary and be sure we don't invest too much in them. Then we must identify what has eternal value and make sure our lives are wrapped up in these things.

|||||| **Seismic Shift Suggestion** ||||||

A View from the Throne. Imagine you have the chance to sit next to God on his throne. From there, you can watch the world and all that people are doing. Now imagine you get to watch your own life for one week. What are you doing that will last forever? And what are you doing that will not make an eternal difference? From this vantage point, decide to shift your time and energy away from some transitory activity and toward a big-K Kingdom investment.

The third stake that defeats the money monster is adopting a heavenly understanding of riches. This involves learning to look at our lives and investments from God's perspective. When we do this, we begin to see what matters, what lasts, what has eternal value.

In the movie *The Dead Poets Society*, there is a scene in which a new teacher at a private prep school helps a group of students see the world from a new vantage point. He invites them to walk to the front of the class, step up on his chair, and from there, stand on top of his desk. The school has rigid rules and does not encourage risky or anti-establishment behavior. But one by one, the boys line up and take their turn climbing up on the desk and looking at the classroom from a new perspective. The camera zooms in on the face of each boy as he looks across the room. Each face tells a story. Some are fearful, others are bold, some seem confused, but all of them see life differently from this perch.

God invites us to climb up on his heavenly throne, stand on tiptoes, and look over the clutter and lies the world has piled up in front of us. From this new vantage point, we can see that many of the things we spend endless hours investing in have very little eternal value. As we strain to see life from God's throne, we discover there are some things that matter a great deal. We should invest our hearts, resources, and strength in these things and not in the accumulation of material treasures.

Fleeting Wealth

Jesus says, "Do not store up for yourselves treasures on earth, where moth and rust destroy, and where thieves break in and steal. But store up for yourselves treasures in heaven, where moth and rust do not destroy, and where thieves do not break in and steal. For where your treasure is, there your heart will be also" (Matt. 6:19–21).

I would very loosely paraphrase Jesus' words this way: "If it can be eaten by moths, if it can rust, or if a thief can steal it, don't make it a big priority in your life." If we take this advice, much of what we do with our time will change. Jesus warns that investing in material things is an unwise use of our lives. He sits on the throne of heaven and has a much better look at this world than we do. He can see what matters most, and wealth is not even near the top of the list.

What Jesus taught two thousand years ago continues to ring true today. Many of the wealthiest people who have walked the earth have discovered that the meaning and purpose they longed to find in life could not be gained by accumulating more of this world's stuff. Reflect on the words of some people who knew quite a bit about stockpiling earthly wealth:

I have made many millions, but they have brought me no happiness.

—**John D. Rockefeller**

Millionaires seldom smile.

—**Andrew Carnegie**

I was happier when I was doing a mechanic's job.

—**Henry Ford**

Many people have studied the relationship between happiness and the accumulation of wealth. The conclusion is that more wealth does not equal greater satisfaction. In an article in the *Grand Rapids Press*, Alison Grant writes that the bottom line is more stuff does not lead to greater happiness. Economist Richard Easterlin talks about "hedonic adaptation and social comparison." This is a fancy way of saying that once we get the thing we thought would make us happy, we notice that others still have more than we do. We end up wanting more. In a short time, we are just as dissatisfied as we were before our most recent acquisition or conquest. Sadly, instead of breaking this vicious cycle, most of us just set our sights on the next goal or acquisition and go through the cycle over and over again.

It would seem that at some point in this endless cycle, we would catch on and invest in something else, but most of us don't. Gregg Easterbrook wrote a book called *Progress Paradox: How Life Gets Better While People Feel Worse*. He explores the sad reality that even though our pursuit of material things often leads to getting the possessions we always dreamed we wanted, once we have them, we are less satisfied and happy.

The key for followers of Jesus is to realize that the amassing of wealth and stuff will not lead to the joy it promises. These treasures fade and rust and get eaten by moths. They don't satisfy. And they will certainly not last forever. It is time to identify the riches and true wealth that will last long after our time on this earth. God wants us to discover how to add eternal investments to our portfolio.

Eternal Investments

Jesus has already helped us see what matters most and lasts forever. True wealth is wrapped up in how we love God and people. The two greatest commandments were given to help us know how to invest our lives so they won't be squandered on toys and counterfeits.

If you watch TV or get spam in your e-mail box, you know that lots of people have discovered the "best-kept investment secrets ever!" For a small price, you can send away for their book. When it arrives, you will read about how easy it is to get rich selling real estate with no money down, or by placing little classified ads, or even by applying for government money that is just waiting to be given to anyone who fills out the right forms. I have never tried any of these "great investment secrets," but I have a feeling they might not be quite as easy and lucrative as advertised.

On the other hand, God has some wonderful investment strategies anyone can use. You don't have to pay "four easy flex-payments of only $29.99 plus shipping and handling." You might even have a copy of his investment guide already: the Bible. For thousands of years, God has given clear investment advice for anyone who will listen. And when we follow his counsel, the seismic shift from fleeting wealth to true wealth takes place.

Here are five key investment principles we can use to invest in things that last forever.

Investment Secret 1: A Heart in Love with God

Every investment program has a philosophy that guides how we use our resources. This philosophy acts as the foundation for the program's whole strategy. In God's investment program, the primary rule for success is found in the book of Deuteronomy: "Love the LORD your God with all your heart and with all your soul and with all your strength" (Deut. 6:5). If we miss this, the rest will never fall into place.

Why is loving God the cornerstone of all investments that last forever? The answer is simple: as we grow in love with God, he shapes our hearts to be more like his. Our values, passions, and lifestyles begin to look more like Jesus'. And the result is that we live the way God intended. Our perspective changes, and the stuff of this world becomes little more than ways to help accomplish God's eternal purposes.

Investment Secret 2: Helping Christians Grow in Faith

Once we are growing to know, love, and worship God, we can discover other investment secrets. One of the most valuable things a follower of Christ can do with their life is invest in those who are seeking to grow in their faith.

You can make this investment in many ways. You could mentor a new believer as they learn to follow Jesus in their daily life. Your prayers, encouragement, and friendship will bless this person, and the eternal impact will be greater than you will see in this life. You might lead a small group for new believers or people who need spiritual encouragement. As this group studies the Bible, prays for each other, offers a place of accountability, and celebrates steps toward growth, an investment will be made in heaven. Perhaps God has given you a gift for teaching and a love for children. You can invest in eternity by leading a Sunday school class for little children. If you volunteer as a youth leader in your church and spend time pouring yourself into the lives of students, the dividends mount up to heaven. Anytime you leverage your time and abilities to help others grow in their faith, the return will be greater than dollars and cents. It will be recorded in a celestial ledger.

||||| **Seismic Shift Suggestion** |||||

Enter the Dream. Imagine that every follower of Jesus is investing in the life of one person who seeks to grow in faith. What might God do to bring maturity and growth among his people? Pray about a specific Christian whom God has placed in your life who needs encouragement to help them keep growing. Identify one way you can invest in this person.

For those who have the honor and responsibility of being parents, one of your most important investments is passing on the faith to the next generation. Your prayers, example, and teaching will make an impact that goes well beyond the boundaries of this life. This is why God gives these instructions in the book of Deuteronomy: "These commandments that I give you today are to be upon your hearts. Impress them on your children. Talk about them when you sit at home and when you walk along the road, when you lie down and when you get up. Tie them as symbols on your hands and bind them on your foreheads. Write them on the doorframes of your houses and on your gates" (Deut. 6:6–9).

The modern notion that children should be left to find their own spiritual pathway is unbiblical and utter folly. God calls parents to teach, talk, and model. It is a parent's God-given responsibility to pass on the faith.

If you look back over your life, you can probably identify people who gave of themselves in a way that aided your spiritual journey. You know the difference their time, love, and care made in your life. You understand that there is no way to calculate how much their investment is worth.

God wants each of us to have this same impact on others. He wants us to see that when we invest in people who are seeking to grow in their faith, we are giving ourselves to something much bigger than we can see. We are investing in eternity.

⚃ Investment Secret 3: Caring for the Poor, Outcast, and Forgotten

All through the Bible, God teaches that he has a special place in his heart for those who are broken, hurt, outcast, and forgotten. In the Old Testament, special provision is made for people who were easily overlooked. They were the "foreigner, the fatherless and the widow" (Deut. 24:19 TNIV; see also Jer. 7:6; Ezek. 22:7). It is not that God loves these people more. He just knows that they are often overlooked, so he calls us to hold them in our hearts and care for them as he does. Jesus reinforces this idea when he says, "Then the righteous will answer him, 'Lord, when did we see you hungry and feed you, or thirsty and give you something to drink? When did we see you a stranger and invite you in, or needing clothes and clothe you? When did we see you sick or in prison and go to visit you?' The King will reply, 'I tell you the truth, whatever you did for one of the least of these brothers of mine, you did for me'" (Matt. 25:37–40).

Again we hear the message loud and clear: we are invited to enter into God's ministry of caring for those who are marginalized, broken, and unable to help themselves.

||||| Seismic Shift Suggestion |||||

Eye Opener. God is the great opener of eyes. Often we want to clench our eyes shut and see no evil. God pries them open so we can see what he sees, even when it is hard. Invite God to open your eyes to see the outcast and forgotten in your community and in the world. Then think of one way you can serve or support a specific person or group of people who need to feel God's love through God's people.

In our day and age, this caring takes on new and challenging forms, but the call is the same. Followers of Jesus can invest in eternity as we serve, love, visit, give to, help, and support those who need a touch from God. Maybe you will be called to take part in a prison ministry, leading worship services for inmates or forming a friendship with a prisoner. God might prompt you to regularly visit a nursing home. Perhaps your investment will come in the form of giving to a ministry that offers relief and support to nations in Africa, where almost half the population has HIV/AIDS. It might be that the Holy Spirit will move you to open your arms to one of the more than three million orphaned girls in China who are waiting for someone to love them. Maybe you will go on a mission trip to the Dominican Republic, Mexico, or India and serve among the poor of these nations. The Lord could call you to serve soup in a local mission or sort clothes to be handed out to families who have lost everything and are living on the streets. There are countless ways we can make an eternal investment in the forgotten people of our day.

Investment Secret 4: Strategic and Consistent Giving

What we say is, "The only treasure we can take to heaven are the spiritual investments we make on earth." As we've noted, we are called not only to tithe but also to be ever ready to invest the other 90 percent of the resources we have in ways that will bless the heart of God and make an eternal impact. Along with supporting the ministry of the church you attend, it is important for followers of Jesus to be intentional and strategic about finding ways to give to ministries, missions, community projects, and people who are in a time of need. When we give away our resources under the leading of the Holy Spirit, we make an eternal investment.

|||||| Seismic Shift Suggestion ||||||

My Investment Plan. Set aside about fifteen minutes to evaluate your personal investment plan. Draw a line down the middle of a blank sheet of paper. On the left side near the top write, "Investments that are valuable in this life alone." On the right side write, "Investments that will last forever." List all of the investments you are making on both sides of the line. If your portfolio is out of balance, make a shift.

Investment Secret 5: Sharing the Good News of Jesus

One of the greatest eternal investments we can make is sharing the love and message of Jesus with those who don't yet know him as their Savior. Nothing is more valuable than a human soul. When we pray for those who are lost, when we build loving relationships with those outside of God's family, when we open our mouths and tell the amazing story of Jesus, we make an investment greater than any earthly treasure.

Some people check their stocks every day to see how their investments are faring. Some keep a close eye on their bank accounts to be sure that their financial stability is assured. Some people spend a large portion of their time and energy seeking after treasures that will end up in the recycling centers of this world.

God invites us to make a seismic shift. We can broaden our investment portfolio to include more than stocks, bonds, and dollar signs.

A Word to the Church: Invest Wisely

An elder came to the church board and said, "I think we should hire another pastor so that we can reach out to our community. There is wonderful growth in the ethnic diversity of our neighborhood, and we should expand our ministry so we can share God's love with some of the folks most of the other local churches are not reaching at this time." This elder met massive resistance. He was informed that the church could not afford such an investment. They just did not have the money or the people to do it.

He pointed out that they owned their building, the land, the parsonage, and even the church bus, free and clear. He also pointed out that over the decades, a number of people had died and left large sums of money to the church. That money was in accounts that were paying a tidy sum in interest. He wondered if they might want to use that money for ministering to their neighborhood.

You would think he had suggested turning the church sanctuary into a brothel. The answer was "No!"

Many years later, the church still owns all of their buildings. My guess is they have some nice savings accounts. But the congregation has dwindled, and they are not offering a vibrant ministry to their community. There is a good chance they will close their doors altogether in a few years.

Churches like this look a lot like the man in a parable Jesus tells:

> The ground of a certain rich man produced a good crop. He thought to himself, "What shall I do? I have no place to store my crops."
>
> Then he said, "This is what I'll do. I will tear down my barns and build bigger ones, and there I will store all my grain and my goods. And I'll say to myself, 'You have plenty of good things laid up for many years. Take life easy; eat, drink and be merry.'"
>
> But God said to him, "You fool! This very night your life will be demanded from you. Then who will get what you have prepared for yourself?"

This is how it will be with anyone who stores up things for himself but is not rich toward God.

—Luke 12:16–21

Jesus emphatically taught that we are not to hoard the resources God gives us; we are to invest them in eternity. Churches, much like individuals and families, can become greedy and hold onto their resources. But this was never God's plan. God gives resources to our congregations so we can share them freely, not so that we can build bigger and bigger barns.

It is tempting for individuals and churches to spend a lifetime gathering and protecting wealth. But like Solomon said, "I have seen all the things that are done under the sun; all of them are meaningless, a chasing after the wind" (Eccl. 1:14). He accumulated more wealth than any of us could ever imagine, and at the end of the day, he said it was like chasing the wind. As individuals and as churches, it is time to make the seismic shift from the things that pass away to the investments that will last forever.

FOR REFLECTION

- If I had only one month to live, what eternal investments would I make with this limited time? What can I do to begin living with the same urgency?
- Who are the outcasts and the marginalized in my community? What can I do to share God's love with these people? What can my church do?

FOR PRAYER

- Ask God to help you love people the way he does. Pray for deeper compassion and concern for people.
- Thank God for the people he has placed in your life who have invested in the development of your faith over the years.
- Pray that your church will develop the vision for investing in things that last forever. Ask God to protect your congregation from getting caught up in things that won't have an eternal impact.

Part 6

Shifts That Will Help You
Impact Your Community
and the World

Things were not going well. Not by a long shot. I was traveling to Scotland with some friends, and it looked like I'd be spending the first day of the trip sleeping on the floor of the airport in Chicago instead of walking the lush hillsides of the Old Country. The weather was not cooperating, and flights were being cancelled left and right. Ours had already been delayed twice, and every time the airline agent's voice came on the loudspeaker, I tensed up, anticipating bad news.

I travel a fair amount, so I have learned to be flexible, but this particular night, I was not feeling real cheerful or understanding. Eventually the flight was rerouted through London, and we were assured we would be on the plane and off the ground soon. But because of the change in planes and connections, my friends and I lost our adjoining seats, and the airline jammed us in wherever they could find room. When I finally found my spot on the plane, I planned to settle in, go to sleep, and try not to interact with those around me.

Now, don't get me wrong; there are many times I get on a plane and look forward to meeting people, chatting, and even praying for a natural opportunity to talk about my relationship with Jesus. This was not one of those times! Honestly, interacting with my shoulder-to-shoulder neighbor was the last thing on my mind. I just wanted to buckle my seatbelt, put on my headphones, and go to sleep!

A young woman in her early twenties sat next to me. She was warm, friendly, and eager for a conversation. I shot up a quick prayer: "Lord, please give me patience and grace." I sat up and began to interact with her. Her name was Gretchen, and she was from the former East Germany. As she shared her story, my sleepy disinterest was soon swept away by a conversation I will never forget.

It turned out Gretchen was a communist. She worked with high school students at a camp. The goal of this camp was to help young people maintain their atheistic worldview amid the flood of Christianity streaming into the former East Germany. I was riveted!

I asked her about her core beliefs as an atheist and a humanist. I listened for over an hour. She spoke passionately about her love for the young people of her nation and her deep concern that they not be corrupted by the hate-mongering small-mindedness of Christianity. I have to say, I liked this young woman's honesty and passion. Although misinformed and misguided, she was filled with an undeniable love and concern for young people.

Finally, after more than an hour of telling me about her world, dreams, and passions, Gretchen turned to me and asked, "So what do you do?"

I responded with a lighthearted chuckle, "Kind of the same as you, except the exact opposite!" Her eyes got real big, and she stared at me waiting for an explanation.

"This might come as a surprise, but I am a Christian! Actually, I am a Christian pastor." She stared at me with a look of puzzled skepticism. I went on, "I spend my life trying to help people learn about the love of God and the great news of Jesus Christ. I guess I am one of those people you are trying to keep away from the youth of your country."

An awkward silence hung in the air. I was not sure how she would respond to this revelation. But to my surprise, Gretchen thanked me. She thanked me for listening and not condemning her. She told me that she had never had a conversation with a Christian that lasted more than five minutes. She said that once a Christian found out she was a communist, the conversation ended abruptly. They would tell her she was going to hell and walk away. She seemed genuinely grateful I had listened to her whole story and not prejudged her.

Gretchen thanked me for being interested in her even though I disagree with her beliefs. I assured her that the vast majority of Christians I know would have treated her just the way I had. I told her that, for the most part, the followers of Jesus I know are gentle, loving, and warm people. She looked at me skeptically but did not try to refute me.

I asked Gretchen if she would like to hear my story and my worldview. She said yes, with no small measure of excitement. So I spent the next hour telling her about how I had come from a nonbelieving family, and that my mother was a math and science teacher and my father was a computer programmer. I told her about my journey from the borderlands of unbelief into the arms of a loving God. I told her how Jesus had become my best friend and how I embraced faith in his life, death, and resurrection as historical realities. I took a risk and shared that I believed my sins are all washed away because of what Jesus did on the cross. I explained, as best I could, how the community of believers I am part of is filled with loving and warm people that I thought she would really enjoy meeting. I even told her that many of her beliefs as a humanist indicated that her heart was not far from the heart of God. Earlier in our conversation, Gretchen had said, "I am a humanist because I believe there is value and dignity in every human life. Everyone matters!" I told her that this is Jesus' message. It is why he came to this earth.

Gretchen was fascinated. After more than two hours of conversing, she agreed we were much closer to each other than she had ever dreamed. I encouraged her to investigate Jesus' message to see if her heart might be drawn to him. I also invited her to pray and to ask God that, if he really is out there, he reveal himself to her. She seemed intrigued by the thought of praying to a God she did not believe in and asking him to show himself.

I wish I could say Gretchen made some kind of radical commitment to Jesus on that flight. She did not. But she heard a personal testimony of faith and the gospel of Jesus for the first time. She had some of her stereotypes about Christians seriously challenged, and she made a new friend, a Christian pastor from America. Before we got off the plane, Gretchen gave me her e-mail address and a standing invitation for me and my family to stay in her home any time we might be in Berlin.

Since that day, I have heard the words of Jesus in a whole new way. Now when I read these words, I think of Gretchen: "Then he said to his disciples, 'The harvest is plentiful but the workers are few. Ask the Lord of the harvest, therefore, to send out workers into his harvest field'" (Matt. 9:37 – 38). Jesus was so right when he said the harvest is plentiful. People are more open to talking about Jesus than we realize. Hearts are longing for the truth in a world that often claims there is none. If someone like Gretchen, a communist who works at a camp to protect young people from Christians, is open to hearing my story of faith and a presentation of the gospel, I have to believe almost anyone is open to listening. What we need today is what was needed in the days of Jesus: followers who are ready to enter the harvest fields of the world and share the life-transforming message of God's love. This must be done with joy and passion. When this seismic shift takes place, the whole world will shake!

Chapter SIXTEEN

The Seismic Shift from Us to Them

Then Jesus came to them and said, "All authority in heaven and on earth has been given to me. Therefore go and make disciples of all nations, baptizing them in the name of the Father and of the Son and of the Holy Spirit, and teaching them to obey everything I have commanded you. And surely I am with you always, to the very end of the age."

—**Matthew 28:18–20**

He said to them: "It is not for you to know the times or dates the Father has set by his own authority. But you will receive power when the Holy Spirit comes on you; and you will be my witnesses in Jerusalem, and in all Judea and Samaria, and to the ends of the earth."

—**Acts 1:7–8**

Then he said to his disciples, "The harvest is plentiful but the workers are few. Ask the Lord of the harvest, therefore, to send out workers into his harvest field."

—**Matthew 9:37–38**

In my first few years as a pastor, I heard the same thing over and over. Church members would come to me and say something that really concerned and even irritated me. It was almost like a mantra they had learned in childhood and had used ever since. With time, I noticed a pattern, and

229

I realized these words had been spoken to every pastor who had led this church.

The persistent chant came each time we tried to broaden the focus of our congregation to include those who were not yet part of the church family. Anytime our church began to make the shift from us (people already in the congregation) to the world (those who do not yet know the love of Jesus), I had to brace myself to hear it one more time! These dear church members came to me and said, "But pastor, what about us? Don't forget us!" I have heard these words more times than I can remember over my two decades as a pastor.

It is clear to me that these people really believe that if a community of Christ-followers makes serious efforts to reach out to those who have not yet come to know the love of Jesus, the community will be forgotten and their needs won't be met. These words reveal fundamental misunderstandings about God, the church, and the call to share God's love with the world. Early in my ministry, I would listen to these people and try to sympathize with their concerns. But along the way, I began to take a very different approach. I would engage them in a conversation that has often led to seismic shifts in the lives of people in the churches I have served.

When someone comes to me and says, "What about us? Don't forget us!" I ask, "What do you need that you don't already have?" I am not talking about physical needs like clothes, a car, or a place to live. I am talking about the spiritual blessings and eternal inheritance we have in Jesus. I remind them that the apostle Paul writes, "Praise be to the God and Father of our Lord Jesus Christ, who has blessed us in the heavenly realms with every spiritual blessing in Christ" (Eph. 1:3).

If they don't connect with what I am trying to communicate, I simply list what we have as children of God. I say, "We have eternal life through a loving Savior. We have the passionate attention and care of a heavenly Father, the grace of Jesus, and the power of the Holy Spirit. The fruit of the Spirit, including love, joy, peace, and patience, and so much more are ours. We have been gifted by the Holy Spirit and given purpose in this life. We have the fellowship of God's people, the wonderful community of the church. The truth is, as followers of Jesus, we have everything we could ever need and more."

Sometimes as I speak about these truths, tears come to my eyes. As a matter of fact, as I am writing these words, tears have welled up once again. This response comes from a profound awareness of how good God has been. They flow when I remember the great grace God has lavished on us and the sacrifice he made to show us his love. These tears are also a gift from God because they remind me that he weeps when he sees his children forget about those who are wandering like sheep without a shepherd. God's heart breaks for those who are lost, and he longs for our hearts to be broken with his.

Once we have reflected on all we have as God's children, I look at them and repeat the question: "What do you need that you don't already have?"

The answer is always the same. "Nothing!"

||||| Seismic Shift Suggestion |||||

Sometimes Comparisons Are Good. Draw a line from top to bottom down the middle of a blank sheet of paper. Then at the top of the left-hand side of the paper write, "What I have that will last forever because I know Jesus as my Savior." At the top of the right-hand side write, "What people who don't know Jesus have that will last forever." Then fill out the lists, comparing those who know Jesus with those who don't. Fold this paper and put it in your wallet, your purse, or Bible. Take it out and read it occasionally. Use it as a reminder to love, reach out to, and pray for those who don't yet know the grace of Jesus Christ.

In this moment, these well-meaning church members experience the profound awareness that Jesus has already given us everything we will ever need. In light of this staggering reality, I ask one more question: "What do those outside of God's family have that really matters, that will last forever, and that brings eternal joy, hope, and security?" Many people become quiet as they ponder this question. Finally they say, "Nothing! They have nothing!" and I have actually seen tears in their eyes. You see, they never really stopped to reflect long enough to realize that those outside of faith in Jesus have nothing of lasting value and that they are heading for an eternity separate from God.

At this point, not much more needs to be said. But to make sure we are clear about the purpose of the church, I will ask, as tenderly as I know how, "What is it that our church is doing to reach lost people that you want us to stop? What is it that we are doing that has too high of a cost?" The look in their eyes tells the whole story. A seismic shift is occurring! In this sacred moment, their hearts begin to beat with the heart of God, and they begin to care more about those who are lost than they care about themselves.

Love That Risks ●

In Jesus' day, there were many cultural barriers between various groups of people. Jews had no dealings with Gentiles. Most men would not speak with women in public. No one wanted to be seen with a tax collector. And no right-thinking person would speak with or dare to touch a person with leprosy. In other words, there was a huge "us versus them" mentality. Since Jesus was an aspiring Jewish rabbi, everyone knew that for him, some people were off limits if he was to maintain a good reputation in the religious community.

But in full view of the public, Jesus systematically knocked down the dividing walls. He questioned the norms of his day. He took a tremendous risk when he had a theological conversation with a Samaritan woman who had a questionable moral history (John 4:4–42). He went out on a thin limb when he touched and healed a man with leprosy (Matt. 8:1–4). When Jesus called Levi, a tax collector, as one of his followers, he crossed the line. It was one thing to invite a common fisherman to be your disciple, but inviting a tax collector was going too far!

Then to top it off, Jesus spent time in intimate table fellowship with tax collectors and sinners. The religious leaders of the day were both baffled and outraged by this behavior. They were upset that Jesus spent time with these people, but they were even more outraged when they saw that these common people were fond of Jesus, that they were drawn to him. Worse, Jesus appeared to authentically love the outcasts, half-breeds, and sinners of his day.

The gospel writer Matthew, whose name was also Levi (the tax collector), records one such encounter:

> As Jesus went on from there, he saw a man named Matthew sitting at the tax collector's booth. "Follow me," he told him, and Matthew got up and followed him.
>
> While Jesus was having dinner at Matthew's house, many tax collectors and "sinners" came and ate with him and his disciples. When the Pharisees saw this, they asked his disciples, "Why does your teacher eat with tax collectors and 'sinners'?"
>
> On hearing this, Jesus said, "It is not the healthy who need a doctor, but the sick. But go and learn what this means: 'I desire mercy, not sacrifice.' For I have not come to call the righteous, but sinners."
>
> —Matthew 9:9–13

Love compelled Jesus to cross every boundary to reach out to those who were lost and wandering far from God. His choice to reach out to, care for, identify with, and relate to "outsiders" did more than raise a few eyebrows. It brought responses of slander, judgment, and even hatred. This is why Luke writes, "The Son of Man came eating and drinking, and you say, 'Here is a glutton and a drunkard, a friend of tax collectors and "sinners" ' " (Luke 7:34).

It would have been safest for Jesus to minister only to those who were on the cultural and spiritual inside track. In the same way, it is easier and safer for us to extend our love and compassion to those who are already part of God's family. We can lock the doors of our churches, gaze at our spiritual navels, and forget the broken world Jesus died to save. But where is the fun in that? Where is the adventure? How does this put us in a place where we have to cry out for the wisdom and power of the Holy Spirit?

Jesus took huge risks when he moved his attention from the "us" of his day to "them." He calls each of his followers to enter into this same risky journey. When is the last time you were accused of being a friend of drunkards, tax collectors, and sinners? If the answer is never, maybe it is time for a seismic shift.

Rolling a Large Stone Up a Steep Hill

The work of reaching out to our world is hard. Let's be honest, although every biblical Christian in the world declares that sharing the message of God's love is a priority, most of us have a hard time keeping this on the front burner. Keeping our focus off ourselves and on those outside of God's family is like rolling a large stone up a steep hill. This might sound a little fatalistic, but it is true. Few things we do as Jesus' followers are harder than keeping our hearts revved up for evangelism.

It has been said that vision leaks. When it comes to evangelism, it would seem there is a bigger hole than in most areas. We can be fired up and committed to share God's message of love with others, and a month later, our evangelistic prayers and efforts have come to a screeching halt.

Why is this? If sharing the Good News of Jesus is such a high value for Christians, why do we struggle to fulfill the Great Commission of our Savior? In his final words on this earth, Jesus told his followers, "All authority in heaven and on earth has been given to me. Therefore go and make disciples of all nations, baptizing them in the name of the Father and of the Son and of the Holy Spirit, and teaching them to obey everything I have commanded you. And surely I am with you always, to the very end of the age" (Matt. 28:18–20).

There are a number of reasons we struggle to make the shift from us to others. First and foremost is the spiritual reality that all the forces of hell are thrown against the work of evangelism. There are lots of things the church does that Satan is not all that concerned about, but evangelism is not one of them. Of all that Satan hates, evangelism is on the top of the list. Why is this? Because his desire is to take as many people to hell with him as he can. He is more hate-filled and evil than we could ever dream. His desire is the destruction of all of creation, and top on his list is people. He is a roaring lion, prowling around seeking someone to devour (1 Peter 5:8). Every time a person becomes a follower of Christ, not only does Satan lose someone he had captured in sin but he also gains an enemy who begins to work against him.

Making the shift from us to them is challenging and difficult. But this should not discourage us. We serve a Savior who has broken the power of sin, the threat of death, and the back of Satan. He who is in us really is greater than the Devil, who is at work in this world (1 John 4:4). The challenge of evangelism should drive us to our knees in prayer. It should move us to action. There are some specific shifts we can make to propel us into the world with the good news of salvation.

From Clean to Messy

We must learn to live with a balance of order and chaos in our lives if we are going to reach out with the message of God's love. Leonard Sweet, in his book *Soul Tsunami*, uses the word "chaordic." This word embraces the reality that so much of what we do in this life puts us in the tension between chaos and order, between clean and messy. This applies in every area as we seek to reach out with God's love. One such area is in our homes.

|||||| **Seismic Shift Suggestion** ||||||

Mini Home Makeover. Take a walk through your home. Ask yourself, Is there something I could do to make my home warmer and more inviting for those who enter? It could mean fixing something up. Or it could mean toning something down. The real issue is creating a space that is attractive to others. Do one thing in your home to make it a place where your unchurched friends feel welcome and at home.

Years ago my wife, Sherry, and I decided our home would be a place with doors wide open to people from any and every walk of life. Our friendships and our boys' relationships cut across all kinds of people groups. We decided we would be intentional about decorating our home so that it would be warm and inviting and not put people off. For instance, when we put in carpet, we did not get the most expensive carpet or even our first choice of carpet. We picked a durable carpet that was a mix of beige and tan so dirt stains would not stand out. We wanted the neighborhood kids and our three boys' friends from school to be able to run through the house and not worry about an occasional spill or stain.

When our boys approached adolescence, we decided to finish our basement. Up to that point, it had been a box with a cement floor and walls. Mostly it was used for playtimes and roller hockey. When we finished the basement, we made it a place where friends could gather for fun. One day some of the boys were playing something called Airsoft, a scaled-down version of paintball, only without the paint. Because someone brought an extrapowerful Airsoft rifle, we ended up with about a hundred dents and chips in our basement walls and in the woodwork. This forced us to make a serious decision. Was our house really a place for outreach into our community, or would it be a showplace where kids felt uncomfortable? We talked with the boys to make sure that future damage would not occur, but no one got in trouble, no heads rolled, and no bill was sent to anyone's parents.

From "You Come" to "We Go"

Many people will not set foot in a church building. Even a contemporary structure without all the steeples, organ music, and gargoyles can still seem threatening. The very idea of "going to church" puts some people off. But here is the good news: Jesus never said, "Go therefore and invite people to church." After Jesus had died on the cross, was laid in the grave, and rose on the third day, he met his followers: "Then the eleven disciples went to Galilee, to the mountain where Jesus had told them to go. When they saw him, they worshiped him; but some doubted. Then Jesus came to them and said, 'All authority in heaven and on earth has been given to me. Therefore go and make disciples of all nations, baptizing them in the name of the Father and of the Son and of the Holy Spirit, and teaching them to obey everything I have commanded you. And surely I am with you always, to the very end of the age'" (Matt. 28:16–20).

Jesus' message was not for the church to build big structures, set up signs, and say, "Come on down!" He called his disciples to go out and share his love in the highways and byways of the world, from Jerusalem (their hometown), to Judea (the surrounding region), to Samaria (the land of their enemies), to the ends of the earth. The people of Jesus are still called to bear his message of love and forgiveness, from our hometowns, to our regions, to our enemies, to the ends of the earth. If we listen closely, we can still hear our Savior giving this great commandment: "Go!"

Where will you go this week? Will you be traveling through the grocery store? If you do, go as one bearing Jesus' message. Will you find yourself in a place you would rather avoid, with people you don't particularly like? See this place as a mission field and know God is sending you there because he loves people. He even cares about those who tend to get under your skin.

From My World to Your World

Through the years, I have spoken with many Christians who have said things like, "I would love to tell others about Jesus, but everyone I know is already a believer!" Some have declared this with sadness in their voices and others with a sense of joyful contentment. In both cases, these words reveal a huge problem. Too many followers of Jesus are isolated from unchurched people. We circle our relational wagons and hunker down to protect ourselves and those we love from the world. Jesus did not give this as an option for his followers. He called us to go out, take risks, and share his gospel to the ends of the earth.

|||||| **Seismic Shift Suggestion** ||||||

Schedule Assessment. Look over your schedule from the past seven days. Identify when you have spent time with people who are not part of God's family. If you see numerous times, thank God for this and commit to keep these kinds of connections in your life. If you can't identify times when you were with people who are not Christians, pray for opportunities in the coming week. Commit to regularly schedule time with friends who are spiritual seekers.

But where do we start? What seismic shifts can we make to move out into the world and connect in a natural way with people who have not yet discovered the joy of knowing Jesus?

Why not make a commitment to open a new world of relationships? Maybe you enjoy painting ceramic figures or making pottery. If so, take a class in your community and watch as God helps you build new relational connections. If you play bridge, join a club in your area. Maybe you are into making scrapbooks. If so, invite people over to your house once a month. If you like softball, soccer, basketball, or some other sport, look into joining a team in your area. If you are an avid reader, call your library to find out if they have book clubs. The key is to find something you like to do and engage in this activity in your community.

Aside from starting a new hobby or activity, you can also begin to connect with people you already see regularly. There are often people in our lives who need, and want, to know about God's love, but we have never been intentional about connecting with them. If you dine at a particular restaurant frequently, make an effort to build relationships with the people there. Do you know the servers' names? Have you asked about their lives? Have you been praying for them and asking the Lord to give you natural opportunities to share his love with them? These are natural relational bridges we can all build. This is also true of the places where we buy our gas, groceries, or any other product we get regularly. The seismic shift involves slowing down, looking into people's eyes, and noting that the person who bags your groceries is loved by God. The fact that you bump into them once a week is no coincidence. It is a God-ordained appointment.

I received a call from a pastor in our community. He knew about my passion for building a church of people who have a deep love for those outside of the church family. So he called and asked if we might meet to talk about how he could help his church grow in its focus on the world. As we sat down for lunch, he flipped open a notepad and began to run through a pretty extensive list of questions. We had never met before, and it became clear, very quickly, that this man was a sharp, gifted leader. He was serious about helping the people in his church engage in the ministry of outreach to their community. He rifled question after question at me, and I did my best to give answers I thought might be helpful in his ministry context.

Then out of nowhere, I felt prompted to say, "Can I ask you one question?"

He looked a little surprised, since he was only halfway through his list of questions, but he said, "Sure."

I asked, "In a typical week, how much time do you spend with friends, neighbors, and family members who don't yet know Jesus?"

There was a moment of silence as he looked down at his salad. As I waited, I imagined him running through the past week in his mind and trying to reconstruct the various times he had interacted with folks outside of his church and outside of the family of faith. After a few more moments, he looked up at me with a sober and sad gaze. He said nothing, but he held up his right hand and formed a circle with his thumb and fingers. Zero, no time at all. We spent the rest of our lunch talking about structuring our days and lives to enable us to rub shoulders with people who still need to hear about the love of Jesus. We had a wonderful conversation about how easy it is to get pulled into church stuff and how we need to consistently evaluate our lives and schedules to make sure we connect with lost people.

We are called to be salt, but salt does no good when it is just sitting in the saltshaker. Jesus made it clear that we are to be the light of the world, and that a lamp must be placed on a stand and not under a bowl (Matt. 5:14–15). It is time for God's people to get serious about living more of our lives outside of the church, outside of our Christian subculture, and outside of the safe haven of our small circle of friends who already have their eternal issues worked out.

The Heart of the Church

Not only do we need to make seismic shifts to move our personal lives from us to them but we also need to do this in the church. Entire congregations can function in a way that says, "We are here for us. Everyone else stay away." Or they can establish patterns that show warmth and an inviting spirit that says, "Everyone is welcome!" A church in Texas has the motto, "No perfect people allowed!" This is their way of saying, "Yes, you are welcome."

Every church needs to take an honest look at how they function and discover if there are patterns that are counterproductive to reaching out to those who are not yet part of the family. I can still remember a decisive moment when I came on staff at a church which had some unhealthy patterns in how they viewed their facility. The first week of work, someone told me there was a coffee break in the midmorning and that I should drop in. I am not a big coffee drinker, but when I got there, I discovered they also served delicious cookies, so I hung around for a while. I chatted with the staff members for a bit, and then everyone got up, with some kind of unspoken awareness that break time was over, and headed back to their desks. As I walked out of the room, I wadded up my napkin, which was filled with bits of cookie rubble, and tossed it into the trash can by the door. I made the shot from a good ten feet away, so I was quietly reveling in my fine trash-can basketball skills.

As I was walking out the door, I felt a tap on my shoulder. It was another leader in the church, and he had a look of concern on his face. "What's up?" I inquired. With awkward reluctance, he whispered, as if a little embarrassed, "We don't use the trash cans during the week. The custodians like us to carry our trash back to our offices and use the trash cans in the building only on Sundays and Wednesday nights."

I looked at him with amusement because I thought he was joking. But when I looked into the trash can, I knew he was serious. There at my feet was the cleanest plastic trash can I had ever seen. Either it had rarely been used or someone scrubbed it regularly. It looked up and screamed, "Don't throw trash in me!" At the bottom of this spotless can were two items. First, I saw a paper towel that had been neatly folded and set squarely in the bottom of the can. I have no idea what purpose this thin buffer served, but I would soon learn that a folded paper towel was placed in the bottom of all the trash cans in the church classrooms. Second, I saw the cause of this whole uncomfortable confrontation: the heinous wad of paper filled with dirty little bits of cookie.

||||| Seismic Shift Suggestion |||||

A Welcoming Church. Take a walk through your church building and across the grounds. Try to look at things as if you were a first-time visitor. Imagine you knew nothing about faith, the location of the nursery, or religious language. Could you find your way around the campus? Could you find your way through a church service without feeling out of place? If you think of any ideas that will make your church more inviting to visitors, pass it on to a staff member. If you are willing to help make this change, let them know they can call on you.

I stood there looking at the sparkling trash can and the wadded-up napkin. An awkward silence hung in the air. I had to make a decision. So I said, "I'm leaving the napkin where it is." The other staff member looked at me like I had just told him that I eat kittens for breakfast. Then he did something that shocked me. He bent over to remove the solitary piece of trash from the forbidden zone.

I swallowed hard and said, "Please don't." I explained that there is a fundamental problem when you can't use trash cans for trash. I am not sure he understood what I meant, but he agreed to leave the napkin where it was and assured me that I would be called to account for my defiance. I promised him I was up to the task, and we both walked away.

That day I was reminded of the powerful temptation to forget that we exist not to build nice structures, protect our way of life, or keep the trash cans clean but to share the best news ever with the people in our community and around the world. The church should never be just about us. Jesus left the glory of heaven, took on human flesh, suffered on the cross, died, and rose again. He did all of this to make a way for lost and sinful people to come back home to their heavenly Father. He calls us to care so much about people that we will pray, work, and sacrifice so others can hear the same amazing news that has changed our lives. It is time to make the seismic shift from us to them.

FOR REFLECTION

- What is one way I can adjust my lifestyle or schedule to spend more time with people who are outside of God's family?
- How can I help my church be a place where people know, right when they enter, they are welcome?

FOR PRAYER

- Pray for your heart to expand to be more like Jesus' heart for lost people. Ask for eyes to notice those who are far from God. Then invite the Holy Spirit to give you the boldness to reach out to these people with God's love.
- Ask God to make your church a place with a warm welcome, open arms, and a genuine love for people who come from any and every walk of life.

Chapter SEVENTEEN

The Seismic Shift from "One Size Fits All" to Your Outreach Style

But in your hearts set apart Christ as Lord. Always be prepared to give an answer to everyone who asks you to give the reason for the hope that you have. But do this with gentleness and respect.

—1 Peter 3:15

It is true that some preach Christ out of envy and rivalry, but others out of goodwill. The latter do so in love, knowing that I am put here for the defense of the gospel. The former preach Christ out of selfish ambition, not sincerely, supposing that they can stir up trouble for me while I am in chains. But what does it matter? The important thing is that in every way, whether from false motives or true, Christ is preached. And because of this I rejoice.

—Philippians 1:15 – 18

Then Jesus told them this parable: "Suppose one of you has a hundred sheep and loses one of them. Does he not leave the ninety-nine in the open country and go after the lost sheep until he finds it? And when he finds it, he joyfully puts it on his shoulders and goes home. Then he calls his friends and neighbors together and says, 'Rejoice with me; I have found my lost sheep.' I tell you that in the same way there will be more rejoicing in heaven over one sinner who repents than over ninety-nine righteous persons who do not need to repent."

—Luke 15:3–7

If you are a good husband, you know all about "the chair." If you are a boyfriend or a man engaged to be married, you will learn about it soon enough. There will come a day when you will sit in the chair and be asked a series of challenging questions.

In this chair, some marriages are strengthened, fortified, solidified; other marriages are strained and tested. In this chair, a man learns some big life lessons, lessons about diplomacy, about speaking the truth in love. And the essential lesson that one size does not fit all. In few other places are a man's honesty and tact tested as severely as they are in this chair.

You will find the chair in the same location in every department store. It is just outside of the women's dressing room. And when a man sits in this chair, he will hear questions like, How does this look on me? Do you think this is the right size? And does this make my hips look big?

Making the right response to these questions is essential for a healthy relationship. And to the surprise of many people, grace-filled honesty is the key! The truth of the matter is, not every outfit looks good on every person. A husband who sits in the chair and refuses to tell the truth does more harm than good. If he sees his wife in an outfit that does not fit well or looks bad on her, but he still says, "I love it. It's beautiful. It fits you perfectly," he is not acting in a loving way. He would do better to say, "Why don't you try on a few other options?" The world needs more people who will speak the truth to those they love.

In the classic story "The Emperor's New Clothes," it takes an honest little boy to finally point out that the emperor is parading down the middle of main street buck naked! In this children's story, no one wants to speak the truth to the emperor. He has convinced himself, with the help of some deceitful tailors, that he is wearing the finest and most beautiful robes ever made. The problem is, the conniving tailors have stolen all of the money for the clothes and dressed the emperor in a lie.

In a similar way, many followers of Christ have been sold a lie. They believe there is only one way to share Jesus' message. Most Christians believe they need to be confrontational, extroverted, and highly verbal to do the work of evangelism. They have bought into the one-size-fits-all mentality that says evangelists are the type that can stand on a street corner and preach to the masses with unwavering confidence. Only those with velvet tongues like Billy Graham or testimonies like Corrie ten Boom, who survived the Holocaust, can do effective outreach. When the average person in the church looks at evangelism this way, the natural response is to say, "That outfit does not fit me! I can't—and I won't—wear it!"

|||||| Seismic Shift Suggestion ||||||

Check Your Wardrobe. One of the best sources for an evangelism wardrobe is your church. Most churches have programs and opportunities to help believers participate in the work of outreach. In the coming week, look over your church's wardrobe. Use the style-based categories explained later in this chapter to help you identify the evangelism opportunities in your church. Then try one on. Show up for an outreach-oriented class or event. If it fits, great. Wear it. If not, try on something else. But make the commitment to try on some of the options to see how they look on you.

It is time for someone to speak the truth. The emperor has no clothes. One size does not fit all! There is not one right way to share the good news of Jesus with all people at all times in all places. The Bible gives models of many ways we can enter into the joy of sharing God's message with those who desperately need to hear it. Most followers of Jesus are overjoyed when they finally realize there is a way they can naturally and comfortably share their faith.

Just like in a department store, we need to try on various options to see how they fit. There are many styles of evangelism and various expressions of the different styles. We need to start trying them on. If one does not fit us, no problem. Try another. But all who are followers of Jesus have a unique God-given style of evangelism. It is our calling and responsibility to discover, develop, and use it in our daily lives.

A New Revolution • • • • • • • • • • • • • • • • • • •

In the 1990s, a quiet revolution began. A team of leaders at Willow Creek Community Church—Mark Mittelberg, Lee Strobel, and Bill Hybels—wrote a book and curriculum called *Becoming a Contagious Christian*. The message in this book is biblical and clear: every follower of Jesus is uniquely gifted with a particular evangelistic style that fits them and can make the work of outreach natural and enjoyable. These leaders sounded the trumpet and started a revolution. They declared, "The emperor has no clothes!" and told the church that a one-size-fits-all approach to evangelism was not working.

> |||||| **Seismic Shift Suggestion** ||||||
>
> **Become a Revolutionary.** If your church offers classes using the *Becoming a Contagious Christian* curriculum, sign up for the next one. Even if you have taken the training before, a refresher is always good. If your church does not offer this class, suggest that they begin one this year. And if your church needs to raise the bar in terms of their commitment to evangelism, consider using *Becoming a Contagious Church* as a model for moving your whole congregation into the evangelistic revolution Jesus began two thousand years ago.

In 2000, one of these leaders took this biblical message to a new level. Mark Mittelberg wrote a groundbreaking book titled *Building a Contagious Church: Revolutionizing the Way We View and Do Evangelism.* In this book, Mark presents a six-stage process to move congregations from being inwardly focused to becoming highly evangelistic. He also reinforces the reality that not all people who follow Jesus are called to evangelize in the same way. We are called to live with "contagious diversity," as Mittelberg puts it. When we do so, the revolution continues and spreads.

Do It with Style ●

As Mark was writing *Building a Contagious Church,* I had the honor of being his research assistant. Over the course of six months, I did research, interviewed leaders, and studied over a hundred of the most outreach-oriented churches in the United States and Europe. I discovered that the biblical model of multiple evangelistic styles was being followed all over the place. In the following pages, I will give a snapshot of what this style-based approach looks like. Although these varied styles are found in the Bible, I want to give credit to Mittelberg, Strobel, and Hybels for their excellent work in presenting this model in a way that has made a huge difference in the church. If you want to dig deeper into this topic, I would highly recommend both of the books I've mentioned. The summary that follows has been heavily influenced by these books and authors. As this quiet revolution explodes, the lives of believers, church cultures, and the entire world will be changed.

A Confrontational Approach

In Acts 2, the apostle Peter stands up and gives us a great example of the confrontational style of evangelism. He looks into the eyes of a crowd of people and boldly presents the case for believing in Jesus as the long-awaited Savior. He challenges them and calls them to respond. In short, Peter was confrontational. If you wonder if this approach was effective, just read what happened at the end of Peter's presentation of the gospel: "With many other words he warned them; and he pleaded with them, 'Save yourselves from this corrupt generation.' Those who accepted his message were baptized, and about three thousand were added to their number that day" (Acts 2:40–41).

Some people think this bold approach is outdated, but they are wrong. At Corinth Church, we have a team of people who are trained in street evangelism. They go downtown or to the malls and pray for opportunities to engage others in spiritual conversations. As the Lord opens doors, they present the message of God's grace. This approach is not for everyone, but it is for some. Every church should make sure there are opportunities for people with a confrontational style to connect with spiritual seekers in a direct, face-to-face manner.

An Intellectual Approach

Some Christians will discover that the way they evangelize naturally is by using an intellectual style. The apostle Paul is an example of this. In Acts 17, we read of how he reasoned with people in the places of worship as well as in the cultural and intellectual centers of his time. Paul was a student of the Scriptures and of culture. He was comfortable presenting a rational, thoughtful, and compelling case for faith.

Many people today have this style. Lee Strobel is an excellent example. He is a former atheist who became a follower of Christ through a process of intellectual investigation. Using his skills as a journalist, he did his homework and came to the conclusion that faith in Jesus Christ not only has intellectual integrity but makes more sense than any other worldview. Through his studies and the gentle work of the Holy Spirit, Lee became a follower of Jesus and has since helped others work through their intellectual roadblocks. Writing books like *The Case for Christ*, *The Case for Faith*, and *The Case for a Creator*, Lee has helped many nonbelievers grapple with their questions, and he has become a mentor for many people who have an intellectual style of evangelism.

A Testimonial Approach

In the gospel of John, we find a surprising example of a testimonial style of evangelism. A man who has been blind from birth is healed by Jesus and places his faith in the Savior. When he is questioned about what happened, he speaks these words: "One thing I do know. I was blind but now I see!" (John 9:25). This man did not have a confrontational spirit or intellectual answers. What he had was his story of how Jesus had touched him and changed his life. This is what he communicated to those who asked him about Jesus.

Many people today have experienced enduring transformation through faith in the Savior. These people can tell their stories. They can testify to the reality of Jesus' love and his power to change lives. These people can use their style naturally in daily conversations. They can also be invited to tell their story publicly. At our church, we capture personal testimonies on videotape and include them in worship services. This inspires those who know Jesus to share their stories, touching the hearts of spiritual seekers.

An Interpersonal Approach

Many of Christ's followers discover that their evangelism style is built on the ability to relate with others, connect people, and extend authentic love. This interpersonal style is modeled by Matthew in the New Testament. When Matthew became a believer, he realized he had two different relational worlds. He had all of his old friends, who were tax collectors, prostitutes, and sinners (Matthew clearly had a rough past), but he also had a new group of friends, a bunch of Christians that included Jesus and his disciples. Matthew exercised his interpersonal approach to evangelism by pulling both groups together at a big party in his home (Luke 5:27–32). This made perfect sense to Matthew because his natural style of evangelism was the interpersonal approach.

I know a woman who exercises this interpersonal style with grace and tenacity. Everyone calls her Grandma Lois. She has a powerful radar system that helps her lock onto almost every new visitor who walks in the door. She is like a heat-seeking missile. Once she sees a visitor, there is no way they are getting out of her sights. She meets them, greets them, hugs them, and introduces them to others in the church. Every weekend, she uses her interpersonal style to show God's love to others, as well as to build relational bridges.

I always knew Grandma Lois did this at church, but one day I discovered it went much deeper. I was with a team that was visiting all of the homes in a new housing tract that happened to be across the street from Grandma Lois's house. As I knocked on doors and delivered a small gift and an invitation from our church, numerous people said to me, "Oh, you go to Grandma Lois's church." I said, "I sure do!" Although the homes had been there only a short time, this dear woman, with her interpersonal style, was already connecting, loving, and reaching out to others.

An Invitational Approach

In every church, there are people who thrive on inviting people to places where they can learn more about Jesus. This could be a dinner party with some believing friends, a church service, a Christian concert, a neighborhood small group, or anyplace where the message of Jesus is lifted up. In the gospel of John, we meet a woman who had this style of evangelism. She had met Jesus and had been transformed by his message of truth, his grace, and his love. In response to this life-changing encounter, she "went back to the town and said to the people, 'Come, see a man who told me everything I ever did. Could this be the Christ?'" (John 4:29) and many came to meet Jesus. Her invitation impacted the whole community because she dared to extend an invitation. What is even more shocking is that this woman was a social outcast. Yet her invitation flowed naturally because this was the unique way God had designed her to share her faith.

ⅠⅠⅠⅠⅠ Seismic Shift Suggestion ⅠⅠⅠⅠⅠ

Start a Bag-People Ministry. Consider using the model of invitational evangelism. Plan to deliver invitation bags before Christmas, before Easter, and maybe near the end of the summer. It is a great way to connect in your community and to be sure new people know they are welcome at your church.

Every year at the church I serve, we gather a group of people who have the invitational style of evangelism. We send them out to a couple of hundred homes of people who have recently moved to our community. They give out gift bags with an invitation letter, some seasonal candy, a pen with our church phone number, a refrigerator magnet, and a book.

We have used books such as *Finding a Church You Can Love*, written by my wife and me, and *The Case for Easter* by Lee Strobel. These teams of people knock on doors, welcome people to the community, and give a heartfelt invitation for people to visit the church if they are not already part of a Christian fellowship. We even bring a bag of doggie treats because we have discovered that we are often greeted at the door by a dog before a person gets there. We always ask permission to give the dog a treat. It is amazing how people respond when they realize we thought ahead and brought a treat for their pet. If no one is home, we hang the bag on the doorknob, say a quick prayer, and head to the next house. This is just one way we help people with the invitational style engage in outreach every year.

A Serving Approach

In Acts 9, we meet a woman who had a heart to serve others. Her name was Dorcas. Her servant's attitude became a bridge to evangelism. Her acts of mercy and kindness opened the door for the gospel. In the same way, many people today love to help others in need. They have compassion and naturally serve their neighbors and even people they have never met.

Those who have this kind of evangelistic style love to do things like serve at a soup kitchen, help build a home with Habitat for Humanity, pass out clothing at a city mission, and participate in countless other types of local and global service projects. It is essential that churches create opportunities for people with a service style to engage in this kind of outreach. One unique and powerful service opportunity is Last Call Ministries. It is all about helping people who have had a few too many drinks and need a ride home from a bar. Teams of Christians shuttle people home. Often those needing a ride are feeling pretty loose, and they ask the driver, "Why are you spending your Saturday night doing this?" When they ask why, the door is open to talk about God's love.

No matter what your evangelism style, God has a plan to use you to be his light in this world. The experience of outreach does not have to be uncomfortable or fear-filled. It can be natural and joyful. The key is learning that we each have a unique way to reach out. In the same way that our DNA and fingerprints are distinct, so is our evangelism style. We are called to discover our God-given approach and to join the outreach revolution.

Faith Comes by Hearing • • • • • • • • • • • • • • • • •

Over the years, I have heard people say things like, "Serving is not evangelism. It is a great thing to do, but serving alone does not present the message of the gospel." Or, "Inviting a person to church or to a Christian concert is not evangelism. It is pre-evangelism." I have even heard people say, "Sharing your story is not enough. We must tell Jesus' story." To these comments and many others like them, I say, "I agree 100 percent!"

In the book of Romans, the apostle Paul says, "Consequently, faith comes from hearing the message, and the message is heard through the word of Christ" (Rom. 10:17). Paul makes it clear that it is not enough just to love and care for people; we are called to communicate the life-changing message of Jesus Christ. Over the years, I have heard many variations on the statement, "Proclaim the gospel wherever you go. Use words when necessary." I understand the spirit of this quote, which has been attributed to many different historical figures, but I feel it is misleading. A more biblical version would be, "Proclaim the gospel wherever you go. Words will always be necessary." The apostle Paul puts it this way: "But in your hearts set apart Christ as Lord. Always be prepared to give an answer to everyone who asks you to give the reason for the hope that you have. But do this with gentleness and respect" (1 Peter 3:15).

There are many approaches to evangelism, but all of them include the wonderful moment when we tell the story of God's gift of salvation. When we serve someone and they ask us, "Why do you care so much?" we let them know how much God has cared for us. We articulate that God cared for us so much that he sent Jesus as a sacrifice for our sins. We tell them our service flows out of this understanding. When we invite someone to a church service or a faith-based event and they ask us, "Do you really believe all this stuff about Jesus?" we have an open door to share how we came to faith, what we believe, and how God has transformed our lives. We are given an opportunity to articulate the message of the gospel. No matter what our personal style, we all should be trained and ready to express the core message of the gospel, and we should know how to lead people to commit their lives to Jesus Christ.

The Power and Place of Prayer • • • • • • • • • • • • •

Along with using our unique and God-given styles of evangelism and being ready to articulate the message of the gospel, we need to be people of prayer. No matter what we say or do, if God's Holy Spirit is not at work, lives will never be changed. All through the Bible and in history, we see that prayer precedes revival and great works of God. In the book of Acts, we read, "Then they returned to Jerusalem from the hill called the Mount of Olives, a Sabbath day's walk from the city. When they arrived, they went upstairs to the room where they were staying. Those present were Peter, John, James and Andrew; Philip and Thomas, Bartholomew and Matthew; James son of Alphaeus and Simon the Zealot, and Judas son of James. They all joined together constantly in prayer, along with the women and Mary the mother of Jesus, and with his brothers" (Acts 1:12 – 14).

The amazing evangelistic revival and work of the Holy Spirit that comes in Acts 2 is clearly connected to the prayers of God's people. What a joy to see a biblical portrait of God's people, men and women, together in passionate prayer, and then to discover that the Spirit descended in power, the gospel was proclaimed, and over three thousand people gave their hearts and lives to Jesus!

Seismic Shift Suggestion

Keep a Seismic-Shift Prayer List. One of the most powerful things you can do to grow in your personal commitment to outreach is to pray for those who are not yet followers of Christ. Make a list of friends, family members, and acquaintances who are not Christians. Put this list where you will see it and pray for one or more of these people each day. Then be sure to ask God to help you be responsive to the opportunities he gives you to use your unique evangelism style to connect with them, love them, and speak to them about Jesus.

Prayer must bathe everything we do, especially when it comes to the ministry of outreach. Every follower of Jesus should be praying for their friends, family members, and acquaintances who don't know Jesus. We also need to undergird all of our outreach efforts with prayer. When Corinth Church goes out to deliver invitation bags to new people in the community, we always cover these events in prayer. We have pairs of people walk through the neighborhoods we will be visiting, and they pray for doors and hearts to be open. When we take worship teams downtown to lead worship services on the streets, we always have prayer teams interceding for them. We try to make prayer an integral part of all of our outreach.

Along with praying for our churches' outreach efforts, it is critical that followers of Jesus discover the power of praying for and with those spiritual seekers God has placed in our lives. Through the years, I have asked many nonbelievers, "Can I pray for you?" So far no one has said no. It is amazing how people who don't have faith in God can still hunger for prayer.

One winter I was on the island of Saint Martin and experienced just how much people hunger for prayer. I was returning a rental car at the end of our family vacation. I had just picked up some ribs and chicken in town, and my youngest son was sitting in the back seat holding our bag of dinner as the owner of the rental company was driving us back to our hotel. As we drove, the owner shared some struggles he was facing and told me a little about his spiritual journey. I shared my testimony of how I came to faith in Jesus and encouraged him in his search for God. I told him the Bible says, "You will seek me and find me when you seek me with all your heart" (Jer. 29:13). He was very open to the message of faith I shared and expressed great interest.

All of a sudden he pulled to the side of the road and turned off the car. We were not back at the hotel, so I wondered what was happening. He was quiet for a moment and then asked, "Do you mind if we just sit and talk a little more?" I glanced back at my son holding our quickly cooling dinner and knew he would understand. "That would be great," I said. So there we sat, talking about life, faith, Jesus, the struggles of relationships, and personal finances. In these sacred moments, this gentle-spirited and spiritually hungry man got to hear the message of Jesus Christ. He was not ready to make a commitment to faith, but he was seeking with all of his heart.

After a time of rich conversation, he said, "Your dinner is getting cold," and fired up the engine. As we drove up the hill toward the hotel, I felt a strong prompting to pray for him. I asked for permission, and he said, "Yes!" After he parked the car at the hotel, we bowed our heads. As strange as this might sound, I felt like I wanted to hold this man's hand as I prayed, but I did not feel I knew him well enough. But as I prayed, he reached across the car and took hold of my hand. He clasped it like a vise, as if holding on for dear life.

God met us in that car as we prayed together. When I got home, I sent him a number of Christian resources. We have communicated by e-mail since then, and I continue to pray that he will one day take that final step of faith and take hold of Jesus' hand with the same intensity he held mine as we prayed. In my heart, I am confident this will happen.

FOR REFLECTION

- How has God used people with various evangelism styles to influence my journey of faith?
- What is one outreach ministry or training opportunity offered at my church that I can participate in sometime over the coming months?

FOR PRAYER

- Pray that the people on your Seismic-Shifts Prayer List will be open to the work God wants to do in their lives. Also ask God to help you connect with these people in a way that reflects the love of God and opens doors for spiritual conversations.
- Pray for the church you attend to become a powerful place of outreach. Ask God to move in ways that will lead your congregation to reach out to those in your community who are far from God.

Chapter EIGHTEEN

The Seismic Shift from Closing the Deal to Making a Journey

What, after all, is Apollos? And what is Paul? Only servants, through whom you came to believe—as the Lord has assigned to each his task. I planted the seed, Apollos watered it, but God made it grow. So neither he who plants nor he who waters is anything, but only God, who makes things grow. The man who plants and the man who waters have one purpose, and each will be rewarded according to his own labor. For we are God's fellow workers; you are God's field, God's building.

—**1 Corinthians 3:5–9**

The Son of Man came eating and drinking, and you say, "Here is a glutton and a drunkard, a friend of tax collectors and 'sinners.'"

—**Luke 7:34**

It was a battle. A wrestling match. A test of wills.

Every day, at exactly the same time, Margaret would go to the bathroom cabinet, open it, and take out a huge bottle of castor oil. Then she would head to the kitchen to get a tablespoon. At the sound of the drawer opening and the silverware rattling, Patches, her Yorkshire terrier, would run and hide—sometimes under the bed, at other times in the bathtub or behind Margaret's recliner. Patches knew what was coming.

Someone had convinced Margaret that her beloved dog would have strong teeth, a beautiful coat, and a long life if she gave him a spoonful of castor oil every day. So as an act of love, every twenty-four hours, she cornered Patches, pinned him down, pried open his mouth, and, as he whimpered, squirmed, and fought her with all his strength, poured a tablespoon of castor oil down his little doggie throat. Neither Patches nor Margaret enjoyed their daily wrestling match.

Then one day, in the middle of their battle royal, with one sideways kick, Patches sent the dreaded bottle of castor oil flying across the kitchen floor. It was a momentary victory for the canine, as Margaret let him go so she could run to the pantry and grab a towel to clean up the mess.

When Margaret got back, she was utterly shocked. There was Patches licking up the spilled castor oil with a look of satisfaction only a dog can make. Margaret began to laugh uncontrollably. In one moment, it all made sense. Patches liked castor oil. He just hated being pinned down and having it poured down his throat.

Welcome to the world of evangelism!

Over the years, many people have been pinned down and had the message of Jesus poured down their throats. And reflexively they have wretched it back up. It is not the message of God's love that most people resist; it is the way many followers of Jesus try to administer it.

Evangelism Snipers

You know the guy. I'm sure you have seen him on the street or on TV. He stands on the corner and screams religious slogans at everyone who passes by. Usually he has a big sign that says something like "Repent, the End Is Near!" Or maybe he wears a giant sandwich board that says "Turn or Burn" on one side and "Get Right or Get Left" on the other. People like this usually don't enter into relationships that help lost people on their journey toward God. They are not patient and engaging. They don't build relationships based on vulnerability and trust. Instead, their aggressive tactics force people to make an immediate decision. Sadly, in most cases, these evangelism snipers push people away from the Lord and do more damage than good.

As a young believer, I was accosted on a street corner by a man who stepped into my path and blurted, "Are you washed in the blood of the Lamb?"

I knew what he meant, but he still startled me. I paused and asked him, "What do you mean by that?"

He looked at me and clarified by asking, "Are you born again?"

> ||||| **Seismic Shift Suggestion** |||||
>
> **Do a Language Assessment**. In the coming week, practice present-ing the gospel to a Christian friend. Invite them to do a language assessment. Have them point out any words you use that might be unfamiliar or confusing to a spiritual seeker, and ask them how you might word things so that your articulation of the gospel would make more sense. You might want to review the gospel presentation in ap-pendix 4 of this book. It has been written so that a unchurched per-son can understand the whole message.

I understood the question but was dumbfounded by his approach. Although I respected his boldness and commitment, I also sensed that his highly religious language and aggressive approach were counterproduc-tive. So I said, "Are you asking me if I have come to God through a rela-tionship with Jesus? Are you asking if I have admitted to God that I have messed up my life and there is no way I can make things right on my own? Are you asking if I have invited Jesus to forgive me and lead my life?"

He got very excited and said, "Yes, that's what I'm saying!"

At that point, I told him I was a Christian. We then had a meaning-ful conversation about how the use of overly religious language can be a roadblock to telling others about Jesus. As we chatted on the street corner, I discovered this man's heart was right, but his approach was suspect.

I am not saying a confrontational style of evangelism is wrong. In the previous chapter, we looked at the apostle Peter and how some people have an effective confrontational outreach style. There are times when this is appropriate. But someone using this style should also extend grace and speak in a way that makes sense to those who are not hip to church lingo.

The real problem comes when followers of Christ use superspiritual language and try to force others to make an immediate decision. Like a pushy salesperson, some Christians feel the best approach is to get a foot in the door, give the full sales pitch, and then demand a response. Their goal is to close the deal and close it now. These folks are convinced that if they don't call people to make a decision at the end of every spiritual conversation, they will end up living with heart-piercing guilt if this person leaves their conversation, wanders into the street, and gets run over by a truck.

It's a Journey

In most cases, people do not come to faith in Jesus because of a random contact with a Christian who presents the gospel for the first time and demands a response. This can happen, and sometimes it does, but the vast majority of people come to an authentic and life-changing relationship with Jesus over time. They enter a journey of seeking, learning, and discovering that God uses to draw them closer and closer. Often even those who seem to respond to a spontaneous presentation of the gospel had already been on this journey without realizing it.

Rudy is a great case in point. He visited our church because a neighbor had extended a personal invitation to him. He had an authentic friendship with this family and knew they loved and cared about him. Rudy had never been in a church service and carried some scars because he had been rejected by some "Christian" neighbors when he was growing up. It seems Rudy's father had committed an unpardonable sin in the eyes of his highly religious neighbors. He mowed the lawn on Sundays. And as a response, many of the parents on the block told their children they could not play with Rudy. This created feelings of rejection that pushed him away from the church and Christians for many years.

When he finally walked into the church, Rudy had no idea what to expect. But he was pleasantly surprised to discover that the people were warm and the worship service made sense. He, his wife, and their children felt at home and accepted almost immediately. He began asking lots of questions and started reading the Bible. Then he jumped into a class about core Christian beliefs. When Rudy came to talk with me, he had finished the class and was holding a notebook full of questions about the Christian faith. We started going through his list of inquiries, and I discovered that Rudy had a sharp analytical mind. As a computer programmer, he liked understanding the details and wanted all of the blanks filled in.

We met for many weeks and had conversations about theology, the Bible, football, computer programming, parenting, the new menu at Taco Bell, and much more. Finally, I asked Rudy, "Do you think you are ready? Are you at a place where you can put your trust in Jesus and ask him to forgive you and lead your life?"

He looked at me and said, "I don't know. This is a huge decision." I could see it in his eyes. Rudy was struggling with the magnitude of this choice. He continued, "This decision is even bigger than getting married or having children. This is the most important decision of my life."

I agreed and asked Rudy if he was ready to step across that line of faith and say yes to Jesus.

He paused and said, "I need more time. I'm not ready yet."

Something in my heart sank. But on the outside, I smiled and said, "No problem. Do you want to meet again next week?"

He assured me that he did, and we agreed on the same place and time. Rudy committed to continue his reading through the gospel of John and to keeping detailed notes on what he was learning about Jesus. As we parted, I lifted up a quiet prayer thanking God for letting me be part of this amazing journey with Rudy as he walked closer and closer to Jesus.

The next week, when Rudy walked in the door, I saw a glow on his face and a bounce in his step. Something was different. We chatted for a few moments, and then I asked, "So what's up? Where are you with this whole Jesus thing?"

He said with confidence, "I'm ready! What do I need to do?"

I told him that he needed to talk to Jesus in prayer and tell him what was on his heart. We had walked through the whole gospel a number of times over the past couple of months, so I knew he understood. So Rudy prayed.

In his prayer, he acknowledged that he had done a lot of things that would separate him from God. His confession of sins came from a broken and repentant heart. He admitted there was no way he could get to God on his own. And then he asked Jesus to forgive him and make the sacrifice of the cross count as the payment for all of his wrongs. Next, Rudy asked God to enter his life and give him a whole new beginning. He told Jesus that he needed him to lead his life and be in charge from that moment on. Finally, he prayed for his wife and his children and thanked God for the many ways he had proved his love over the years.

When Rudy was done praying, there was a holy quiet in the room. He looked at me and asked, "Can I tell you something?"

I said, "Anything."

He said, "You might think this is weird, but I feel light, like a huge weight has been lifted off of me."

I told him that the weight of sin, guilt, and death had been lifted and his feeling was both natural and supernatural. We talked about John Bunyan's great book *The Pilgrim's Progress* and how when Pilgrim came to the cross, he laid down the burden of sin. This all made sense to Rudy; he realized he was also a pilgrim. Finally, we discussed the journey ahead and how, in many ways, Rudy was just beginning his adventure with God.

||||| Seismic Shift Suggestion |||||

Thank Someone. Look back on your journey of faith and identify the people who really walked with you along the way and showed you God's love. Then pick one of them and write a note or send an e-mail telling them how much their time, care, and love has meant in your life.

I suppose the very first week I met Rudy I could have tried to force him to make a commitment to Jesus. I could have worried that he might be hit by a truck the next day. I could have tried to close the deal. But I sensed the Holy Spirit was at work in his life, and I knew my part was to walk with him on his journey toward God. Over those months, many other people were praying for Rudy and encouraging him along the way. And we all trusted that God's grace and sovereign power were great enough to protect him and move him toward the Savior.

Keeping Things in Perspective • • • • • • • • • • • • •

Sometimes we need God to give us perspective on our role in the work of evangelism. There are times when we devalue our contribution to God's work in the lives of spiritual seekers. But there are also times we esteem our part too highly. The apostle Paul addresses this when he writes, "What, after all, is Apollos? And what is Paul? Only servants, through whom you came to believe—as the Lord has assigned to each his task. I planted the seed, Apollos watered it, but God made it grow. So neither he who plants nor he who waters is anything, but only God, who makes things grow. The man who plants and the man who waters have one purpose, and each will be rewarded according to his own labor. For we are God's fellow workers; you are God's field, God's building" (1 Cor. 3:5–9).

Paul gives some crystal-clear reminders that we need to hear. We can plant seeds of the gospel. We can water these seeds as we walk with people on their spiritual journey and extend God's love to them. Our role of being a friend, extending grace, answering questions, praying fervently, serving humbly, and loving passionately are all very important. But only God can bring the growth. Only the Holy Spirit can change a heart.

This reality should not discourage us or make us feel like our contribution in the work of outreach is unimportant. Rather, it should give us a sense of confident freedom. We can walk with people on their faith journey, but we are not ultimately responsible for their eternal choices. We can't be. This is God's domain.

When a person responds to the gospel and makes an authentic commitment to Jesus Christ, God gets the glory, not us. We don't enter the faith journey of others for the sake of collecting spiritual trophies. We don't get the credit and praise when someone receives Jesus as Savior. And by the same token, we do not have to live with fear, guilt, and remorse over those who resist the message of God's grace. Our role is to joyfully plant seeds, faithfully water them, and give God all the glory every time a man, woman, or child comes to Father through the blood of Jesus Christ.

It's about People

We live in a world full of people who feel depersonalized and marginalized. Most of us are known less by our name and more by a number. To many people, we are a Social Security number, a credit card number, a checking account number, a frequent-flyer number, a PIN, or an offering-envelope number. Into this impersonal world, Jesus wants to speak the same message he has declared from the beginning. He loves and cares about people. He wants us to do the same.

It takes just a quick survey of Jesus' life to learn how much he cared about human beings. In the gospel of Matthew, we read that "little children were brought to Jesus for him to place his hands on them and pray for them. But the disciples rebuked those who brought them. Jesus said, 'Let the little children come to me, and do not hinder them, for the kingdom of heaven belongs to such as these.' When he had placed his hands on them, he went on from there" (Matt. 19:13–15). Jesus loved even the little ones. In the midst of full days of ministry, high demands on his time, and countless responsibilities, Jesus made children a priority.

In the gospel of John, we see Jesus encountering a woman who was a social outcast and a religious leper. He was a Jewish rabbi, and she was a

Samaritan half-breed who had been married five times and was living in sin with a sixth man. Yet Jesus reached out to her and said, "If you knew the gift of God and who it is that asks you for a drink, you would have asked him and he would have given you living water" (John 4:10). This woman was shocked that Jesus had spoken to her and asked her for a drink of water from the well. In the first century, no right-minded Jewish rabbi would have acknowledged a woman in public, much less a Samaritan woman who was known to have a bad reputation. Jesus astounded her by offering the gift of eternal living water. Jesus' love for people built a bridge across all social, religious, and gender gaps.

When he called Levi to be his follower, Jesus showed his love for one of the most hated groups of his day, tax collectors (Mark 2:14). This love was reemphasized when Jesus reached out to a chief tax collector named Zacchaeus (Luke 19:1–9). Over and over, Jesus extended a hand to the broken, outcast, sick, and forgotten. He went so far as to reach out and physically touch the untouchable: lepers (Matt. 8:2–3). Jesus' life stands as a model for all who call themselves his followers. We are to love people as he did. We should not see them as obstacles or projects. Through the eyes of Jesus, we need to see people as valuable, important, and worthy of God's love and ours.

People, Not Projects

I was speaking at an evangelism conference in Chicago. After a session that focused on reaching out into the community with God's love, we had a question and answer time. A man came to the microphone and asked a heartfelt question. He said, "What do I do if I am trying to reach out to someone, but I have very little in common with this person?" He went on to clarify, "I actually don't really enjoy being with him!"

I paused, reflected, said a quick prayer, and then asked, "Do you love this person?"

The man stood for a moment in quiet reflection.

I went a little deeper and asked, "If this person never came to faith in Jesus, would you still be his friend, would you hang out with him, would you still love him?" The man swallowed hard and said, "I'm not really sure if I would still connect with him if I was not trying to win him to Christ."

I encouraged the man to consider staying away from this person. This might seem a little harsh, but I believe we can do considerable damage when we make people our personal outreach projects but don't really love them. If our goal is to declare the message of the gospel revealed in the love of God poured out through the blood of Jesus shed on the cross, but we are not incarnating a life overflowing with love, we can actually push people away from Jesus. I was not trying to be mean-spirited or judgmental; I just wanted this man to know that making a person an evangelistic project can be counterproductive.

> |||||| **Seismic Shift Suggestion** ||||||
>
> **Who Will I Walk With?** Identify one person God has placed in your life who is on a journey toward Jesus. Ask the Lord to use you to encourage them along the way. Also, commit to spending time with this person. Listen for the leading of the Holy Spirit as you continue on a journey with this friend. When the Spirit prompts you to share your faith, be ready to respond.

I closed by telling the audience that if we are reaching out to someone strictly because they are a "project," we should consider stepping away from them for a time and pray for our hearts to change. Evangelism must grow out of a posture of authentic concern for others. When we reach out to people only out of a sense of guilt or duty, they will feel it, they will smell it, and they will know that we see them as a chore on our checklist of things to do. However, when we walk with people on their spiritual journey because the love of God overflows in our hearts and because we see them through the eyes of Jesus, this is powerful. Through an authentic relationship like this, people outside of the family will know they are loved and cherished by God long before they enter a relationship with Jesus.

A Battle in and with the Church • • • • • • • • • • •

Every church exerts a gravitational pull on its members. When a church has effective programs, a strong youth ministry, opportunities to serve, warm fellowship, and Spirit-filled worship services, the force of attraction can be powerful. What tends to happen is that church members find themselves spending all of their extra time doing church activities. They might teach Sunday school, help with youth group, participate in a small-group Bible study, and attend weekly worship. Sometimes the gravitational pull of the church takes on the force of a black hole: followers of Christ find themselves so drawn to things happening at church or among their believing friends that they have no time for those outside of God's family. And what's worse, they find it almost impossible to escape the pull to invest their whole lives in those who already know Jesus.

> |||||| **Seismic Shift Suggestion** ||||||
>
> **Create a Connection Point.** Think about a hobby or activity you really enjoy. It might be something you have not done for years. Then investigate how you can participate in this activity on a community level. You might begin playing bridge every week, join a softball league, take a pottery class, find a book club, or become part of a community orchestra. The key is that you do this outside of the church setting. Pray for the Lord to open the door to new friendships with people who need someone to walk with them on their journey toward God.

This temptation to become isolated from the world is just as powerful for pastors as it is for anyone else. Every person who loves God and hears his call to walk with spiritual seekers on their journey of faith must learn to break free of the gravitational pull of the church and make time to be in the world. Jesus made it clear that his followers were to be in the world, though not conformed to it (John 17:13–19; Rom. 12:2). We need to learn from his example.

What does it take to propel us out of the gravitational pull of the church and into the world? Think about the rocket thrusters needed to push a space shuttle out of the earth's atmosphere. It takes a similar level of energy.

First, we need the profound conviction that it is God's plan for his children to engage with those who are outside of his family. We must live with the ever-present awareness that the same Savior who touched lepers, shared meals with tax collectors, had a theological conversation with a morally questionable woman, and called people like you and me to be his followers calls us to love people the way he does. When we remember that God so loved the world, we will be moved to do the same.

Also, pastors and church leaders should start encouraging and affirming believers who are devoted to engaging with the world. When we see people who have moved out of the gravitational pull of the church and discovered natural ways to connect with lost people, we should hold them up as examples. The problem is we tend to point out and praise those who are so immersed in the life of the church that they have no time to walk with people outside of the community of faith.

In addition, the church needs to be structured in a way that not only pulls believers in but also pushes them out. We need to look at our church calendars and be intentional about leaving open time for people to be in their neighborhoods, hang out with friends, and to spontaneously interact with those who are still finding their way to God. Sometimes we pack our church schedules so full that we make engagement with the world almost impossible. If we don't have church-related programs planned for every day of the week, we feel like we are not offering enough. But sometimes the most strategic thing a church can do is leave open space on the calendar. If your church is pathologically busy, consider recommending a reevaluation of the schedule.

Another wonderful way to help Christians escape the gravity of the church is to start seeker small groups. These are small group gatherings designed to bring believers and spiritual seekers together. Willow Creek Church has led the way in this movement. For many years, they have invited nonbelievers to be part of their small groups. The community and relationships that are forged naturally advance people on their journey toward God. Willow Creek has also developed small group resources designed to appeal to people who are not yet part of God's family. These materials avoid overly religious language. One of the best ways to move people out of the church atmosphere and into the world is connecting them with a small group in which they interact with other believers and seekers at the same time.

||||| Seismic Shift Suggestion |||||

Begin a Seeker Small Group. Identify four or five people you know who are not yet followers of Jesus. Also, think of a couple of strong Christians you know and respect who might connect well with these friends. Then invite the whole group over for dinner or a dessert. Watch the interactions and connections that are generated. If people seem to relate well, pray about inviting this whole group to be in a small group for six weeks. Pick up one of the Willow Creek *Tough Questions* small group guides to help you. You might also want to get a copy of Garry Poole's book *Seeker Small Groups*.

Finally, congregations need to plan more opportunities for people to connect off of the church campus. Take advantage of every chance you can to use space in the community when you get together. The Crossroads Church in Amsterdam, Netherlands, does not have their own building for weekly worship. Although they have been a healthy and influential church in their community for over a decade, they still meet in a rented school facility. This forces them to interact with people in their community on their own turf and terms. Think about holding small group meetings at a coffee shop or in a community center. Plan a special church service in a school or a movie theater. Plan an outreach event in which you actually go out as a church rather than inviting people to come to you. By being intentional about connecting off of your church campus, you will have many unplanned contacts with people in your community.

Which Doctor Would You Want?

In one of my favorite movies, *What about Bob?* we meet Dr. Marvin. He is caught up in his career, his new book, and his ego. He sees patients not as people to engage with but as clients for whom he renders a service. The boundary of his interaction with them begins when they walk into his office and ends after exactly fifty minutes.

This is all turned upside-down when he meets Bob. Bob has some serious boundary issues and ends up following Dr. Marvin to his vacation home. Through a humorous series of events, Bob makes his way into Dr. Marvin's home and also into the hearts of his wife and children. When his family points out that he is not treating Bob very kindly, Dr. Marvin blurts out, "He's a patient," as if this explains his insensitivity. Dr. Marvin is all about doing his job, closing the deal, punching the proverbial clock, and then being done with his patients.

In another movie, we meet a doctor who goes by the name Patch Adams. In this movie, titled *Patch Adams*, we encounter a man who is struggling against the norms of the medical profession. Many doctors in his day are trained to render their medical services without letting their hearts engage with their patients. This professional distance is supposed to keep the lines between the medical practitioner and the client clear. In the story, Patch Adams allows himself to care about people. He refers to patients by their names and not their illnesses, he encourages laughter, and he even allows his heart to be broken and tears to flow for those who are hurting. When I need a doctor, I definitely want someone who cares and who engages with me as a person, not as a case number.

In the same way, Jesus, the Great Physician, calls us to extend his care in this broken and hurting world. We are not called to stand at a safe distance, throw out an occasional religious slogan, punch the clock for a fifty-minute session, and declare, "I did my part and now I'm done." Rather, we are called to walk with people the way Jesus did. We are to enter their journey, welcome their questions, feel their pain, and even sacrifice of ourselves. This is what Jesus did for us; we can do no less for others. When we follow our Savior and walk with spiritual seekers on their journey toward God, we discover some of the greatest joys in this life.

FOR REFLECTION

- Who has God called me to walk with as they continue their journey toward Jesus? What can I do to extend more of God's grace to them?
- What can I do to free up my schedule and make more time to connect with people who are not yet in God's family?

FOR PRAYER

- Lift up prayers of praise and thanks for all of the people God used in your life to show his love and draw you to Jesus.
- Pray for the people in your life who do not yet know God's love. Ask the Holy Spirit to give you patience, boldness, and tenderness as you walk with these people on their journey toward the Savior.

Conclusion

From Glory to Glory

Now the Lord is the Spirit, and where the Spirit of the Lord is, there is freedom. And we, who with unveiled faces all reflect the Lord's glory, are being transformed into his likeness with ever-increasing glory, which comes from the Lord, who is the Spirit.

—2 Corinthians 3:17–18

The sign was posted beside a major dirt road in the outback of Australia: "Choose your rut carefully. You will be in it for the next 200 miles." This fatalist mindset rules the lives of far too many Christians. We act as if change is impossible.

In this book, you have discovered that God offers the power you need for radical life transformation. You do not have to stay in your rut. God invites you to make seismic shifts that will wake you, shake you, and jolt you out of your old way of life and set you on a new path. He wants to take you on a lifelong journey that leads from glory to glory as you draw closer to his heart.

Seismic shifts are little changes that make a big difference in your life. But no one can make these shifts for you. God invites you to make little changes that will make a big difference as you:

- experience deep and lasting joy.
- engage in a growing and dynamic relationship with him.
- feel healthy, rested, and peaceful.
- build intimate relationships marked by honest communication.
- attain financial security and contentment.
- enjoy sharing your faith naturally and consistently.

May the God of all glory reveal his presence and power as you make seismic shifts that lead to powerful changes in your life. May you feel his glorious presence each and every day. And may his glory so fill your life that it overflows to each person you encounter. Amen.

Weekly Reading Guide

Week 1: Shifts That Bring Greater Joy Than You Can Imagine

☐ Day 1   Psalm 4–5
☐ Day 2   Psalm 30
☐ Day 3   Ephesians 4
☐ Day 4   Psalm 139
☐ Day 5   Philippians 3
☐ Weekend   Romans 8

Week 2: Shifts That Expand Your Faith

☐ Day 1   Hebrews 11–12:3
☐ Day 2   Isaiah 6:1–8; Revelation 5
☐ Day 3   Psalm 119:1–88
☐ Day 4   Psalm 119:89–176
☐ Day 5   John 17
☐ Weekend   Matthew 6:5–15; Colossians 1:1–14

Week 3: Shifts That Bring Health and Rest

☐ Day 1   Genesis 1:1–2:3; Exodus 20:8–11
☐ Day 2   Mark 2:23–3:6; Luke 6:1–11
☐ Day 3   1 Corinthians 6:12–20; Matthew 6:25–34
☐ Day 4   Psalm 139
☐ Day 5   Philippians 4
☐ Weekend   John 14

Week 4: Shifts That Build Dynamic and Lasting Relationships

☐ Day 1   Proverbs 12
☐ Day 2   Proverbs 18
☐ Day 3   John 13
☐ Day 4   Philippians 2
☐ Day 5   Mark 10
☐ Weekend   John 19

Week 5: Shifts That Open the Floodgates of True Riches

☐ Day 1   Malachi 3
☐ Day 2   Matthew 6:19–24
☐ Day 3   1 Timothy 6
☐ Day 4   Luke 12:13–34
☐ Day 5   2 Corinthians 8
☐ Weekend   2 Corinthians 9

Week 6: Shifts That Will Help You Impact Your Community and the World

☐ Day 1   Matthew 28; 9:35–38
☐ Day 2   Acts 1
☐ Day 3   Acts 2
☐ Day 4   Philippians 1
☐ Day 5   1 Corinthians 3
☐ Weekend   Luke 15

Appendix 2

Praying the Lord's Prayer
Matthew 6:9 – 13

The purpose of the Lord's Prayer is to give direction, a starting point, a springboard for meaningful prayer. In this prayer, Jesus gives us basic categories to help us, as we pray, to keep our focus on what matters most. Here are some prompts to give you direction as you use the Lord's Prayer in your spiritual life.

Prayers of Adoration

Our Father in heaven, hallowed be your name.

- Lift up prayers of praise for who God is.
- Meditate on the names of God found in the Bible and reflect on what you learn about his character.
- Express thanks and deep appreciation to God for being your perfect Father.

Prayers of Submission

Your kingdom come, your will be done, on earth as it is in heaven.

- Yield your life, relationships, habits, and decisions to God's will.
- Pray for God's will to break into national and international politics.
- Pray for God's purposes and plans to be understood and adopted in the life of your church.
- Ask the Holy Spirit to move in the hearts of people who are far from God's kingdom that they might see and receive Jesus as the leader of their life.

Prayers of Supplication

Give us today our daily bread.

- Ask for your daily needs (physical, emotional, relational, etc.).
- Pray for those who are close to you and for their needs.

Prayers of Confession

Forgive us our debts, as we also have forgiven our debtors.

- Confess your sins to God and tell him how you feel about these areas in which you have rebelled against his will.
- Ask God to help you extend grace and forgiveness to those who have hurt you.
- Praise God for the greatness of his love and grace in your life.

Prayers of Protection

And lead us not into temptation, but deliver us from the evil one.

- Ask the Holy Spirit to protect you from the attacks and temptations of the Devil.
- Think about sins with which you have struggled, and pray for power to resist and overcome them.
- Pray, in the name of Jesus, that the power of Satan in this world and in your life would be broken.

Daily Health Sheet

Date:

Area of Focus	Plan for the Day	Notes
Breakfast: Write down what I will eat before I eat. Pray before I eat. Stop when I am satisfied!		
Lunch: Write down what I will eat before I eat. Pray before I eat. Stop when I am satisfied!		
Dinner: Write down what I will eat before I eat. Pray before I eat. Stop when I am satisfied!		
Snacks:		
Exercise or Activities:		
Rest and Refreshment:		
Other Health Goals: • Number of glasses of water each day. • Stop all eating after ____ p.m.		

Lord, I eat this food with thankfulness to you
and with the awareness that it is a gift from your hand.
I eat it so that my body might be healthy,
an acceptable temple for you.
Let this food strengthen my body that I might serve you
and live each moment for you. Amen!

Key Reminders

- Stop eating when I am satisfied.
- Taste and enjoy my food. Eat slowly and deliberately.
- Sit down and enjoy meals. Stay away from fast food or fast meals of any kind.

Do you not know that your body is a temple of the Holy Spirit, who is in you, whom you have received from God? You are not your own; you were bought at a price. Therefore honor God with your body.

—1 Corinthians 6:19–20

Since we have these promises, dear friends, let us purify ourselves from everything that contaminates body and spirit, perfecting holiness out of reverence for God.

—2 Corinthians 7:1

Appendix 4

The Best News Ever

*G*od's love for people is huge and amazing. The Bible teaches that God loves you more than words can express. The whole story of the Bible is filled with God's love. The starting point of salvation is love. No matter how you feel about yourself and no matter how others treat you, God's love is constant. God longs to be in an intimate relationship with you.

> But you, O Lord, are a compassionate and gracious God, slow to anger, abounding in love and faithfulness.
>
> **—Psalm 86:15**

> How great is the love the Father has lavished on us, that we should be called children of God! And that is what we are!
>
> **—1 John 3:1**

Human beings have broken their relationship with God by sinning. Sin is the word the Bible uses to describe anything you do that is not consistent with God's plan. Any thought that does not honor God, any word that is unkind, and any action that hurts others or is against God is called sin. The Bible also teaches that when we know there is something good we should do and we fail to do it, this is sin. In light of this definition, it becomes clear very quickly that we all sin quite a bit, every day.

Sin destroys our relationship with God. He still loves us, but our sin drives a wedge between us and him. God loves us and wants a restored relationship with us, but he can't just look the other way and pretend we have not sinned. Because God is perfectly pure (holy), he can't ignore sin. Because he is perfectly fair (just), he must punish sin. The Bible makes it clear that there is only one punishment for sin. It might sound harsh, but sin demands the death penalty. God's absolute holiness and unparalleled justice demand that this ultimate punishment be paid.

This is the worst news imaginable! Because of our sin, we are all separated from the God who loves us. And we are condemned to death because of our sin. This bad news can seem overwhelming until we realize what God did so that we could be restored to relationship with him and be freed from the punishment and the death sentence that hang over us.

All have sinned and fall short of the glory of God.

—**Romans 3:23**

For the wages of sin is death, but the gift of God is eternal life in Christ Jesus our Lord.

—**Romans 6:23**

God did something about this problem, and what he did is the greatest news ever. God offers to pay the price for us. He came to this earth as a man, Jesus. This is what we celebrate on Christmas. Jesus was God in a human body. Jesus lived a real life, with real joys, pain, and temptations, and he experienced everything we face. But here is the difference: Jesus never sinned. He did not have one thought, motive, or action that dishonored his Father. He never spoke a word that was hurtful or wrong.

Then, one day, he was accused of crimes he did not commit and was condemned to death. He was nailed to a cross and executed as a common criminal. He was stripped, beaten, mocked, and killed. Jesus suffered this brutal death so that we would not have to pay the price for our sins. His death was the payment. We have sinned and deserve to die. Jesus sacrificed himself on the cross in our place. His death became ours. He did not deserve to die. We deserve to die, but we don't have to—if we accept Jesus and enter a relationship with God the Father through him.

The gospel is called the Good News because we are offered a pardon for all of the wrongs we have ever done and ever will do. We can have new life and a restored relationship with God through Jesus. We don't earn it or deserve it, and we can't take credit for it. All we can do is accept it.

For God so loved the world that he gave his one and only Son, that whoever believes in him shall not perish but have eternal life.

—**John 3:16**

This is love: not that we loved God, but that he loved us and sent his Son as an atoning sacrifice for our sins.

—**1 John 4:10**

How can a person accept Jesus, have their sins washed away, and enter a restored relationship with God? The Bible makes it clear that salvation through Jesus is a free gift; it is not earned by checking the boxes on some to-do list of good works. Salvation can be received only by faith in Jesus. This faith begins by praying and asking Jesus to be the one who forgives you and is the leader of your life. This step of faith means you are admitting you have sinned against God and that you are sorry for your sins. It means asking God to help you live a new and changed life that honors him.

You don't have to know a lot of fancy religious terms. Just tell God that you know you have sinned. Express your sorrow over your sin and ask for the forgiveness that comes through the price Jesus paid when he died on the cross. Then invite Jesus to enter your life and to lead you from this moment on, all the way into eternity. You can express this prayer in your own words, or you can use the following prayer:

> Dear God, I am coming to you to express that I need you, that maybe I need you more than I have ever known. I want to admit my sins. I have thought things, said things, and done things that do not please you. [At this point, you might want to specify some of the sins you are sorry about.] I realize that my sins cause me to be under a death sentence. I have also come to know you sent Jesus, your only Son, to pay the price for my sins by dying in my place. Jesus, I thank you for paying the price for me. I need your forgiveness, and I want you to enter my life and become my leader from this moment on. Thank you for all you have done and all you will do in my life. Amen!

When you have lifted up this prayer, you can be confident that you are now in a restored relationship with God and that all of your sins are forgiven.

> If we confess our sins, he is faithful and just and will forgive us our sins and purify us from all unrighteousness.
>
> —1 John 1:9

> As far as the east is from the west, so far has he removed our transgressions from us.
>
> —Psalm 103:12

> If you confess with your mouth, "Jesus is Lord," and believe in your heart that God raised him from the dead, you will be saved.
>
> —Romans 10:9

Study Guide

Part 1: Shifts That Bring Greater Joy Than You Can Imagine

1. In the introduction to *Seismic Shifts* are numerous examples of little changes or movements that make a big difference, such as movement along a fault line, a spoon taped to a pen, a person's attitude about worship styles, a domino being pushed over, and a husband's commitment to say "I love you." Tell about a seismic shift you have experienced in some area of your life and how this small change made a big impact.

2. As you anticipate spending six weeks learning about seismic shifts, which area of change are you most excited about experiencing?

   - Shifts that bring new levels of joy
   - Shifts that help you grow deeper in your faith
   - Shifts that lead to physical health and rest in your soul
   - Shifts that build strong and lasting relationships
   - Shifts that lead to true riches and contentment
   - Shifts that prepare you to share God's love with the people you meet each day

   What changes do you hope to experience in this area of your life?

3. Read the introduction to part 1 of *Seismic Shifts* (pp. 16–18). What might it look like when a person is content "playing with mud pies in the slums" when God offers "a holiday by the sea"? How do you think God feels when he sees his children living this way?

4. Read Ephesians 4:14–15 and Hebrews 5:12–6:1. What is God's message to those who are comfortable staying in the same place spiritually and who don't desire to mature in their faith?

5. Read the story about Zach learning to swim (p. 21). What is one area of your life in which God is trying to get you to swim but you won't let go of the chain-link fence? What do you believe God wants to say to you about letting go and making a seismic shift in this area of your life?

6. In chapter 1, we looked at key indicators that we are taking joy-filled steps forward in spiritual maturity. Below is a list of all seven. Identify where you are in your spiritual growth in each area of your life.

Learning to Feed Ourselves (Studying the Bible)

1	2	3	4	5	6	7	8	9	10
first steps			walking			jogging			running

Learning to Talk and Listen (Developing a prayer life)

1	2	3	4	5	6	7	8	9	10
first steps			walking			jogging			running

Sharing (Growing in generosity)

1	2	3	4	5	6	7	8	9	10

first steps   walking   jogging   running

Helping Others (Serving others and entering into ministry)

1	2	3	4	5	6	7	8	9	10

first steps   walking   jogging   running

Loving People (Fulfilling God's call to love your neighbor)

1	2	3	4	5	6	7	8	9	10

first steps   walking   jogging   running

Loving God (Loving God with all your heart, soul, and mind)

1	2	3	4	5	6	7	8	9	10

first steps   walking   jogging   running

Living in a Bigger World (Caring for those outside of God's family)

1	2	3	4	5	6	7	8	9	10

first steps   walking   jogging   running

Identify one area in which you are doing well and showing signs of growth and tell your small group how you are experiencing joy as you grow in this area of spiritual maturity. Identify an area in which you desire to take a step forward in spiritual maturity. What is one shift you can make that will help you grow up in faith in this area?

7. Read Psalm 139:1–16. What do you learn about how God sees you and feels about you from this passage?

8. Read the story at the beginning of chapter 2 about nap time in kindergarten (pp. 31–32). Tell about a time when you discovered that a large part of your value (in the eyes of some people) was based on how you behaved or performed, and describe how this impacted the way you viewed yourself.

9. Read John 3:16–17; Romans 5:8; and John 15:13. How does God's message of love fly in the face of what the world teaches us about our value?

10. Read 2 Corinthians 11:23–28; 2 Corinthians 4:16–18; and Romans 8:18. The apostle Paul wrote all of these passages. The same man who suffered through the things listed in 2 Corinthians 11:23–28 was able to live with deep and lasting joy. How is it possible for a person to face deep suffering and still live with enduring joy?

11. What is one Seismic Shift Suggestion from part 1 that you have decided to try in the coming days? How can your small group members pray for you

and keep you accountable as you seek to experience transformation in this area of your life?

Part 2: Shifts That Expand Your Faith

1. Read Isaiah 6:1–8 and Hebrews 12:1–3. Then read the story about Cameron in the introduction to part 2 (p. 56). How did Cameron find strength, peace, and confidence in a situation that felt scary to him? Tell about a time when taking your eyes off yourself and focusing on God brought confidence.

2. How do you see the disease of spiritual myopia spreading through our culture and even the church?

3. Why is it so challenging to keep our eyes on God through the course of the day?

4. What is one thing you can do to focus more on God and less on you as you walk through the day?

5. Imagine a person who comes to your worship service with the following mindset: "I am here to receive. I want music that inspires me, a sermon that grips my attention, and elements of the worship service that fit my taste and style. If there is something in the service that does not meet my needs or hold my attention, I will be quick to critique it and tell people that I am not happy with that part of the service."

   Respond to one of the following questions:

   1. How might this attitude impact this person's worship experience?
   2. How might this person's disposition impact other people?
   3. What advice would you give this person?

6. Imagine another worshiper who comes to church with this attitude: "I am here to give praise and honor to God. This service is not about me but about God's glory. No matter what the music, prayers, or sermon are like, I will do all I can to lift up the name of Jesus and be an authentic worshiper."

   Respond to one of the following questions:

   1. How might this attitude impact this person's worship experience?
   2. How might this person's disposition impact other people?
   3. What shifts can you make to have an attitude more like this person?

7. In chapter 5, we saw five images of how the Bible works in our lives:

   - A *lamp* to illuminate our way (Ps. 119:105)
   - Sweet *honey* (Ps. 119:1–5)
   - A *training manual* that equips for ministry (2 Tim. 3:16–17)
   - A *surgeon's scalpel* that cuts to heal (Heb. 4:12–13)
   - A *sword* for spiritual warfare (Eph. 6:17)

   How have you experienced the Bible working in one of these ways in your life?

8. Read John 10:1–6. As Jesus teaches about his relationship with his followers, he uses the image of a shepherd and sheep. Jesus says, "His sheep follow

him because they know his voice." In chapter 6, we reflected on some of the
ways God speaks to his children:

* The Bible
* Other people
* Circumstances
* A still, small voice
* Dreams and visions
* Other ways

How have you learned to recognize his voice?

9. What is one Seismic Shift Suggestion from part 2 that you have decided to
try in the coming days? How can your small group members pray for you
and keep you accountable as you seek to experience transformation in this
area of your life? Read the section "In the Arms of Jesus" (pp. 95–96).

Part 3: Shifts That Bring Health and Rest

1. Read Exodus 20:8–11 and Matthew 11:28–30. In a culture that is busy and
hurried and in which many people feel perpetually tired, what message do
these two passages speak to our hearts?
2. Read the story about Robert (pp. 101–2). How have you experienced the
Robert Syndrome in your life? How do you see this syndrome impacting
our society?
3. Why do you think God is so serious about his children learning the secret
of Sabbath?
4. Jesus made it clear that the Sabbath was designed not to imprison us with
legalism but to set us free. Respond to one of the following statements
about the Sabbath:
   1. Taking a weekly Sabbath is a declaration of trust that God can run the
   universe without me.
   2. Taking a weekly Sabbath is a living parable that I know God will provide all I need in six days of labor.
   3. Taking a weekly Sabbath is a regular reminder that I know meeting
   with God's people for worship is a priority for my spiritual health.
5. What are some things you could do that would be restful, refreshing, and
nourishing to the soul on your Sabbath day?
6. Read 1 Corinthians 6:18–20 and Romans 12:1–2. What implications does
truly believing that the Holy Spirit dwells in us have on how we view and
treat our bodies?
7. In chapter 8, there are eight suggestions for maintaining our bodies and
treating them as dwelling places of the Holy Spirit. They are shifts from:

* Stuffed to satisfied
* Gulping to tasting
* Guilty to thankful
* Random to planned
* Fast food to sit-down meals
* Many drink options to water

- Anytime eating to planned times
- Passive to active lives

What is one shift you would like to make in how you care for your body? What steps can you take in the coming days to make this a part of your lifestyle?

8. What is one roadblock standing in the way of your committing to care for your body? What can you do to remove this barrier?

9. Read Philippians 4:6–7 and Matthew 6:25–27. What does God want to say to those who allow their lives to be overrun with anxiety?

10. Read the story in chapter 9 about Laura and her family (pp. 131–32). Tell about an anxious time when you experienced the peace of God come over your life as you prayed and cried out to God.

11. What is one situation in which you tend to experience a high level of anxiety, and how can prayer act as the antidote to worry at this time?

12. What is one Seismic Shift Suggestion from part 3 that you have decided to try in the coming days? How can your small group members pray for you and keep you accountable as you seek to experience transformation in this area of your life?

Part 4: Shifts That Build Dynamic and Lasting Relationships

1. Read the following three quotes:

> We humans are like hedgehogs in winter. We try to stand close enough for warmth, but not too close—for fear of being pinched by each other's quills.
> **—German philosopher Schopenauer**

> We don't live alone. We are members of one body. We are responsible for each other. And I tell you that the time will soon come when, if men will not learn that lesson, then they will be taught it in fire and blood and anguish.
> **—J. B. Priestly, British writer**

> Our world has become a neighborhood without becoming a brotherhood.
> **—Billy Graham**

Which of these quotes speaks to your heart? Explain.

2. Read the introduction to part 4 (pp. 142–43). If our relationships are a priority, why don't we do regular checkups and maintain them so they won't break down?

3. Read Proverbs 18:21; Proverbs 12:18; and James 3:3–12. What are some of the warnings God gives about the power of our words?

4. How have you experienced the power of words to cut, burn, and bring pain?

5. How have you been blessed, built up, and encouraged through the words of another person?

6. Read 1 Corinthians 10:6–10. The Bible warns against the serious dangers of grumbling. Why do you think God takes this sin so seriously?

7. In chapter 10 there is a discussion about establishing Zero Tolerance Zones for grumbling (pp. 152–54). What might happen if you established your home, church, workplace, or neighborhood as a ZTZ for grumbling? What steps could you take to create a climate free of grumbling?

8. Just as words can burn, they can also bless and build others up. God wants us to use this great power to strengthen and affirm people. What is one action you can take to begin blessing others with your words?

9. Read John 13:1–17 and Mark 10:45. What message is Jesus sending to those who want to be his followers?

10. In Jesus' day, washing feet was one of the humblest forms of service. What are some modern-day examples of foot washing? Who is one person you believe God wants you to serve more faithfully, and what service can you extend to this person?

11. When is it most difficult for you to serve?

12. What is one Seismic Shift Suggestion from part 4 that you have decided to try in the coming days? How can your small group members pray for you and keep you accountable as you seek to experience transformation in this area of your life?

Part 5: Shifts That Open the Floodgates of True Riches

1. Read the introduction to part 5 about the money monster (pp. 184–85). How has the money monster caused damage in one of the following areas:

   • In our culture
   • In the church
   • In your life
   • In the life of someone you love (please do not use names)

2. Read Matthew 6:19–21; Matthew 24; and 1 Timothy 6:10. How is Jesus' view of material things in opposition to our culture's view of things?

3. Read Malachi 3:8–12. In this passage, what does God ask and what does he promise?

4. Read the story about Dustin in the introduction to chapter 13 (pp. 187–88). Tell about a Smarties hero in your life who modeled a lifestyle of joyful generosity.

5. What are some of the things that cause us to hold onto our Smarties and not share them?

6. Read the section titled "What Is a Tithe or Tithing?" (p. 195). If we truly believed that everything we have belongs to God, how might this change the way we use our resources?

7. Read the introduction to chapter 14 (pp. 202–3). How do you see the hamster spirit at work in the world today?

8. Read 2 Corinthians 9:6–8. What does this passage teach us about God's part in giving, and our part?

9. Read the section titled "Is *Cheerful Giver* an Oxymoron?" (pp. 205–7). What lessons can we learn from the little boy in this story?

10. Read Matthew 6:19–21 and 1 Timothy 6:17–19. What are the differences between earthly wealth and heavenly wealth?

11. What is one step you can take to invest in things that will last forever?

12. What is one Seismic Shift Suggestion from part 5 that you have decided to try in the coming days? How can your small group members pray for you and keep you accountable as you seek to experience transformation in this area of your life?

Part 6: Shifts That Will Help You Impact Your Community and the World

1. Read Matthew 9:35–38. In this passage, Jesus uses the image of a harvest and harvesters. The harvest is people who have not yet come to faith in Jesus Christ. The harvesters are those who already know Jesus and are called to go out and share his love and message. What does Jesus teach about the harvest and those who are sent to bring it in?

2. Read the introduction to chapter 16 about people who say, "What about us? Don't forget us!" (pp. 229–32). What can happen to a church that spends all of its time and energy caring for those who are already in God's family and neglects those outside?

3. One of the ways we make the shift from focusing on ourselves to caring for the world is by remembering what we have because of Jesus. Working as a group, list all of the enduring things we receive when we become children of God through faith in Jesus. Now list all of the things those who are not followers of Jesus have that are of eternal value.

4. How should these two lists impact the way we set priorities in our lives and in the church?

5. What were some of the risks Jesus took to reach out to people who were outcasts, lost and wandering like sheep without a shepherd? What were some of the consequences of the risks Jesus took?

6. Reaching out to those who are not followers of Jesus can be messy and costly. But it is always worth the investment when God brings in a harvest of people who come to faith in Jesus. What risk is God calling you to take so that you can share his love more effectively? What risks might God be calling your church to take?

7. Part of entering into God's call to reach the world is learning to get out of the church and live outside of our comfortable Christian circles. This happens as we enter into the lives and worlds of those who do not know Jesus as the leader of their lives. What is one step you can take to connect more closely in your community and with those outside of God's family?

8. Read 1 Peter 3:15 and Matthew 5:13–16. Every person who follows Jesus is called to let their light shine. Our lives are to be like salt that causes people to thirst for the living water that only Jesus can offer. We are to be prepared to tell others about the hope we have in Jesus Christ. But we each do this in different ways with styles that are unique to us. Discovering your evangelism style is like trying on an outfit. Some fit and others don't. The key is that we try various evangelism styles until we find one that fits us. In chapter 17, we looked at six distinct evangelism styles:

- Confrontational (like Peter in Acts 2)
- Intellectual (like Paul in Acts 17)
- Testimonial (like the blind man in John 9)
- Interpersonal (like Matthew in Luke 5)
- Invitational (like the woman at the well in John 4)
- Serving (like Dorcas in Acts 9)

Tell about how you have tried on one or more of these styles. Which one do you think fits you best?

9. Read the introduction to chapter 18 about Patches the dog (pp. 253–54). Most of us have met people who have tried to force the message of Jesus down our throats like it's a tablespoon of castor oil. We have also known people who have walked with us in a patient and loving relationship and shared Jesus in the natural flow of that relationship. Describe how you feel these two approaches to evangelism impact those who are not yet followers of Jesus.

10. Read 1 Corinthians 3:5–9. What is our part in the process of evangelism, and what is God's part? How can a clear understanding of our role lead to confidence, peace, and freedom?

11. What is one Seismic Shift Suggestion from part 6 that you have decided to try in the coming days? How can your small group members pray for you and keep you accountable as you seek to experience transformation in this area of your life?

Notes

Part 1: Shifts That Bring Greater Joy Than You Can Imagine

16   *We are far too easily pleased.* C. S. Lewis, *The Weight of Glory* (Grand Rapids, Mich.: Eerdmans, 1977), 1–2.

16   *Through tears and times of joy.* In his book *A Tale of Three Kings*, Gene Edwards tells the story of how David honored God as the King of Israel during a time when Saul (the king before him), who wanted him dead, and David's own son Absalom tried to take the throne from David.

32   *... an APGAR rating.* APGAR scores are based on five things: heart rate, respiratory effort, muscle tone, reflex irritability, and color. Each category is scored with a 0, 1, or 2. This test is given one minute after birth and also at five and ten minutes. The higher the number, the healthier the baby. Along with this, infants are weighed and measured.

35–37   *I give my life to you!* Over the years, I have heard the story of the geese in many versions. I am not sure who authored this story or first told it. But it communicates a powerful message of why God came in human flesh.

47   *... the most heart wrenching prayers of all time!* In his book *Out of the Depths* (Westminster Press, 1970), Bernard W. Anderson does a wonderful job of explaining the content and structure of these powerful psalms.

48   *... recapture the glory of his past.* The movie *Napoleon Dynamite* became a surprise hit in 2004 and 2005. This quirky story looks at high school students' longings, loves, and desire to belong.

49   *... vows never to look back again.* The movie *Chariots of Fire* captures themes of faith, commitment, devotion, and friendship as seen through the lives of Olympic athletes in the 1920s.

Part 2: Shifts That Expand Your Faith

60   *... the condition of their eyes.* Richard J. Foster deals with some of these themes in his Renovare materials.

61–62   *It just said it.* C. S. Lewis, *The Silver Chair* (New York: Macmillan, 1953), 17.

63   *... and make them happy.* I have lived in Orange County, the greater Chicago area, and the Grand Rapids area and have seen the Church Hopper Syndrome at work. As I have talked with leaders from around the country, I have discovered that these dynamics apply anywhere there is a large number of churches.

70–71   *... in the pages of this glorious book.* At Corinth Church, we invest thousands of dollars a year purchasing Bibles that people from our congregation can give to friends. We always have shelves of good hardback Bibles available that are appropriate for people of various age groups and places in their spiritual journey, and for those who have varied needs. I would commend this practice to any congregation that desires to get the Word of God into people's hands and hearts.

Part 3: Shifts That Bring Health and Rest

98   *... between 1987 and 2000.* These statistics were taken from the website of the *Journal of Medical Affairs,* http://www.kaisernetwork.org/daily_reports/rep_index.cfm?DR_ID=25428.

104   *... one day of Sabbath rest.* John Ortberg deals with the theme of Sabbath and rest in some creative and wonderful ways in his book *An Ordinary Day with Jesus,* as well as in *The Life You've Always Wanted.*

107   *... Sabbath observances as they were growing up.* Various parts of the country and the world approach the Sabbath in very different ways. In Orange County, where I grew up, there was very little legalism, but there was also no sense of what Sabbath meant for followers of Jesus. In Grand Rapids, there is still a concern for observing Sabbath, but it often takes on legalistic tones.

107   *... different from what we do on the other days of the week.* Theologian John Calvin emphasized that doing things that were distinctly different on the Sabbath is a central theme of Sabbath observance.

123   *... programs that help people plan their meals are so helpful.* If you need help in this planning process, two reputable programs are Jenny Craig and Weight Watchers.

124   *... the lost value of the convivium.* I cover the topic of sit-down meals very quickly in this chapter. Randy Frazee digs into this at much greater length in his book *Making Room for Life.* If you want to be challenged to make meals with family and friends a priority, I would encourage you to read chapter 10 of Randy's book.

133   *In the movie Roxanne ...* This movie has some humorous moments and illustrates some points, but its themes are inappropriate for most young people.

139–40 *Ken Davis, a Christian speaker ...* Ken has not only come up with a clever concept for a T-shirt; he also has books and videos that communicate the message of faith in creative, humorous, and life-changing ways.

Part 4: Shifts That Build Dynamic and Lasting Relationships

161   *Nancy, Nancy, Nancy.* In this story, as in many others in this book, I have changed the names of the people to protect their privacy. The stories are real, but the names are not.

162   *On his website, The Sideroad, Neil Payne ...* Neil Payne works in the area of business etiquette and is a specialist in cross-cultural communication for the business community.

168–69 *... spiritual gifts class in your church.* The *Network* training resource was developed by Bruce Bugbee, Don Cousins, and Bill Hybels. It is published by Zondervan and is an excellent tool for training people to discover and develop their spiritual gifts.

172–73 *She never admitted any wrongdoing.* The facts in this story were drawn from four different newspaper articles about the Boston Marathon in 1980. The goal of this story is not to condemn Rosie Ruiz but to shed light on the temptation to lie that we all face.

175   *... authentic community and healthy relationships.* If you are part of a small group that wants to dig deeper into this topic, I suggest you use the discussion guide in the Interactions series titled *The Real Deal: Discover the Rewards of Authentic Relationships,* published by Zondervan.

Part 5: Shifts That Open the Floodgates of True Riches

188 *You remember Smarties* ... A friend who reviewed this chapter informed me that in Canada, Smarties (made by the same company) are little candy-coated balls with a chocolate center. Just for the record.

200 ... *the resources God had placed in his care.* This story is found in D. James Kennedy's book *Character and Destiny* (Zondervan, 1994).

203 ... *learned quite a bit about Mesocricetus auratus.* I could not find that little book I received with the purchase of our first two hamsters, so I am not able to credit those who wrote it and who first taught me so much about hamsters. But I found some good hamster information on a number of internet sites all about these furry little rodents.

205 ... *humorous lists of oxymorons?* Many of the oxymorons on my list were found at http://www.topskills.com/oxymorons.htm.

218 ... *the relationship between happiness and the accumulation of wealth.* The article by Alison Grant mentioned in this chapter was published in the *Grand Rapids Press* ("Rich Get Richer, but Not Happier," February 6, 2005, H4). The quotes from Richard Easterlin and Gregg Easterbrook were taken from the article.

Part 6: Shifts That Will Help You Impact Your Community and the World

234 ...*uses the word "chaordic."* Sweet presents a case for the chaos that comes from the necessary change the church must make if it is going to survive in the new millennium. We must be ready to face chaos and also maintain a level of order. The combination is a chaordic church.

238 ... *the motto, "No perfect people allowed!"* John Burke pastors Gateway Church in Austin, Texas. The message of this church resonates with so many: no perfect people allowed. This theme is expanded in John's book by the same name, *No Perfect People Allowed: Creating a Come-as-You-Are Culture in the Church* (Zondervan, 2005).

243 *In the 1990s, a quiet revolution began.* I would highly recommend both books mentioned in this chapter: *Becoming a Contagious Christian* and *Building a Contagious Church.* Both are published by Zondervan. The survey of evangelism styles in this chapter is drawn from these two resources, as well as from my own experience helping mobilize people for outreach based on their unique and God-given styles.

Recommended Reading

There are many helpful books and resources that can help you dig deeper into the topics discussed in this book. Here are some suggestions.

Part 1: Shifts That Bring Greater Joy Than You Can Imagine
Boomerang Joy by Barbara Johnson (Zondervan, 1998). Sixty devotions on joy.
The Christian's Secret of a Happy Life by Hannah Whitall Smith (Revell, 1952).
The Divine Conspiracy by Dallas Willard (HarperCollins, 1997).
The Life You've Always Wanted by John Ortberg (Zondervan, 1997). The entire book is excellent, but chapter 4 is very helpful on the topic of joy.

Part 2: Shifts That Expand Your Faith
Celebration of Discipline by Richard Foster (Harper and Row, 1978).
Deepening Your Conversation with God by Ben Patterson (Bethany House, 1999).
Experiencing God by Henry T. Blackaby and Claude V. King (Broadman and Holman, 1994).
How to Listen to God by Charles Stanley (Thomas Nelson, 1985).
Listening for God by Marilyn Honts (Tyndale, 2004).
Prayer Devotional Bible by Ben Patterson (Zondervan, 2004). With devotions by Ben Patterson.
Too Busy Not to Pray by Bill Hybels (Zondervan, 1988).

Part 3: Shifts That Bring Health and Rest
Food for Life by Pamela M. Smith, R.D. (Creation House, 1994).
The Life You've Always Wanted by John Ortberg (Zondervan, 1997).
Making Room for Life by Randy Frazee (Zondervan, 2003).
The Purpose-Driven Life by Rick Warren (Zondervan, 2002).
Ten Essentials of Highly Healthy People by Walt Larimore, M.D. (Zondervan, 2003).
Thin Within by Judy and Arthur Halliday (W. Publishing, a division of Thomas Nelson, 2002).

Part 4: Shifts That Build Dynamic and Lasting Relationships
Boundaries Face to Face by Dr. Henry Cloud and Dr. John Townsend (Zondervan, 2003).
The Connecting Church by Randy Frazee (Zondervan, 2001).
Doing Life Together by Brett and Dee Eastman, Karen Lee-Thorp, Denise Wendorff, and Todd Wendorff (Zondervan, 2002). This is a series of small group resources that include a DVD teaching component.
Safe People by Dr. Henry Cloud and Dr. John Townsend (Zondervan, 1995).

Part 5: Shifts That Open the Floodgates of True Riches

Answers to Your Family's Financial Questions by Larry Burkett (Focus on the Family, 1987).

Good Sense Budget Course by Dick Towner and John Tofilon (Zondervan, 2002).

Your Money Counts by Howard Dayton (Crown Ministries, 1996).

Part 6: Shifts That Will Help You Impact Your Community and the World

Building a Contagious Church by Mark Mittelberg (Zondervan, 2000).

The Case for Christ by Lee Strobel (Zondervan, 1998).

The Case for Faith by Lee Strobel (Zondervan, 2000).

Rumors of Another World by Philip Yancey (Zondervan, 2003).

Sharing the Truth in Love by Ajith Fernando (Discovery House, 2001).

The Unchurched Next Door by Thom S. Rainer (Zondervan, 2003).